Praise for

Camelot and the Cultural Revolution

"Mr. Piereson [shows that] the assassination of Kennedy was more than a shot heard round the world. It was a shot that blasted into the liberal *Weltanschauung*, bringing on the enormities of the sixties and seventies. Mr. Piereson earns the gratitude of curious people, whom he fascinates." —William F. Buckley Jr.

"It is one of the best accounts we have of why liberalism—which 'owned the future' in 1963—fell from grace and has yet to recover." —*The Wall Street Journal*

"James Piereson has written an idiosyncratic, provocative, and quite brilliant book. He puts the Kennedy assassination—or, rather, the left's rewriting of history occasioned by the Kennedy assassination—at the center of liberalism's crackup in the 1960s in a way that no one, so far as I know, has done before. I'll go so far as to say this: Piereson's study will be indispensable to anyone, from now on, who seriously tries to come to grips with the last half-century of our history." —William Kristol, *The Weekly Standard*

"In his book *Camelot and the Cultural Revolution*, Mr. Piereson has brilliantly added a new dimension to the bitter controversy that still rages over the JFK assassination: political perspective. It is much needed, if only to make some sense of the disputation over evidence that has gone on for over forty years." —Edward Jay Epstein, author of *Inquest: The Warren Commission and the Establishment of Truth* and *Legend: The Secret World of Lee Harvey Oswald*

"Provocative and innovative . . . Piereson has made a major contribution to the literature on the Kennedy assassination." —Mark Moyar, *National Review*

"A brilliant new book [that] makes us think again about events or personalities . . . to rethink again an entire era." —*Catholic Light*

"[An] intriguing explanation of how . . . liberalism declined into the adolescent anger that is now its essence."
—R. Emmet Tyrrell Jr., *The American Spectator*

"James Piereson has succeeded in providing a fresh and persuasive way of understanding the political and cultural history of America's last half-century." —*First Things*

"A brilliant analysis . . . one of those rare works that actually change people's minds." —John O'Sullivan, *The American Conservative*

"Brilliant." —Jonah Goldberg, *National Review Online*

"The book is a stunning success [that] reveals amazing historical facts." —Brian Domitrovic, *Intercollegiate Studies Institute*

"Every now and then you come across a book that is so interesting, so clearly written and so carefully reasoned (and so brief) that you marvel at it. . . . This is a fine little book, deserving a wider audience."
—Jim Delmont, *Omaha City Weekly*

CAMELOT AND THE CULTURAL REVOLUTION

How the Assassination of
John F. Kennedy
Shattered American Liberalism

JAMES PIERESON

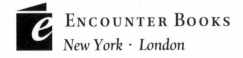

ENCOUNTER BOOKS
New York · London

Paperback edition published in 2009 by Encounter Books,
an activity of Encounter for Culture and Education, Inc.,
a nonprofit, tax exempt corporation.
Encounter Books website address: www.encounterbooks.com

Manufactured in the United States and printed on acid-free paper. The paper
used in this publication meets the minimum requirements of ANSI/NISO
Z39.48-1992 (R 1997) (Permanence of Paper).

PAPERBACK EDITION ISBN: 978-1-59403-258-5

FIRST EDITION

THE LIBRARY OF CONGRESS HAS CATALOGED
THE HARDCOVER EDITION AS FOLLOWS:

Piereson, James.
Camelot and the cultural revolution : how the assassination of John F.
Kennedy shattered American liberalism / James Piereson.
p.   cm.
Includes bibliographical references and index.
ISBN-13: 978-1-59403-188-5 (hardcover : alk. paper)
ISBN-10: 1-59403-188-6 (hardcover : alk. paper) 1. United States—Politics
and government—1945-1989. 2. Liberalism—United States—History—20th
century. 3. Political culture—United States—History—20th century.
4. Kennedy, John F. (John Fitzgerald), 1917-1963—Assassination. I. Title.
E839.5.P54 2007
306.20973'09046—dc22
2007008529

10 9 8 7 6 5 4 3 2 1

CONTENTS

FOREWORD TO
THE PAPERBACK EDITION

THE QUESTION OF "Who killed Kennedy?" has dominated the literature on the Kennedy assassination from the moment the first book on the event appeared in 1964. Unfortunately, the now voluminous literature on the assassination has failed to produce any public consensus as to what happened on that day in Dallas in 1963, despite the official report of the Warren Commission, which concluded that Lee Harvey Oswald was the lone assassin of President Kennedy, and several subsequent studies of the evidence that reached the same conclusion. The public, however, notwithstanding the overwhelming evidence pointing toward Oswald, has never accepted this version of the assassination, preferring instead to believe in one or another theory suggesting that President Kennedy was a victim of a conspiracy engineered by right-wing businessmen, organized crime, or rogue elements of the CIA or the FBI. Judging by opinion polls and the continuing interest in conspiracy theories, the public is still as divided and confused as ever about the identity and motives of Kennedy's assassin. Because the public never fully came to terms with the event, the debate over the assassination remains stuck more or less where it was when it began in the mid-1960s.

Camelot and the Cultural Revolution takes a different approach to the Kennedy assassination. Instead of asking "Who killed Kennedy," the book begins from the factual premise that Oswald was the assassin, and then develops various implications from this premise. The evidence against Oswald was overwhelming at the time and continues to be so as new information has come to light. This evidence has been ably assembled again in recent years by Gerald Posner and Vincent Bugliosi in comprehensive studies of the assassination.* In view of the evidence, it is an interesting question why the Kennedy assassination should have been the focus of such a long-running controversy. There are other questions that deserve an explanation as well: How was the assassination interpreted at the time and how was it placed within the context of the politics of the period? In what ways did the event challenge received assumptions? What were its political and cultural consequences? In what ways might the assassination have been linked to other events in the 1960s—in particular to the revolution in cultural ideas that divided the nation in the late 1960s? The Kennedy assassination was the single most important political event of the 1960s, while the cultural revolt was among the most important social developments of the period. It is plausible to think that the two must have been connected in some way.

Regarding the latter point, *Camelot and the Cultural Revolution* sets forth a political interpretation of the Kennedy assassination by linking it to the disintegration of the postwar liberal consensus. That consensus, which developed in response to the New Deal, World War II, and the Cold War, was reflected in the policies and aspirations of Kennedy's administration and, indeed, in those of the Johnson administration which succeeded it. Kennedy, along

---

See Gerald Posner, *Case Closed: Lee Harvey Oswald and the Assassination of JFK* (New York: Random House, 1993); and Vincent Bugliosi, *Reclaiming History: The Assassination of President John F. Kennedy* (New York: W. W. Norton & Co., 2007).

with his liberal allies, accepted without question the assumption that the United States played a benign and progressive role in the world and that the American past was a story of steady progress in the direction of democracy and widening prosperity. By 1968, liberals increasingly disputed the old faith, emphasizing American misdeeds abroad and the oppression of minority groups at home. Kennedy's death, especially in the way that it happened and the way it was interpreted, was one of the catalysts for the new skepticism about widely held ideals. The assassination and its aftermath also produced a profound irony: Kennedy in life was the exemplar of the old liberalism, but after his assassination he was viewed as the torchbearer for the new.

The book makes two general claims:

First, though President Kennedy was assassinated by a communist, few were prepared at the time to say that the event was linked to the Cold War. Instead, Kennedy's death was interpreted by national leaders, both in government and in the press, within the framework of the civil rights movement. Kennedy, it was claimed, was a victim of hatred and bigotry, and (like Lincoln) was a martyr to the cause of civil rights and racial justice. National leaders deflected responsibility for the act away from Oswald and in the direction of domestic groups and forces such as "the radical right," a spirit of lawlessness in the nation, or a climate of hatred and bigotry that had been expressed in acts of violence against civil rights workers in the South. One will search in vain for any prominent leader at the time who linked Kennedy's assassination to communism or the Cold War. Oswald may have pulled the trigger, as many were forced to acknowledge, but a deeper domestic sickness was finally responsible for the president's death. Yet, as a matter of fact, the assassination had nothing whatever to do with civil rights or domestic politics and everything to do with the Cold War. Oswald did not shoot President Kennedy because he was unhappy with his administration's civil rights policies but because he opposed Kennedy's Cold War policies, especially as they related to Cuba. Kennedy's assassination was thus a highly anomalous event within the context of the time, because every thoughtful liberal in the early 1960s was convinced that the danger of violence in American life came from the far right rather than from the far left. The facts notwithstanding, they proceeded to interpret the assassination in terms of the established expectation. This misinterpretation was one of the factors responsible for the long-running confusion surrounding the assassination. If President Kennedy had in fact been shot by a right-wing fanatic whose guilt was established by the same evidence as condemned Oswald, there would have been no protracted controversy about "who killed Kennedy."

The book's second major claim is that this interpretation of the assassination was incorporated into the unfolding radical narrative of the 1960s, which saw American society as "sick" and the United States as an out-of-control colossus on the world scene. This latter point was, of course, an elemental aspect of the opposition to the war in Vietnam. Thus, Kennedy's assassination came to be viewed by both radicals and liberals as an item in a broader indictment of American society and of America's role in the world. Vietnam, civil rights, racial prejudice, violence at home—all were implicated in the indictment. Despite the contradictory identity of the assassin, it turned out to be all too easy to fit Kennedy's death within that critical narrative, since (as it was argued) he was a victim of the same forces that were responsible for the war in Vietnam, racial bigotry, and other ills of American society. It was this general indictment which shattered the postwar consensus and thus brought about the end of the liberal era that began in the 1930s. The optimism that had marked liberal thought from the time of the New Deal could not be sustained against this cultural attack, which gained strength year by year through the 1960s. The oppositional themes that had long been bubbling on the margins of American life burst into the mainstream of liberal thought, redefining and redirecting liberal assumptions in the process. The Kennedy assassination was not the single cause of this development, but it must be viewed in retrospect as one in an unfolding series of events that contributed to it, much in the way that the Kansas-Nebraska Act, the Dred Scott decision, and John Brown's raid combined to bring about the Civil War.

The first of these general points is validated by the historical evidence outlined in the book. The second is more interpretive in nature and thus far more controversial. Yet the two themes are closely linked because the interpretation of the Kennedy assassination as an event in the civil rights movement provided a basis for incorporating it into the critical narrative that emerged from the 1960s. It would not have been possible to do so if Kennedy had been properly viewed as a victim of the Cold War—or, more precisely, as a victim of communism. Yet such an interpretation was never developed, even though the evidence indisputably pointed to Oswald as the assassin.

I am not the first author to have made such claims about the wide-ranging political effects of the Kennedy assassination. The journalist Theodore H. White and the novelist Norman Mailer traced the negativism that they associated with the 1960s to the shocking ramifications of Kennedy's death. Both agreed that Kennedy's death undermined the optimism of the postwar era and introduced a negative mood into American life. *Camelot and the Cultural Revolution* develops in some detail the process by which this took place.

Reviewers, quite naturally, set forth mixed judgments of a book containing such a disturbing theme. Some found the arguments compelling as regards both the misinterpretation of the assassination and the importance of the event in the disintegration of the liberal consensus. Some were shocked to learn about the extent of Oswald's communist connections and activities, which established the motive for his attack on President Kennedy. Many appreciated the book's somewhat novel approach to the assassination—that is, the effort to get beyond the question of "Who killed Kennedy?" to address the political dimensions of the event. Conspiracy theorists, obviously, could not accept the premise that Oswald alone killed President Kennedy, convinced as they are that every effort to point the finger of blame at Oswald must be part of an effort to cover up the truth about the assassination. Liberal commentators, meanwhile, have had difficulty accepting the claim that liberal leaders at the time created the long-running controversy over the assassination by placing it within the context of the civil rights struggle

instead of the Cold War. Nor are they prepared to accept the judgment that the liberal consensus was broken apart in the 1960s,
because they look back on that period as one of hope and idealism
rather than one of shattered ideals and loss of faith. They still tend,
moreover, to accept the judgment of the time that the assassination
was a product of domestic ills justifying further reform and enlightenment. These are signs that the Kennedy assassination is still a
subject that evokes partisan and ideological passions. It will be for
a later generation to give some perspective to the event and fold it
into a dispassionate history of the time.

Camelot and the Cultural Revolution has been called a "revisionist"
history of the Kennedy assassination. There is a sense in which this
is true, since it challenges the version which holds that Kennedy
was shot by a "nut" who just happened to be a communist but
whose deed arose more from the ills of American society than from
his dedication to communist ideology. This idea is plainly wrong as
to the facts, and so in this respect there is not much revisionism to
undertake except to set forth those facts. The problem, however, is
that this view of the assassination became entangled in broader
ideological commitments such that any attempt to revise it necessarily challenges those commitments. The claim that national leaders engineered the assassination for covert purposes proved easy
for many to accept, while the truth that national leaders deflected
responsibility from communism and toward the national culture
proved difficult for many even to consider. Thus, as in other sensitive cases, it is not the facts that are difficult to accept but rather
their implications.

Somewhat lost in these arguments were other themes developed in the book, such as the important role played by Jacqueline
Kennedy in formulating the civil rights interpretation of Kennedy's
death and in devising the symbolism of Camelot to reinforce that
interpretation. If any single person was responsible for creating the
Kennedy myth, it was Mrs. Kennedy, who in the grief-filled days
following her husband's death came up with the images by which
he would be remembered: the eternal flame, King Arthur and
Camelot, the association with Lincoln, and the claim that President

Kennedy was a martyr for civil rights. These images defined the assassination for the American people and, once they were inscribed in the public's mind, rendered impossible a fully rational interpretation of the event.

A few reviewers wrote under the misimpression that my aim in the book was to discredit John F. Kennedy and his legacy. That is a misreading of what I wrote. It is true that the book disputes the myth that grew up around Kennedy after his death that he was some kind of liberal idealist who entered politics to set right the problems of the world. The real Kennedy, as opposed to the idealized image, was more of a pragmatic politician than a starry-eyed idealist. Kennedy was reluctant to get too far ahead of public opinion, especially in the area of civil rights, wherein his hand was eventually forced by developments beyond his control. The book is, if anything, laudatory toward Kennedy as an articulate spokesman for postwar liberalism and as an effective leader in the areas of civil rights and the Cold War. It was the effort to create a legend around Kennedy that contributed so greatly to the confusion surrounding both his life and his death. Kennedy in life was a far more attractive and interesting figure than the Arthurian image erected by his friends and allies after his assassination. At the same time, the myths surrounding Kennedy may have served the deeper purpose of keeping alive within a liberal polity the vision of the ideal statesman. The tangled history of the Kennedy assassination may thus be taken as proof that liberal nations–and perhaps liberal nations most of all–have need for consoling myths and legends, even when they have unwholesome consequences.

This edition of the book is only slightly revised from the hardcover edition, which was published in 2007. The new edition appears, however, following the election to the presidency of Barack Obama, who during the election campaign was identified by prominent members of the Kennedy family as the new representative of the Kennedy ideal. That is a burden that no president should want. Much has been written in recent months about the similarities between the two men, and there has even been some commentary about their differences (which are substantial). There is little point in entering into that controversy here. Suffice it to say that this book suggests that our new president would be better off by taking his bearings from the reality of President Kennedy's tenure in office than from the myths and legends that grew up around him after his death.

New York, July 2009

INTRODUCTION

IT IS NOW closing in on a half-century since President John F. Kennedy was assassinated on the streets of Dallas on November 22, 1963. No other event in the postwar era, not even the terrorist attacks of September 11, 2001, has cast such a long shadow over our national life. The murder of the handsome and vigorous president shocked the nation to its core and shook the faith of many Americans in their institutions and way of life. The repercussions from that event continue to be felt down to the present day. Looking back through the decades, it seems clear that Kennedy's death marked an important turning point in American life, after which time events began to move in strange and unexpected directions. This was the moment, if there was a particular moment, when the cultural consensus of the 1950s began to give way to the oppositional and experimental culture that we associate with the 1960s.

Barely a month passes without some reminder of the assassination appearing in the news. In recent years, several new biographies of President Kennedy have been published, including a highly praised volume by the historian Robert Dallek, who had access to much new information about Kennedy's health and medical history.[1] Jacqueline Kennedy Onassis continues to be a favored subject for biographers.[2] Robert Kennedy's assassination in 1968 was the subject of a recently released Hollywood movie. There seems to be no end to books and articles advancing some new conspiracy to account for the assassination. The Kennedy family is now as prominent as ever and continues to be a subject of keen interest to the American public. In many ways, the very prominence of the Kennedys is a continuing reminder of the assassinations that tore the nation apart a generation ago.

Those who were living at the time and old enough to recall them today will never forget the moving scenes associated with President Kennedy's death: the Zapruder film depicting the assassination in a frame-by-frame sequence; the courageous widow arriving with the coffin at Andrews Air Force Base still wearing her bloodstained dress; the throng of mourners, many of high school or college age, lined up for blocks outside the Capitol to pay their respects to the fallen president; the accused assassin himself gunned down two days later while in police custody, and in full view of a national television audience; the little boy saluting the coffin of his slain father; the somber march to Arlington National Cemetery; the eternal flame affixed to the gravesite. These scenes, repeated endlessly on television at the time and then reproduced in popular magazines and, still later, in documentary films, were marked indelibly on the nation's memory, where they served as a dark backdrop to the tumultuous decade that followed.

After all these years, there is little new or even different that might be said about this sad event. There remain, of course, many unanswered—and unanswerable—questions which have by now nourished several decades of fruitless speculation about who actually killed the president and what might have happened (or not happened) had he lived. Such speculation is perhaps the clearest sign that the assassination was never fully digested by the generation that lived through it. Lincoln's assassination in 1865 had both immediate and lasting political consequences, yet it never generated the level of sustained public fascination as the Kennedy assassination precisely because the public at that earlier time had little difficulty understanding why a Southern partisan would wish to kill the leader of the Union cause. For many reasons, Kennedy's assassination proved more confusing and less intelligible to the American people, so much so that despite compelling evidence showing that Lee Harvey Oswald was the lone assassin, more than two-thirds of Americans still believe that President Kennedy was the victim of an organized conspiracy.[3]

The ongoing controversy over the causes and ultimate meaning of the assassination has largely taken place among liberals and leftists, who had the greatest difficulty coming to terms with it. Most of the notable books on the assassination over the years have been written from this general point of view, an acknowledgment that for Americans on the left the assassination represented an especially shattering and confusing event. Conservatives, in contrast, have generally played the role of spectators in these polemics, perhaps because they have been satisfied with the official explanation that Oswald was the assassin or because they have viewed the whole subject as another of those intellectual swamps patrolled by sentimental leftists and conspiracy theorists of various stripes. To a considerable degree, however, the rampant speculation about conspiracies and "what might have been" has diverted attention from some of the most perplexing and long-running consequences of the Kennedy assassination.

The assassination, in combination with later events, especially the war in Vietnam, drove the nation's political culture sharply to the left during the latter half of the 1960s. To be more precise, it drove liberal culture—led by the universities and the national news media—to the left, and much of the rest of the country to the right in response. Why should this have been so? The assassin, Oswald, was a communist (or a Marxist, as he preferred to call himself) who had defected to the Soviet Union in 1959 but, dissatisfied with Soviet life, returned to the United States with his Russian wife in 1962. By 1963, his political affections had shifted from the Soviet Union to Fidel Castro's Cuba. In the months leading up to the assassination, he was active in a front organization that sponsored protests against the Kennedy administration's aggressive stance toward Cuba. Oswald was a committed leftist but perhaps one of the first of an evolving breed who rejected the Soviet Union in favor of third-world dictators like Castro, Mao, and Ho Chi Minh. In any event, like many leftists of the modern era, he hated the United States and everything it stands for.[4]

The assassination of a popular president by a communist should have generated a revulsion against everything associated with left-wing doctrines. Yet something very close to the opposite happened. In the aftermath of the assassination, left-wing ideas and revolutionary leaders—Marx, Lenin, Mao, and Castro foremost among them—enjoyed a greater vogue in the United States than at any other time in our history. By 1968, student radicals were taking over campuses and joining protest demonstrations in support of a host of radical and revolutionary causes, even going so far as to grow beards and don army jackets in emulation of Castro. Socialism and revolution—causes that Kennedy resolutely fought against —were the watchwords of the New Left that had emerged by the mid-1960s. It is one of the ironies of recent history that many of those young people who filed in shocked grief past the president's coffin in 1963 would just a few years later embrace as political activists the very doctrines that drove Oswald to assassinate him.

It seems plain in retrospect, moreover, that President Kennedy's assassination stalled the advance of twentieth-century liberalism, then the nation's reigning public philosophy and, in the opinion of historians at the time, our only genuine public philosophy. It did this in several ways: first, by undermining the confidence of liberals in the future; and second, by changing their perspective from one of possibility and practical reform to one of grief, loss, and frustrated hopes. It also compromised their faith in the nation because many concluded, against all factual evidence, that in some way the nation itself was responsible for President Kennedy's death. A confident, practical, and forward-looking philosophy, with a heritage of genuine accomplishment, was thus turned into a pessimistic doctrine—and one with a decidedly negative view of American society and its institutions. Such assumptions, far from marking a temporary adjustment to the events of the 1960s, have proved remarkably durable over the decades; indeed, they survive today, unaltered by time or by the terrorist attacks of 2001, as defining characteristics of contemporary liberalism.

How and why this happened remains something of a puzzle, in part because this change in mood and perspective was more of a cultural reorientation than a rational response to Kennedy's death. In addition, the early histories of the Kennedy administration were written in the main by Kennedy loyalists like Theodore Sorensen and Arthur Schlesinger Jr., or by liberals and radicals whose mood was so affected by the event.[5] Among liberals who admired Kennedy and were devastated by his death, there was a tendency to view the event through the prism of loss and disappointment: How could this have happened? What if he had lived? Who was really responsible? Yet one still wonders why the assassination should have had such a perplexing consequence, and what it was about midcentury liberalism that allowed it to be knocked so badly off balance by a single event, shocking though it may have been. Whatever it was, this vulnerability in postwar liberalism opened the way for the revival of conservatism from the 1970s forward.

This, then, is an extended essay on the effects of the Kennedy assassination on the foundational assumptions of American liberalism—and especially on those assumptions that governed liberal thought in the postwar period. It is, as such, more of an interpretative essay than a research study that brings new or unknown facts to the attention of readers. Some of the facts that are emphasized here have been disregarded, it is true, but they are far from unknown. It is, admittedly, a challenging and perhaps an impossible task to tease out the effects of the assassination from overlapping events that also shaped the history of that time. Rather than attempt the impossible, the author has prepared a brief, as it were, for the importance of the Kennedy assassination as a decisive factor behind the unraveling of liberal doctrine in the 1960s.

Kennedy was in many ways an exemplar of the brand of pragmatic liberalism that emerged after World War II. He was tough and realistic, much like his Democratic predecessors Franklin Delano Roosevelt and Harry Truman, yet at the same time idealistic about the prospects for reform and progress in American life. Shortly after the assassination, Arthur Schlesinger Jr. wrote that "The energies he [Kennedy] released, the standards he set, the purposes he inspired, the goals he established would guide the nation he loved for years to come."[6] One wishes that this in fact had been so. Kennedy's assassination, and the ways in which it was interpreted and assimilated by Americans, challenged many of the deepest assumptions of postwar liberalism and dashed the hopes that Kennedy had inspired. The event, as things turned out, set the nation off in a political direction that could not have been foreseen by the wisest and most farsighted of the postwar liberals, including Schlesinger himself. There was no reason, given the facts of the situation, why this should have been so. As with the assassination of Archduke Franz Ferdinand of Austria in 1914, it was the reaction to the facts, rather than the facts themselves, that turned the Kennedy assassination into an event of such far-reaching significance.

The historian Merrill Peterson remarked, in his fine book on *Lincoln in American Memory*, that "the public remembrance of the past ... is concerned less with establishing its truth than with appropriating it for the present."[7] The man or woman on the street does not look back on history or on historical figures with the historian's concern for evidence and objective assessment. The memory of Lincoln was refracted through the lenses of his assassination and the final victory of the Union army. These events turned the politician who eight months earlier was certain that he would lose his bid for re-election into a martyr for the Union. In a parallel way, Kennedy, following his sudden death and solemn funeral, was turned into something different in public memory from how he was understood in life. Like Lincoln, Kennedy too was viewed as a martyr, albeit in devotion to a most uncertain cause. Here was a source of much bewilderment about the man and the event. What exactly did John F. Kennedy stand for? The great difference between Lincoln and Kennedy is that the former died at his moment of victory while the latter was killed before he was able to achieve any great success. Lincoln was assassinated at the end of a civil war, Kennedy at the beginning of a long-running cultural war. Lincoln's assassination united a nation but Kennedy's divided it. Lincoln was mourned but also celebrated for his magnificent achievement; Kennedy was mourned in a spirit of frustrated possibility and dashed hopes. This spirit, as things turned out, infected the liberal movement in America.

It will be said, not without justice, that Kennedy's assassination was but one of many events that provoked the political and social upheavals of the 1960s. The war in Vietnam, the generational bulge that created a vast population of college-age youth, the civil rights movement, the urban riots—all these were at least as important as the Kennedy assassination in shaping the mood of the time and raising doubts about the liberal credo of progress through incremental reform. It is also true that the greatest of liberal victories after the New Deal occurred in 1964 and 1965, following Kennedy's death, when Lyndon Johnson and a Democratic Congress pushed through a Civil Rights Act, a Voting Rights Act, Medicare and Medicaid programs, and countless minor pieces of reformist legislation. If Kennedy's assassination caused a crisis in liberalism, that crisis was not immediately apparent.

Yet Kennedy's murder was the first of these unfolding events and as such it created something of a template for the interpretation of what happened afterwards. Indeed, Kennedy's death itself provided some short-term momentum for the liberal victories that followed in the immediate aftermath of the tragic events in Dallas. These legislative victories in 1964 and 1965 turned out to be the high-water mark for postwar liberalism. Moreover, once the assumptions of postwar liberalism were shaken by Kennedy's death, they were thereafter more vulnerable to attack from those who asserted that they encouraged or indulged any number of political vices, from racism to imperialism. In mounting a defense against such attacks, liberals gradually lost their programmatic emphasis and began to focus instead on cultural factors that were felt to be the ultimate sources of misguided policy.

Conservatives, on the other hand, while pushed into the background by the mayhem of the later 1960s, emerged from all these events with their basic assumptions intact and even strengthened.

Indeed, Kennedy's assassination probably reinforced conservative assumptions every bit as much as it undermined liberal assumptions. Conservatives were hardly shocked or surprised to learn that a communist had killed the president of the United States, for this was precisely the kind of thing they had been cautioning against since the Cold War began. They had been saying for years—and had been ridiculed for saying it—that communism represented not simply an external danger to the Republic, as liberals acknowledged, but an internal danger as well (which liberals denied). As a consequence, conservatives were not inclined to buy into any of the conspiracy theories that later emerged which sought to place the blame for Kennedy's death on organized crime or on right-wing extremists. Nor were conservatives inclined to romanticize Kennedy after his death or to resent his successor, as many liberals did. From the standpoint of conservatives, Kennedy's style and *savoir faire*, which carried great weight among liberals, meant very little; Lyndon Johnson, who had no style at all in the eyes of liberals, was a much more fearful character from a conservative standpoint precisely because of his effectiveness in dealing with the Congress.

Conservative leaders like Barry Goldwater and William F. Buckley Jr., along with conservative writers like Russell Kirk, John Chamberlain, and James Burnham, thus picked up and moved on after Kennedy's assassination without any re-examination of principles or any significant soul searching about the meaning of the event. For them, the assassination, sad and shocking though it was, did not carry the emotional freight that it carried for liberals. In succeeding decades, then, conservatives would contest for power and influence with greater self-confidence and optimism than liberals were able to muster after their worldview was turned upside-down in the 1960s.

The passing of the decades is now providing historians with a somewhat clearer perspective on President Kennedy than was possible in the immediate aftermath of his death. Americans under the age of fifty have little recollection at all of John F. Kennedy and but a hazy memory of the upheavals of the period. For those even younger, John F. Kennedy and the 1960s are subjects studied in the history books and perhaps the topics of lectures given by college professors who came of age during that era. Nearly all those directly involved in the events of November 22, 1963, have passed away, including all the passengers in the presidential limousine and many of the immediate witnesses to the event. The admiring and somewhat hagiographic memoirs of Kennedy loyalists have given way to more objective and dispassionate works of professional historians. Most of the salacious secrets of the Kennedy White House have by now been bared to the public. The dramatic events and the oversized personalities of the time have passed or are passing into history. Many things that were difficult to see at the time now appear more clearly visible from the distance of over four decades; and many things that may have been difficult to express then because they may have seemed insensitive to the Kennedy family or to the memory of the slain president may now be said with less fear of provoking emotional recriminations.

The subject of this essay is less the assassination itself than the political reaction to it and the lasting consequences of that reaction for the political movement Kennedy represented. The main point is not to say something new about what happened on November 22, 1963, because the salient facts are already known, though not in all cases widely accepted. The point is rather to begin the work of placing the Kennedy assassination into the perspective of history, particularly as the event might have been connected to the fortunes of the liberal movement in the United States. For better or worse, liberalism supplied much of the energy that drove our politics forward during the greater part of the twentieth century. It now seems clear that Kennedy's assassination had the effect of draining much of that political energy out of the liberal movement. It was also a catalyst for redefining what it meant to be liberal in the United States. During the 1930s, under the leadership of Franklin Delano Roosevelt, liberalism redefined and re-energized itself, much to the benefit of the nation. The revision and redefinition that took place in the 1960s had profound effects as well, but of a different kind. Much as Roosevelt came to be associated in the public mind with the New Deal, John F. Kennedy and the fortunes of the Kennedy family came to be linked with liberalism in the 1960s. The deaths first of John F. Kennedy and, next, of Robert Kennedy could not have helped but cause disorientation in the ranks of American liberalism.

The essay begins from the not so controversial premise that Lee Harvey Oswald assassinated President Kennedy and in doing so he probably acted alone. What then follows from this factual premise? The various conspiracy theories that arose in the wake of the assassination must be viewed in a different light—not so much as efforts to discover the truth but as aspects of a struggle to find meaning in a seemingly senseless event. The various myths that viewed the New Frontier as a version of Camelot and Kennedy as a modern-day King Arthur must be similarly understood. Most of all, the essay highlights the wide gulf between the liberalism that prevailed before Kennedy's assassination and the version that emerged afterwards. It was Kennedy's assassination, perhaps more than any other single event, that served as a punctuation point for this transition and reorientation.

ONE · LIBERALISM

As THE 1960s BEGAN, liberalism was without doubt the single most creative and vital force in American politics. The liberal movement was riding a wave of accomplishment running back to the Progressive era through the New Deal and into the postwar period. John F. Kennedy, the new representative of this tradition, had just been elected to the presidency, and though there were many doubts as to the depth of his commitment to liberal doctrine, there was little doubt that his administration would advance the still unfinished agenda of liberal reform. Liberalism owned the future, as Orwell might have said, which is to say that liberals looked ahead to a future defined by their ideas of progress through the expansion of democracy and the welfare state. They assumed that the United States would play a decisive role in the world in spreading these hopes and expectations to other lands. By the end of the decade, however, liberal doctrine was in disarray, with many of its central assumptions broken by the experience of the preceding years. It is still trying to recover.

The assassination of a liberal president, along with the circumstances surrounding his death, challenged the assumptions of postwar liberalism as no other event could have done. It brought up, for

1

example, the disquieting political question (raised just a few years earlier by Daniel Bell) as to whether the conventional reform agenda—either of the Progressive or the New Deal variety—was sufficiently compelling to give meaning to liberal politics or to public life generally. Conventional reform appears prosaic unless joined with a sense of historical movement that gives it broader meaning, purpose, and importance. It was commonly said, for example, that reform was a means of perfecting our democratic heritage or of delivering to everyone the promise of American life. Yet in many ways Kennedy's death severed the ties between reform and the idea of historical progress. Reform seemed to point in one direction: toward more hope, more democracy, and more justice and equality in American life; but Kennedy's death pointed in quite another: that is, toward a sense that public life is out of control or subject to direction by conspiracies or crazed individuals. Kennedy's assassination was so shocking and unexpected that to many it made the reform agenda seem small, insignificant, and meaningless.

This confusion was compounded by the peculiar character of postwar liberalism, which supplied the script, as it were, for the interpretation of Kennedy's presidency and his untimely death. By virtue of the doctrines and ideas they had absorbed, liberal Americans, and especially liberal intellectuals, were wholly unprepared to understand or to interpret Kennedy's assassination. Liberal thinkers in the postwar era were convinced that liberalism provided the only rational doctrine of progress available to the American people. At the same time, they were equally convinced that liberalism was under siege by irrational and atavistic elements in the American polity that would roll back the liberal achievements of previous generations. Kennedy's death, and the way it happened, had a shattering effect on this outlook.

Postwar liberalism, because of the new political context in which it operated, took on a somewhat different tone and emphasis from the Progressive and New Deal movements that preceded it. During the decade of the 1950s, thoughtful liberals came to understand that for the first time they represented the political establishment in the United States. Liberals had been in power for the two eventful decades from 1933 to 1953, and to them went the credit for the domestic experiments of the New Deal, the subsequent victory over fascism in World War II, and the creation of the postwar international order. Liberalism, as a consequence of these achievements, had earned the designation as the public philosophy of the nation. Even Republican leaders, like Dewey, Eisenhower, and Nixon, were obliged to accept the liberal framework of ideas, albeit with the hedge that they could carry it out with greater efficiency. The reformers and critics of the previous generation were now insiders placed in the position of defending their status and the achievements of their movement.

Liberalism, a doctrine of reform, thus began to absorb some of the intellectual characteristics of conservatism—a due regard for tradition and continuity, a sense that progress must be built on the solid achievements of the past, an awareness of the threat of Soviet totalitarianism, and a conviction that its domestic opponents were radicals at war with modernity and bent on undoing the hard-won achievements of the previous decades. Richard Hofstadter, Columbia University's prize-winning historian, expressed this mood very well in *The Age of Reform* (1955), his influential account of the reform movement from the 1890s through the New Deal. "For the first time since the 1880s," he wrote, "there are signs that liberals are beginning to find it both natural and expedient to explore the merits and employ the rhetoric of conservatism. They are far more conscious of those things they would like to preserve than they are of those things they would like to change."[1]

The mood that Hofstadter described called forth a distinctively new chapter in the history of liberal reform that contrasted sharply with the ethos of Progressivism and the New Deal. Both of these earlier movements were confident that they represented the views and interests of a majority of Americans; both sought to mobilize the public against the special interests intent on taking advantage of the common man. The leaders of these movements were all too happy to embrace the labels of liberalism and reform. Woodrow Wilson was proud to call himself a liberal and claimed that liberalism was the philosophy of all thinking men. Roosevelt and Truman said much the same thing. These leaders never found it expedient, in Hofstadter's description of the liberalism of the postwar period, "to explore the merits and employ the rhetoric of conservatism." They accepted, albeit in different degrees, the revised idea of liberalism that developed late in the nineteenth century, which held that, in the struggle for liberty, the conflict between the individual and the state had been replaced by one that pitted the individual against the large corporation and the entrenched political machine. In this new struggle, it was argued, the state was obliged to take the side of the individual and the common man against these new aggregations of power.

The Progressives certainly believed that they spoke for the masses of Americans when they fought the trusts, the bosses, and the special interests that they claimed had insinuated themselves into the machinery of American government. Their reform agenda advanced from two distinct directions. There was, first, the presumption that the influence of special interests could be circumvented by returning power back to the people in the form of the direct primary, initiatives and referenda, and the direct election of United States senators. At the same time, they advocated a host of new regulatory bodies, such as the Food and Drug Administration, the Federal Reserve Board, and the Federal Trade Commission, that would be administered by disinterested experts acting in the public interest. The first reflected a traditional theme in American life according to which nefarious interests had infiltrated the temples of government; the second reflected the reality of new industrial combinations that had to be regulated in the public interest. Thus liberal reformism began a century ago with the paired assumptions that the people must rule but that in many areas they can do so only through the agency of disinterested judges, commissioners, and regulators.[2]

The Progressives were animated, as Hofstadter and others have argued, by a moral impulse that sought to restore the influence in American life of the independent worker, farmer, and businessman, which was being overtaken by the emerging urban political machines, labor unions, and large commercial enterprises. The nation had been built on its faith in the yeoman farmer and the independent worker and businessman, but such individuals acting on their own had little chance to compete successfully against such powerful new combinations. The sense among Progressives that they were trying to shore up the traditional foundations of American democracy gave to their movement a certain crusading and moralistic character. They disdained a politics of interest or faction because of its suggestions of partisanship and corruption. They followed instead a politics of moral uplift with appeals to democracy, law, and disinterested leadership. When the arch-Progressive Woodrow Wilson led the nation to war in 1917 he did so not on the basis of national interest but rather to make the world safe for democracy. As Hofstadter wrote in relation to the moralistic aspects of Progressivism, "It is hardly an accident that the same generation that wanted to bring about direct popular rule, break up the political machines, and circumvent representative government was the same generation that imposed Prohibition on the country and proposed to make the world safe for democracy."[3]

The New Deal, however, introduced a different kind of reform politics to the American scene, one that was less moralistic and more programmatic than Progressivism. The New Deal, in contrast to Progressivism, developed in an atmosphere of profound crisis. Unlike Progressivism, which had friends and foes in both political parties, the New Deal was entirely associated with the Democratic Party, which henceforth became the vehicle for liberal reform in American politics. Because it was a response to crisis, FDR and his supporters were far less interested in process and procedural issues than the Progressives; the New Dealers focused almost entirely on substantive measures that might restore the economy to productive functioning and relieve the distress brought forth by the Depression. President Roosevelt, moreover, established a broad base of popular support for New Deal measures that would guarantee their survival far beyond his time in office. The New Deal represented the working man and encouraged labor unions, while Progressivism was more of a middle-class movement. The New Deal, in contrast to Progressivism, institutionalized itself in government and in the party system. As a consequence, a destructive world war, which killed the spirit of Progressivism in 1918, only augmented the appeal of the New Deal after 1945. In perhaps the most important departure from Progressivism, the New Deal accepted the reality of modern industrial organization and sought to respond to it, not by restoring the influence of the individual farmer, worker, and businessman, but by building a parallel capacity in the national government to regulate and direct it.[4]

The New Deal represented a triumph of party politics and administration and to some extent a fusion of the two impulses that the Progressives had felt to be in tension. Party politics was viewed by the New Deal Democrats as a means of advancing and representing the interests of the broad public rather than as an avenue for corruption, patronage, and special interests. The spirit of New Deal liberalism was more administrative and experimental than moralistic; it sought more to establish new levers of power in the American system than to reinvigorate old ones.

In a matter of a few years, Roosevelt and the Democrats had built the foundations for the American welfare state in the form of old age insurance, bank deposit insurance, securities regulation, collective bargaining for unions, price supports for farmers, welfare for widows and orphans, and much more—all administered through a now vastly enlarged national government. When he was finished with his domestic agenda, Roosevelt next led the nation into a world war against fascist tyranny that ended with the United States as the undisputed leader of the democratic world. Most importantly, Roosevelt and the New Deal, in the minds of many, had saved the liberal order itself from the chaos of the 1930s and the totalitarian ideologies that claimed to own the future. By 1945, liberalism, now identified with the Democratic Party, and personified by FDR, had guided the nation through depression and war, along the way laying the foundations for the welfare state and permanent American participation as the leader of the postwar international order.

Postwar liberals were influenced more by the programmatic

ethos of the New Deal than by the more moralistic and procedural approach of the Progressives. Their champion in politics was FDR rather than Woodrow Wilson. Liberalism was now a philosophy more attuned to the challenges of governance than to those of opposition. It saw in the New Deal something to be defended and preserved, but also a roadway into the future through further acts of reform. Hofstadter put it well when he said that the liberals of the postwar period looked more to things they wished to preserve than to those they wished to change. Critics on the left, by contrast, denounced postwar liberalism (or Cold War liberalism, as they called it) on precisely these grounds as being too pragmatic and technocratic, as placing too much faith in incremental measures of reform as opposed to radical change, as far too detached from the struggles of the workers and the poor, and as inappropriately pre-occupied with communism and the Cold War. In a word, the liberals of the 1950s and early 1960s were "too conservative."[5]

The influence of FDR and the New Deal, along with the hopes and expectations of American liberals at the end of the war, were on display in *The Vital Center* (1949), by Arthur Schlesinger Jr., an early and influential liberal manifesto of the postwar era. Schlesinger's book, written before Joseph McCarthy appeared on the scene, urged a continuation of New Deal liberalism as the most effective alternative to communism abroad and stagnation at home. In his view, big-business conservatism, or "plutocracy" as he called it, had discredited itself in the 1920s because it placed private interests above the public interest, an attitude which led ultimately to the stock market collapse and to the Great Depression. The opposition of business interests to price controls and regulation, he wrote, continued to damn them in the eyes of the average citizen. As a consequence, business-oriented conservatism, with its faith in free markets and individualism, could not hope to govern effectively or win the support of a public that had enthusiastically endorsed the programs of the New Deal. On the left, Progressivism had discred-ited itself because it was soft and sentimental, because it sought to restore ideals now buried in the past, and because it tended to view politics as a stage on which to work out emotional grievances rather than as a means of developing practical programs that might make life better for the masses of citizens. Genuine liberalism, Schlesinger argued, requires both a vision of the possible and a practical sense of how it may be achieved.

Schlesinger's critique of conservatism and progressivism was particularly telling because it pointed in the direction of the kind of practical reform implemented so successfully in the New Deal. He wrote,

> We are changing from a market society to an administrative society; and the problem is which set of administrators is to rule. If the decisions are to be made in a directors' board-room or in a government agency, then the political process permits us a measure of access to a government agency. Big government, for all its dangers, remains democracy's only effective response to big business.[6]

Here Schlesinger, no doubt exaggerating the responsiveness of bureaucracy to popular will, expressed some of the fundamental ideas of New Deal reformism—that large organizations are an inextricable part of modern life, that government must regulate private organizations in the public interest because government is responsive to the will of the public while business organizations are not. This was the "vital center" of American politics, an alternative both to self-interested conservatism and to sentimental progressivism.

Schlesinger's book, it should be acknowledged, contained a powerful denunciation of communism and a condemnation of the Soviet Union as a totalitarian state. Schlesinger left little doubt that he, along with liberals in general, regarded the Soviet Union as a threat to the United States and its allies in Europe. Indeed, writing as the Cold War was beginning, he argued that the Soviet Union, not the United States, was responsible for stirring up tensions. Stalin (as Schlesinger wrote) decided even before World War II was over that the wartime partnership with the West was no longer needed to advance Soviet interests. Soviet occupation of Eastern Europe and the imposition of undemocratic governments in that region were aggressive moves that provoked a reaction in the West, setting the Cold War in motion.[7]

It was the rise of Joseph McCarthy and the anticommunist movement after 1950 that as much as anything else contributed to the new conservative mood among postwar liberals. Schlesinger, because he wrote his book immediately after the war and before McCarthy burst onto the scene, wrote with a sense of optimism about the American public and its continued support for liberal initiatives. He could not foresee the implications of McCarthy and the anticommunist movement for the ethos of postwar liberalism. McCarthy, because of his obvious popular support, demonstrated plainly that liberalism was vulnerable to populist attacks and that, indeed, liberalism was not necessarily the preferred philosophy of the masses after all (as Schlesinger and other New Dealers thought it was). The accepted wisdom of the previous generation had now reversed itself: liberalism was about to become the doctrine of the elites and the establishment, while the masses of Americans seemed to be animated by reactionary impulses. The challenge to postwar liberalism was to make sense of this reversal while maintaining its democratic ideals.

McCarthy came to public attention with his famous speech at Wheeling, West Virginia, in early 1950, when he declared that he held a list of 205 employees of the State Department who were members of the Communist Party—a number that he would repeatedly change and adjust in subsequent weeks and months in response to demands for evidence to document his accusations. McCarthy's speech, which created a national sensation, came just weeks after the former State Department official and devoted New Dealer Alger Hiss had been convicted of perjury for denying in sworn congressional testimony that he had known Whittaker Chambers as a member of the communist underground during the 1930s. Hiss's conviction, along with revelations by various ex-communists of Soviet espionage activities in the United States, provided ammunition for McCarthy's claim that communism was advancing in the world because it had been aided and abetted by traitors in our own government. McCarthy said in his speech:

> The reason we find ourselves in a position of impotency is not because our powerful enemy has sent men to invade our shores but rather because of the traitorous actions of those who have been treated so well by this nation. It has not been the less fortunate or members of minority groups who have been traitorous to this nation, but rather those who have had all the benefits that the wealthiest nation on earth has to offer, the finest homes, the finest college education and the finest jobs in government we can give.[8]

With this stroke, McCarthy turned the tables on the liberals and progressives who had earlier made political headway by attacking "special interests" and "malefactors of great wealth" in the name of an aroused and outraged public. The liberals had viewed themselves as spokesmen for the common man, seeking to improve his condition through government action, but the rise of McCarthy confused matters considerably. Now McCarthy himself sought to turn the wrath of the people against the liberal veterans of the New Deal who, he claimed, had looked the other way as communists infiltrated the government. With these attacks McCarthy and other anticommunists were able to steal the mantle of populism from the liberal New Dealers. Their targets, as Daniel Bell later wrote, were elite groups like "intellectuals, Harvard, Anglophiles, internationalists, and the Army."[9]

From this point forward through the 1950s and into the 1960s, liberals were aware that their most pressing challenges came, not from the far left at home or from communism abroad, but rather from the far right at home in the form of anticommunist extremism and allied causes, including especially Protestant fundamentalism and religious and racial bigotry. Such movements seemed to represent, in the context of the time, a collection of forces that might easily overwhelm the liberal establishment and perhaps even begin to repeal the landmark legislation of the New Deal era. In the minds of some, the tactics and rhetoric of these extremists threatened the democratic order itself. According to Bell, "the ideology of the right wing in America threatens the politics of civility. Its commitment and methods threaten to disrupt the fragile consensus that underlies the American political system." While most Americans at the time believed that the greatest threats to the nation came from the Soviet Union and international communism, the liberals argued for something altogether different–that the fundamental challenge to liberal institutions came from extremists on the right. Though this was something of an overreaction to McCarthy and his allies (as became clear later by the collapse of the far right in the 1960s), it nonetheless reflected an awareness of real threats and vulnerabilities.

The danger arose because right-wing spokesmen deployed the incendiary rhetoric of "treason" and "betrayal" to rouse the population against New Deal policies and necessary accommodations with the Soviet Union. Adlai Stevenson, a favorite of liberals because of his facility with ideas and the spoken word, described during the 1952 campaign the paradoxical situation in which liberals now found themselves:

> The strange alchemy of time has somehow converted the Democrats into the truly conservative party in the country–the party dedicated to conserving all that is best and building solidly and safely on these foundations. The Republicans, by contrast, are behaving like the radical party–the party of the reckless and embittered bent on dismantling institutions which have been built solidly into our social fabric. . . .[10]

Stevenson's astute observation reflected the awareness among liberals that they now had a responsibility to defend the institutions and policies their movement had built. There was also the strong implication in these comments, and in liberal writings of the period, that there existed no rational opposition to liberalism–that such opposition as did exist was irrational, extremist, and delusional.

The liberal movement was fortunate to have had during this time a group of intellectual spokesmen whose output in the form of influential books and articles compares favorably with any previous generation of thinkers in the United States, with the exception of the founding fathers. Richard Hofstadter and Daniel Bell, who have already been mentioned, but also Louis Hartz, Lionel Trilling, David Riesman, Arthur Schlesinger Jr., Seymour Martin Lipset—these were the writers who shaped the new liberalism and sought to adapt it to its new circumstances. All wrote or edited important books that contributed to the repositioning of American liberalism as a doctrine of continuity, tradition, and practical reform. Most were academics. One thus finds in their writings an effort to use the theories of historians and social scientists to make sense of their immediate situation. Their persistent focus was on the dangers to the nation, as they saw them, arising from the American right. In contrast to their Progressive and New Deal predecessors, who thought mainly in terms of change, reform, and new policy, these writers focused more on consolidating earlier gains, defending them against new challenges, and reconciling their ideas with the American democratic tradition.

Hartz, a professor of government at Harvard University, offered the most comprehensive statement of the revised liberal outlook in his 1955 book, *The Liberal Tradition in America*, which argued that the American nation was built around liberal assumptions and that, moreover, these are the only ideals Americans really know or understand. Hartz thus emphasized the broad consensus around liberal ideals that shaped the development of the American nation, in contrast to the Progressive historians, like Charles Beard and Frederick Jackson Turner, who saw the conflict between democracy and capitalism as the animating source of national development and progress. The use of the term "tradition" in the title was deliberate, as it implied that there was also a conservative dimension to liberalism.[11]

Hartz's consensus theory of American politics, as it was called, was built upon the historical fact that the United States lacked a feudal background such as in Europe gave rise to class divisions and ideological conflict. The United States, by contrast, was "born free," as Tocqueville had observed, with neither a privileged aristocracy nor a powerful established church. There was thus no need here for a bloody revolution to demolish aristocratic privilege, as occurred in France, England, and elsewhere. America had its own revolution, to be sure, but it was a liberal revolution that reiterated principles about which nearly everyone agreed. As a consequence, Americans inherited liberal ideals as a kind of birthright without having had to fight for them. Since there was little opposition to these ideals, they advanced here in isolation from the forces that challenged and inhibited them in Europe.

This unique historical background created a polity that enjoyed a near universal consensus around the liberal ideas of liberty, private property, and representative government. Yet at the same time, Americans were prone to a loss of perspective owing to their isolation from conflicting philosophies or ideologies. This meant to Hartz and others that Americans were inclined to moralism in politics, precisely because they understood their ideals as universal moral imperatives that cannot be legitimately opposed. Such moralism, they pointed out, can be dangerous or self-defeating when it leads to a phenomenon like McCarthyism or to conflicting urges either to withdraw from the world (as in isolationism) or to declare war against it (as in efforts to "roll back" communism).[12]

It followed from Hartz's thesis that the United States lacked an authentic conservative tradition that might be called upon to restrain radical impulses from the right. Without a feudal tradition, Hartz said, America also lacked a true conservatism of the kind found in Europe, which defended established institutions in the name of continuity and experience. (For the same reason, the United States similarly lacked a class-based socialist movement as found in Europe.) Conservatism, Hartz argued, had no genuine roots in American history and culture, and therefore had little chance of building substantial popular appeal. In America, therefore, attacks on liberalism tended to be radical or populist in nature, rather than conservative in the traditional sense. This is why attacks on liberalism from religious fundamentalists and anticommunists like

McCarthy had a radical or an extremist character that showed little regard either for the practicality of their proposals or for the give-and-take that is essential to democratic politics. Moreover, the rhetoric and literature of the far right came from those who felt weak and dispossessed by modern life, not from groups in possession of power and authority who had traditionally carried the conservative point of view. It was, as Hofstadter wrote, "a literature of resentment, profoundly anti-establishment in its impulses."

Daniel Bell referred to this collection of forces as the "radical right" and, indeed, employed this term as the title of a book of essays that he edited on the subject.[13] Hofstadter, in one of his essays from the period later collected in that book, preferred the term "pseudo-conservative," which he borrowed from Theodore Adorno, the German sociologist, to describe those "who employ the rhetoric of conservatism, [but] show signs of a serious and restless dissatisfaction with American life, traditions, and institutions. They have little in common with the temperate and compromising spirit of true conservatism in the classical sense of the word." Hofstadter went on to say of the pseudo-conservatives that "their political reactions express rather a profound if largely unconscious hatred of our society and its ways—a hatred one would hesitate to impute to them if one did not have suggestive clinical evidence."[14] If liberalism defined the American creed, as Hartz and others suggested, then the pseudo-conservatives, by their overwrought attacks on liberal traditions, were guilty of a right-wing form of anti-Americanism.

The far right, Hofstadter and Bell reminded us, developed out of the politics of prosperity rather than from depression or stagnation. The politics of the 1950s was something far different from the politics of the 1930s. "During depressions," Hofstadter wrote, "the dominant motif in dissent takes expression in proposals for reform or in panaceas. Dissent then tends to be highly programmatic. It is also future oriented and forward looking in that it looks to a time when the adoption of this or that program will materially alleviate or eliminate discontents." On the other hand, in times of prosperity when status politics becomes more important, "there is a tendency to embody discontent not so much in legislative proposals as in grousing. . . . Therefore, it is the tendency of status politics to be expressed more in vindictiveness, in sour memories, in the search for scapegoats than in realistic proposals for positive action."[15] Status politics is often irrational in that it involves the projection into the political world of private and personal anxieties that cannot be relieved by the implementation of any practical program. There was thus in this analysis the suggestion that there was something else bothering the radical rightists other than the concerns they expressed about communists in government and U.S. policy toward the Soviet Union and international communism.

Hofstadter argued that the radical right was a product of the "rootlessness" of American life and the constant movement of Americans from place to place and up and down the ladders of class and status.[16] Where people are uncertain of their status in the community or fear that they and the cultural groups to which they belong are losing status to other groups, they are prone to blame their situation on powerful symbols like "the establishment" or "Wall Street bankers." Supporters of the radical right, he suggested, are those who are most uncertain of their status in a changing society or who fear that they are losing out to new groups that have more recently appeared on the scene. Bell argued along similar lines, suggesting that support for the far right came from "the dispossessed"–that is, the "old middle class" of farmers and small-town businessmen whose values predominated in the nineteenth century but which in the twentieth century came under relentless attack by modern trends such as industrialization, immigration, the rise of the welfare state, and the erosion of religious convictions.[17] Viewed from this perspective, it appeared that the real grievance of the far right was with modernity itself.

The postwar historians saw a link running back from the radical right of the 1950s to other extremist movements in the American past, such as the Know-Nothings of the 1850s, the Populists of the 1890s, the Ku Klux Klan in the 1920s, and the followers of Huey Long and Father Coughlin in the 1930s. All these, argued Hofstadter, Bell, and others, were a product of the dynamism and endless movement of American life that produces a new array of winners and losers every generation or so. Here was a novel historical interpretation, one put forth most convincingly by Hofstadter in *The Age of Reform* but also developed in some of the essays in *The Radical Right*—the claim that extremist groups in American life, whether expressing left- or right-wing ideas, arise in response to challenges to their status caused by the forward movement of American life.[18] Such movements, while developing out of different conditions, had some obvious features in common: in particular, the conviction that their people had been "sold out" by a conspiracy of Wall Street financiers, traitors in the government, or some other sinister group. Such conspiracies are put forward as a ready-made explanation for the loss of status and influence in society. As Bell put it in his introductory essay in *The Radical Right*, "The theme of conspiracy haunts the mind of the radical rightist."[19] This conspiratorial cast of mind, he argued, accounted for the central delusion of McCarthy and the anticommunists—the belief that communism is not merely an external threat to the United States but a grave domestic threat as well.

This thought—the notion that the far right was unhinged from reality—was developed most memorably in Hofstadter's influential article, "The Paranoid Style in American Politics," published in *Harper's* magazine in 1964 but based on a lecture he delivered at Oxford University in 1963 just days before Kennedy was assassinated. The concept of the "paranoid style" seems to have seeped into our political lexicon to the point where it is applied to any number of exaggerated or hyperbolic statements or accusations. Hofstadter, however, tried to capture a broader phenomenon that he saw at work in the rhetoric of the radical right. He was impressed not simply with the wilder statements emanating from such quarters (for example, the claim by the head of the John Birch Society that President Eisenhower was a communist or that Senator Robert Taft, who died of cancer, was actually killed by a radium tube placed in his Senate chair), but by a style of argument that seemed to begin with feelings of persecution and concluded with a recital of grandiose plots against the nation and its way of life. Communism was, of course, a common theme in the rhetoric of the far right, but Hofstadter cited also paranoid fears about fluoride in the drinking water, efforts to control the sale of guns, federal aid to education, and other (usually) liberal initiatives. The paranoid style is one that is inclined to believe in plots and conspiracies as explanations for complex phenomena.[20] The paranoid mind is one that is predisposed to see the world in terms of conspiracies.

The exemplars of the paranoid style, men like McCarthy, Joseph Welch of the Birch Society, and the fundamentalist ministers heard over the radio, may not have seemed irrational to the casual observer because they documented their theories with impressive arsenals of facts and footnotes, which gave a patina of respectability to their accusations of treason and betrayal. "The entire right wing movement of our time," Hofstadter wrote, "is a parade of experts, study groups, monographs, footnotes, and bibliographies."[21] Yet, as he argued, such recitals of facts, statistics, and expert judgments were always accompanied at some point in the far-right narratives by leaps of imagination that brought together apparently disparate events into the form of vast and sinister conspiracies. Though there are conspiracies in history, Hofstadter acknowledged, the paranoid style is one that views conspiracy as the driving force of history. From this standpoint, then, it seems entirely reasonable to ask questions like "Who lost China?" or "Who sold out Eastern Europe?" Important events never happen through coincidence, circumstance, or the unfolding of complex processes, but by the will of some malevolent power.

With this analysis, Hofstadter brought to the surface some assumptions that had long been implicit in the liberal assessment of the far right—namely, that it represented a form of lunacy or irrationality that is best understood in psychological or sociological terms rather than as an ideology or a point of view that might be challenged by rational argument. Unfortunately, in the revised version of his lecture that appeared in *Harper's* after the 1964 election, Hofstadter described Barry Goldwater and his conservative followers as contemporary manifestations of the paranoid style, thereby bringing the Republican Party and the conservative movement generally under indictment for irrationality and paranoia.[22] If this was in fact a valid observation (which it was not), then it followed that any opposition to the liberal worldview was irrational at best, and possibly delusional and dangerous.

Hofstadter's essay is an illustration of the preoccupation of the postwar liberals with "the politics of irrationality" or, put differently, with the dark underside of political life. The triumph of fascism in Europe in the 1920s and 1930s had left a pronounced imprint on their political outlook, as did the rise of McCarthyism and the radical right in the United States after the war. Such examples proved clearly enough, to their minds anyway, that the great challenge to liberal democratic life came not so much from competing ideologies framed in rational terms, but rather from irrational and emotional forces turned loose in the arena of politics.

Hofstadter developed this theme further in another influential book of the period, *Anti-Intellectualism in American Life* (1964), in which he argued that American culture has been consistently hostile to intellectuals and the life of the mind, and that such prejudices have had unwelcome political consequences, most particularly in persistent efforts in the past to mandate conformity, to shut down dissent, or to emphasize practicality at the expense of academic learning.[23] If the Progressive historians had viewed American history as a continuing battle between capitalism and democracy, Hofstadter and his liberal colleagues portrayed a different kind of conflict, one in which the national psyche was divided between a commitment to liberal rationality on the one side and the temptation to engage in emotional and counterproductive tantrums on the other. At different times in our past, they tried to show, one or another of these tendencies has temporarily gained the upper hand, producing a cyclical pattern in which periods of reform are followed by periods of reaction, much of it driven by resentment or irrational yearnings.

Having framed the issues in this way, the postwar liberals came to view ideological thinking, whether of the left or of the right, as an expression of the irrational in politics and thus as something to be discouraged and criticized. Bell made this case most explicitly in an essay titled "The End of Ideology in the West," the final chapter of a book of essays suitably subtitled "On the Exhaustion of Political Ideas in the 1950s." Here he argued that the ideological alternatives to liberal capitalism had been discredited by the horrifying realities of Hitlerism and Soviet communism. The radical passions of the previous generation had been spent in the failed enthusiasms of the 1930s. They could not now be revived except in new and completely different forms. Politics would henceforth proceed according to a more mundane and orderly path defined by the assumptions of postwar liberalism. "In the Western world," Bell wrote, "there is rough consensus among intellectuals on political issues: the acceptance of the welfare state; the desirability of decentralized power; a system of mixed economy and political pluralism."[24] He dismissed socialism and communism as serious alternatives to liberalism, along with those who said that the welfare state placed us on "the road to serfdom," a pointed reference to Friedrich von Hayek's critique of socialism and the welfare state from a free-market point of view. The liberal framework thus seemed to define the boundaries both of the possible and of the rational in politics.

There was, however, a disquieting aspect to the postwar situation for, as Bell and others suggested, the end of ideology meant that politics would now become a rather boring affair, reduced to questions centering on the minimum wage, old age pensions, the price of bread and milk, and the like. Such an agenda, he recognized, cannot provide a unifying appeal to those who seek more from politics than stability, incremental reforms, and material progress. Affluence and prosperity had changed the focus of intellectual criticism from economics and class conflict, the paramount issues of the 1930s, to concerns about cultural issues that do not lend themselves to political solutions. Here he had in mind issues relating to mass taste, conformism, and relations between the sexes. The very success of liberalism in overcoming basic economic conflicts might, paradoxically, lead to new expressions of the radical impulse centering on cultural questions that had hitherto been kept out of the political arena.

Notwithstanding the skepticism of the postwar liberals regarding the popular mind, the liberal reformers from the Progressive era through the postwar period generally accepted an American version of what Herbert Butterfield called "the Whig interpretation of history"–the idea that history is a tale of steady progress in the direction of liberty and democracy. He referred to those British historians of the nineteenth and twentieth centuries who tended "to write on the side of Protestants and Whigs, to praise revolutions provided they have been successful, to emphasize certain principles of progress in the past and to produce a story which is the ratification if not the glorification of the present." The Whig historian, according to Butterfield, sets himself up as the arbiter of past controversies, identifying winners and losers according to their roles in bringing about the present state of affairs. Orwell wrote that this approach to history encourages a complacent attitude toward the present and the future. "Nourished for hundreds of years on a literature in which Right invariably triumphs in the last chapter," he wrote in one of his wartime essays, "we believe half-instinctively that evil always defeats itself in the long run." The belief that everything turns out all right in the end takes away from the past much of its genuine complexity and open-endedness. Things might have turned out differently–and they yet may.[25]

The Progressives, as we have noted, viewed American history as a continuing battle between the forces of democracy and those of capitalism, while the postwar liberals tended to emphasize the enduring struggle between liberalism and the counterproductive and irrational responses to its successes. It may be true (as Butterfield suggested) that the Whig interpretation, and variations on its themes, represents an ideological view of the past in that it takes sides on past controversies in favor of those whose positions point toward the present. Yet, even as this is so, it is also true that every modern political movement has developed its own view of history in order to identify itself as the crucial link between past and future. This is as true of liberalism as it is of Marxism or conservatism—all doctrines which understand the past in terms of their unique struggles, whether on behalf of liberty, or the proletariat, or religious authority. Butterfield makes a case for dispassionate and objective history that does not take sides on the great controversies in the past and avoids association with any of the present political parties or interests. His advice, though often cited, is most difficult to follow, not simply because historians have political biases, but because political movements have need of their own distinctive histories. In America, as in England, history as often as not has found itself placed in the service of political parties or social movements.

It has been observed elsewhere that many of the leading theorists of the reform tradition were historians who sought to place that tradition in a historical context, thereby lending it greater legitimacy and momentum. Progressivism, though focused on political reform, developed its own version of the American past that focused on the emerging commercial forces that it sought to understand and control. The rise of Progressivism as a political movement was greatly aided by the work of an influential group of Progressive historians, led by such luminaries as Charles Beard, Frederick Jackson Turner, and Vernon Louis Parrington, who (in Hofstadter's words) "moved the thinking of American historians . . . into the controversial world of the new century and into the intellectual orbit of the Progressive movement."[26] During the 1940s, Schlesinger weighed in with a book on Andrew Jackson, described by Hofstadter as the final important work of the Progressive tradition, which portrayed Jackson's administration as a forerunner to the New Deal. This was perhaps as good a case as one might find of a reform-minded historian reading the assumptions of the present into the past.[27] Jackson, though certainly a populist reformer, was also a representative of the Southern slave interest, an advocate of states' rights and *laissez faire*, and a foe of Henry Clay's American System—and thus a highly imperfect model for Roosevelt's New Deal. Schlesinger's main purpose in this volume, and indeed in much of the rest of his historical portfolio, was to make a case for the Democratic Party as the instrument of popular reform in America dating back to its origins in the time of Jefferson and Madison. Republicans and, before them, the Whigs were viewed as representatives of business interests and the status quo. Schlesinger's view of Democrats and Republicans was not far removed from the stance of the Whig historians toward the Whigs and the Tories.

Postwar liberalism was just as well represented by eminent historians, among them Hofstadter, Hartz, and Schlesinger, to name just a few. Hofstadter understood the link between history and reform better than most, for one of his finest books was *The Progressive Historians*, a critical appraisal of the historical writings of Beard, Turner, and Parrington, and more generally a reflection on the relationship between politics and the writing of history.[28] Hofstadter acknowledged, both in *The Age of Reform* and in *Anti-Intellectualism in American Life*, that his interpretations of the American past were tinctured by the preoccupations of the 1950s—in particular, the threat from the radical right. Given his description of Goldwater as a manifestation of the paranoid style in American politics, Hofstadter was every bit as committed as Schlesinger to the view that the Democrats are the party of progress in American life and the Republicans the party of reaction. On this point, Hofstadter and Schlesinger spoke for many historians, as well as for postwar liberals in general.

It is something of an irony that such a forward-looking movement as modern liberalism should have been so preoccupied with the past and not a little surprising that its most articulate proponents should have been historians. Their writings reinforced the sense that liberalism was the party of ideas and of the thinking man (and woman), while conservatism was, in the famous words of John Stuart Mill, "the stupid party," or at least, as Hofstadter suggested, the party of anti-intellectualism. The identification of liberalism with intellect reached a culmination following the election of John F. Kennedy to the presidency, for it now seemed that at last a genuine intellectual occupied the White House. Like other liberal con-

ceptions, this one, too, was profoundly challenged by the tragic
events of November 22, 1963.

The liberal thinkers of the 1950s and early 1960s sought to establish their outlook as at once the authoritative liberal *and* conservative position in national politics. This was done, admittedly, through
a certain amount of scholarly legerdemain that ignored real conservative arguments from the likes of Russell Kirk and William F.
Buckley Jr., or by reducing opposing points of view to absurdity by
rendering them in sociological or psychological terms. There was
also a certain irony in their position, as Peter Viereck, the conservative writer and poet, pointed out in a 1955 essay: "The intellectual
liberals who twenty years ago wanted to pack the Supreme Court
as frustrating the will of the masses and who were quoting Charles
Beard to show that the Constitution is a mere rationalization of economic loot—these same liberals are today hugging for dear life that
same court and that same Constitution."[29] The attempted merger
of liberal ideals with conservative methods represented a novel
synthesis in American political thinking. Also new was the idea
that the challenge to liberalism came from irrational elements in
the society, as opposed to capitalists or "special interests." If the
postwar liberals did not entirely succeed in the combative world of
electoral politics, they did very well in the intellectual arena, where
their writings were greatly influential among academics and journalists.

Accompanying the rise of liberalism over the first six decades of
the twentieth century was a countermovement of social radicalism
that had little resonance among the broad public but found adherents among the intellectual and academic classes, and in many
instances among the idle rich. Christopher Lasch called this the
"new radicalism" to distinguish it from the "old" radicalisms of
socialism, anarchism, or extreme individualism.[30] The new radicals owed their intellectual debt more to Freud and Jung than to
nineteenth-century radicals like Marx or Mill, and they identified

the main source of human oppression as lying neither in capitalism nor in any specific acts of tyranny, but rather in the human psyche itself as it was shaped or "socialized" by the wider culture. "The new radicalism differed from the old," Lasch wrote, "in its interest in questions which lay outside the realm of conventional politics. It was no longer his political allegiance alone which distinguished the radical from the conservative. What characterized the person of advanced opinions in the first two decades of the twentieth century—and what by and large continues to characterize him at the present time—was his position with regard to such issues as childhood, education, and sex; sex above all."[31]

The new radicals, from their first appearance early in the last century down to the present time, were preoccupied with liberation—liberation of the child from the restraints of family and conventional schooling, liberation of women from the demands of family and conventional living, liberation of sexual impulses from old-fashioned morality, liberation above all of the human unconscious from the oppressive demands of modern civilization. Among the key figures in this movement were men and women like Randolph Bourne, John Dewey, and Jane Addams from the early part of the century to writers like Norman Mailer, Allen Ginsberg, and the Beat poets in the 1950s and 1960s. The new radicals could not have cared less about run-of-the-mill political issues such as tariffs, taxes, and old age pensions; they moved into politics in order to transform education, the family, religion, relations between the sexes, and attitudes toward life generally. They were preoccupied, in short, with what today we call "cultural politics."

These were the people Schlesinger dismissed because they were sentimental and ineffective and whom other liberals (like Hofstadter) criticized as utopian and contemptuous of the beliefs and attitudes of the common man—all observations which were undoubtedly true. The new radicals, on the other hand, attacked liberalism on opposite grounds—that is, as lacking in vision, as shoring up the status quo through incremental reforms, as too pragmatic to affect far-reaching changes, as too boring to command the interest of creative men and women. If liberals like Hofstadter sought to contain or suppress the irrational element in politics, the new radicals were eager to liberate it for the greater good of human happiness. The liberals held the upper hand on the radicals for the greater part of this period, only to see their respective positions reversed in the 1960s. Naturally, the radicals did not like the Kennedys either, though they would seize on his assassination as an instrument for discrediting the liberals.

Lionel Trilling, the great literary critic and contemporary of Hofstadter, Bell, Schlesinger, and the other postwar liberals, articulated a thoughtful critique of liberalism from the "inside," as it were, from the standpoint of one who was himself a liberal. Trilling wrote, in his introduction to *The Liberal Imagination*, that liberalism in America is prone to brittleness both because of its universality in America and because of its highly programmatic emphasis. There is, on the one hand, no genuine opposition to liberal assumptions in America such as in other countries gives toughness and determination to liberal doctrine as a consequence of disappointment and occasional defeat. Liberalism, moreover, because of its programmatic focus and a near exclusive emphasis on politics, lacks an imaginative dimension that might give it a better sense of the richness and complexity of life. Here Trilling cited an epigraph used by Coleridge as an introduction to the *Rime of the Ancient Mariner*, which implies that it is good that human beings contemplate invisible beings in the universe "lest the intellect, habituated to the trivia of daily life, may contract itself too much and wholly sink into trifles." The point here is not that we should believe in demons, spirits, and fairy tales, but that, as Trilling wrote, "the world is a complex and unexpected and terrible place which is not always to be understood by the mind as we use it in our everyday tasks." Liberalism rejects as false and irrational the old myths and fairy tales that in traditional societies spurred the imagination and supplied meaning and perspective to an unpredictable world. Because liberalism is committed to a rational view of the world, it does not follow that the world must always cooperate.[32]

Trilling's criticism of liberalism was far different in implication from that lodged against it by the various spokesmen (and spokeswomen) for the new radicalism who dreamed of using the imagination as a means of expanding the scope of political life beyond the confines of reformist liberalism. Trilling, who had little sympathy with the ambitious cultural agenda of the new radicals, saw in the imagination a means of bringing perspective to political liberalism by encouraging an appreciation of the complexity of life and the genuine difficulty of changing its terms by political means. Trilling hoped that this imaginative dimension formerly encouraged by myth might now be supplied through art and literature, particularly the novel, which in contrast to political manifestos can portray life in its richness and variety. The essential task of literature is to serve as a corrective to, rather than an expression of, liberal aspirations. The task of the writer and critic, Trilling argued, was "to recall liberalism to its first essential imagination of variousness and possibility, which implies the awareness of complexity and difficulty."[33] Liberalism, he suggested, had become too formulaic, perhaps too worldly, and rather more optimistic about the future than was justified by the real conditions of life. Liberalism, moreover, because of its optimism and the complacency induced by the absence of any genuine opposition to its intellectual assumptions, lacked a sense of tragedy that might help see it through times of difficulty. Liberalism, he suggested with an unusual degree of prescience, was not immune to human tragedy, and he feared that its assumptions may prove too brittle to survive it.

TWO · KENNEDY

IN NOVEMBER OF 1963, as John F. Kennedy prepared for the election campaign of 1964, his approval ratings in the polls hovered around 60 percent, certainly an encouraging sign for his re-election prospects.[1] At the same time, Victor Lasky's broadside against the president, *J.F.K.: The Man and the Myth*, reached the top of the bestseller lists. This book contrasted Kennedy's carefully crafted image of competence and idealism with the actual man, whom Lasky said was shallow, immature, and untrustworthy. Widely read though it was, Lasky's book failed to dent Kennedy's popularity and quickly disappeared from the bestseller lists after the assassination. Stories that came out later about Kennedy's conduct in the White House suggested that Lasky was more right than wrong in his assessment. Nevertheless, the gulf between the man and the myth was magnified many times over following Kennedy's assassination.[2]

Lasky was on target with his main point: John F. Kennedy, with the assistance of his family and loyal associates, paid careful attention to promoting an image of himself that did not necessarily accord with reality. He did so—and they did so—out of the conviction that the public mind attaches itself more readily to images and symbols

than to facts. Numerous Kennedy biographers, following Lasky's
lead, have documented the wide gulf between the popular imagery
of John F. Kennedy and his actual conduct in public office. Yet, as
public opinion polls have shown, President Kennedy remains highly
popular with the American people even as scholars and historians
increasingly discount his importance and influence as a political
leader. Indeed, a Gallup Poll taken in early 2000 revealed that
Americans ranked Kennedy as the "greatest president ever," with
Abraham Lincoln and Franklin Delano Roosevelt coming in second and third.[3]

"Grief nourishes myth," as one of Kennedy's aides later wrote
about the legends that had grown up around the assassinated president.[4] A profoundly sorrowful event, such as the death of a young
leader, nourishes efforts to keep him alive as a cultural ideal. In this
way he becomes an inspiration for others and a standard against
which aspiring leaders are measured. Kennedy, of course, was a real
person, and a contemporary one at that, and thus an awkward subject for myth or legend. Too much was known about the real Kennedy to allow the mythic Kennedy to grow unchecked. In addition,
his violent death was a potent reminder, as Trilling had said, that
"the world is a complex and unexpected and terrible place." Kennedy
in life was held up as a standard of excellence and achievement,
but no one could ignore the fact that his death demonstrated how
ugly, unpredictable, and unfair the world could be. If some looked
to Kennedy as a source of inspiration, others looked on his death as
a reason for despair. Often these conflicting emotions were opera-
tive in the same people.

After his death, Kennedy was soon portrayed by family loyalists
as something of a liberal hero who (had he lived) might have led
the nation into a new age of peace, justice, and understanding. This
was one of the central themes that developed in the years following
the assassination. This portrayal was encouraged by tributes and
memorials inspired by Jacqueline Kennedy and friends and other
family members of the slain president, and by numerous books
published after the assassination, particularly those by presidential
aides Arthur Schlesinger Jr. and Theodore Sorensen, both of whom

portrayed the fallen president as the brightest star of the time and a leader impossible to replace. Sorensen wrote that Kennedy was the equal of any of our earlier presidents. Schlesinger went further to say that "He re-established the republic as the first generation of our founders saw it—young, brave, civilized, rational, gay, tough, questing, exultant in the excitement and potentiality of history."[5] There was a sense in these tributes that the loss of John F. Kennedy had deprived the nation and the world of a new beginning.

This sentimental and overstated image, an understandable byproduct of the grief felt by those close to Kennedy, must have gnawed at Lyndon Johnson, who felt with good reason that his own record of liberal legislative victories dwarfed anything that Kennedy might have been able to achieve. Johnson believed that he had in fact earned the mantle that had been granted posthumously to JFK. Such feelings of resentment merely demonstrated how far out of touch Johnson was with the evolving liberal ethos that had been redefined in the 1960s both by Kennedy and by his shocking assassination. Johnson was a practitioner of the old liberalism at the moment it was being overtaken by the new.

Kennedy, through his life and death, had somehow managed to change the terms of American liberalism from a doctrine of programmatic reform with an emphasis on economic security and national defense to one of cultural change and criticism with an emphasis on liberation and the reform of traditional morals and ways of living. It was in this latter sense that Kennedy came to be viewed, albeit unintentionally on his part, as a liberal visionary and path-breaker, more as a revolutionary cultural figure than, like FDR, as an architect of new policies. The rapidly shifting standards of American liberalism in the 1960s quickly turned Kennedy into a heroic figure at the same time that they made old-style reformers like Johnson and Hubert Humphrey look like boring and tiresome politicians. Kennedy became a liberal prophet because he changed the character of liberalism and helped create new standards according to which he and other leaders were subsequently judged.

Thus it was that veteran politicians who knew Kennedy well and who had followed his career over the preceding two decades, including most especially opponents like Johnson, Humphrey, and Richard Nixon, were taken by surprise by the postmortem tributes to President Kennedy as the inspirational symbol of American liberalism, since neither his career leading up to the presidency nor his actual achievements in office seemed to justify this particular designation. Kennedy was viewed during the 1950s, and even after he was elected to the presidency, as more of a pragmatic and moderate liberal who worked cautiously to extend the legacy of the New Deal without getting too far out in front of public opinion. He was, as he said at the time, "a liberal without illusions," a practical more than a sentimental liberal, whose thinking was very much in tune with the mood expressed by intellectuals like Hofstadter, Schlesinger, and other of the postwar liberals.

There were good reasons why liberal Democrats like Hubert Humphrey, Adlai Stevenson, Harry Truman, and Eleanor Roosevelt, along with liberal interest groups like the Americans for Democratic Action, should have been skeptical about Kennedy's candidacy when the 1960 campaign began. Kennedy had not distinguished himself as a leader of any important liberal causes during his years in Congress, and indeed he usually went out of his way to avoid any such associations. He was known to be friendly to Joseph McCarthy and Richard Nixon—both hated foes in the eyes of liberals at the time. Liberals (with good reason) distrusted Kennedy's father. In his campaigns, moreover, Kennedy carefully positioned himself so as to make it difficult for voters or anyone else to pin him down as either a liberal or a conservative—a tactic designed to highlight his attractive looks and personality.

At times Kennedy disdained the label "liberal" altogether, preferring to say that he was simply "a Democrat." In 1953, in an article in the *Saturday Evening Post*, he was quoted as saying, in response to criticisms of his record, "I'd be very happy to tell them that I'm not a liberal at all. . . . I'm not comfortable with those people." *Time* magazine in 1957 said that he was in many ways a conservative, while *Newsweek* reported at about the same time that he was "an authentic moderate."[6] Herbert Hoover called Kennedy his "favorite" senator. During his tenure in the House and the Senate, Kennedy failed to lead the charge for any important piece of reformist legislation. As a senator, he avoided taking strong positions on the civil rights proposals of that era for fear of antagonizing -southern colleagues.[7] Lasky writes that when in 1957 the liberal Americans for Democratic Action gave Kennedy a highly favorable rating on the votes he had cast in the Senate, he went well out of his way to explain that the ADA's ranking was inaccurate and that he was in truth one of the more moderate members of the Senate.[8] It was left to other political figures like Humphrey and (to a lesser extent) Stevenson to carry the banner of crusading liberalism during the 1950s. The transformation of Kennedy's reputation following his death was thus all the more remarkable because so many aspects of his actual career pointed in a different direction altogether.

An important sticking point for liberals, aside from his legislative record, was Kennedy's association with Senator McCarthy, who had been a friend of the Kennedy family since he and John F. Kennedy were elected to Congress together in 1946. The new senator from Wisconsin was a frequent guest in Kennedy's Georgetown home during those early terms in Congress, and occasionally even dated one of the Kennedy sisters. A few years later when McCarthy emerged as the leader of the anticommunist cause, Kennedy flatly refused to criticize his methods. Kennedy's father, a devoted anticommunist himself, applauded McCarthy's efforts to remove communists (and their sympathizers) from government service. The elder Kennedy contributed financially to McCarthy's re-election campaign in 1952, perhaps (as Lasky and others have suggested) as a way to discourage the popular McCarthy from coming into Massachusetts to campaign on behalf of Senator Henry Cabot Lodge, John F. Kennedy's Republican opponent in the 1952 Senate race. Following the 1952 election, in which both Kennedy and McCarthy were victorious, McCarthy hired Robert F. Kennedy as his staff counsel on the Senate Permanent Committee on Investigations. In 1954, when McCarthy faced censure from his

Senate colleagues, Kennedy was able to duck the vote because at that time he was recovering from back surgery in a New York hospital.[9]

Kennedy was a target of criticism from liberals because of his apparent support for McCarthy, or at least for his reluctance to condemn McCarthy's methods, and for ducking the vote on censure. A few years later, after McCarthy's censure, Kennedy tried to explain his position in terms of his family's personal relationships with the Wisconsin senator. When pressed by a reporter on this point in 1956, Kennedy said, "You must remember that my father was a friend of Joe's, as was my sister, Eunice, and my brother Bobby worked for him."[10] What he did not say, but what many suspected to be true, was that these connections had been deliberately arranged by Kennedy's father.

If his association with McCarthy was a problem for Kennedy, at least in the eyes of the liberal wing of the Democratic Party, it paled in comparison with that posed by his father, Joseph P. Kennedy, the patriarch of the Kennedy family, who deployed his wealth and vast influence in behalf of his son's political career. As the 1960 campaign began, Truman was quoted as saying about the Catholic Kennedy that it was not the Pope he was worried about but rather the Pop.[11] Here he expressed the worries of many in the Democratic Party.

Though today he is viewed as a footnote to history rather than an important figure in his own right, Joseph Kennedy was widely known and remembered in the 1940s and 1950s both for his business investments in film studios and liquor interests and for his own aborted political career, in which he managed to place himself at odds with both Winston Churchill and Franklin D. Roosevelt. Kennedy earned his vast fortune from bootlegging and smuggling liquor during the Prohibition era, activities which brought him into partnership with organized crime but also to the attention of federal authorities. Kennedy, however, was shrewd enough to understand that in order to protect his illicit gains he had to deploy some of his money to establish friendships with gangsters, politicians, and (importantly) journalists. Kennedy put money into FDR's presidential campaign in 1932. He established a business association with James Roosevelt, FDR's son, who helped Kennedy secure appointments in the Roosevelt administration. He nurtured friendships with the columnist Walter Winchell and Arthur Krock, Washington bureau chief of the *New York Times*, to whom he provided information and money in exchange for favorable coverage in the paper. It was Kennedy's experience as a black-market businessman that later made him such an effective behind-the-scenes promoter of his son's political career. As Lasky wrote, "the story of John Fitzgerald Kennedy is not wholly separable from the story of his father."[12]

By the time his son ran for president, Kennedy had earned a reputation, not merely as a crooked businessman, but also as an arch-conservative and anticommunist. He was a Democrat because he was Irish Catholic, not because he was liberal. Kennedy's business and personal affairs make for an inexhaustible reservoir of lurid tales.[13] Yet his own aborted political career was perhaps more important than these other activities in establishing his later reputation as an untrustworthy character. This career was also important as a formative experience for his son's career in politics.

The elder Kennedy came to public attention during the New Deal when he was first appointed chairman of the new Securities and Exchange Commission, much to the dismay of liberals who thought the appointment akin to placing the fox in charge of the henhouse. He secured an even more important appointment in 1938 when he persuaded President Roosevelt to appoint him ambassador to the Court of St. James's. Kennedy was the first Irish Catholic to hold this prestigious post, a distinction of which he proudly boasted in Protestant Boston. In that role he turned in one of the most spectacularly incompetent performances in the history of American diplomacy.

He arrived in London at precisely the time when Hitler's challenge to France and Great Britain was reaching a point of crisis. Once in London, Kennedy made it clear that he supported the

British government's policy of appeasement toward Nazi Germany as the only means of avoiding war. He strongly endorsed Prime Minister Chamberlain's decision at Munich in September 1938 to allow Hitler to annex the Sudetenland in return for a promise of peace. Kennedy claimed, as did others in Britain at the time, that such a policy reflected the wishes of the British people to avoid another war. In any case, he said, Great Britain was far too weak militarily to oppose Hitler, who had deliberately cultivated an exaggerated estimate of Germany's military strength in order to deter a British military response. Kennedy believed that Hitler, if properly managed, might serve as a fortification in Europe against communism. On all these critical points, Kennedy took the position directly opposite of Winston Churchill, who denounced appeasement as a policy that was not only cowardly but also ineffective, since it would only delay the day of reckoning with Hitler, whom he regarded as a more immediate threat to European civilization than Stalin.

Kennedy maintained this position even after Britain declared war on Germany in 1939 following Hitler's invasion of Poland. During these months of the so-called "twilight war," he advised Roosevelt to keep the United States out of the European conflict at all costs. The British position was hopeless, he said, and he judged it likely that the British would be "badly trashed" by the German military machine, a position that hardly endeared him to the British people or their government. Here Kennedy also proved an embarrassment to his own government because his position ran directly counter to Roosevelt's own wish to assist the British. Kennedy, according to observers at the time, harbored ambitions to succeed FDR in 1940 as the Democratic candidate for president, in which campaign he would highlight his role in keeping the United States out of the European conflict. Word of such ambitions naturally got back to Roosevelt. Kennedy was bitterly disappointed—and made no secret of it—when Roosevelt announced his intention to run for a third term.

When Churchill was appointed prime minister in 1940 after the fall of France, Kennedy's already tenuous position in Britain was further compromised. Churchill had little use for the appeasement-

minded ambassador, a feeling that was fully reciprocated by
Kennedy. Late in 1940, after Roosevelt was safely re-elected, Kennedy delivered his opinion to the American press that "democracy
is finished in England" and that the British could not long hold out
against the German bombing campaign then under way. This
tirade, which Kennedy claimed was supposed to be off the record,
was also laced with indelicate comments about Churchill, the queen,
and even the president's wife. Once his comments were published,
Kennedy saw that he had little choice but to resign.[14]

The fiasco in London effectively ended the elder Kennedy's political career and closed the door on any possibility that he might run
for public office on his own. In the span of a few years he managed
to antagonize the two great democratic leaders of the time, while
promoting a position that was soon discredited by events. A reputation for a loose tongue and poor judgment was further stained by
insinuations of anti-Semitism because of his willingness to do business with Hitler.[15] His political career now in shambles, Kennedy
retreated to private life to focus on his substantial business interests, while transferring his political ambitions to his sons. After the
war, he remained politically active behind the scenes, promoting
Jack Kennedy's budding career in national politics and befriending
important national leaders, including Senator Joseph McCarthy of
Wisconsin. All this—and much more—was known about the elder
Kennedy when his son began his run for the presidency in 1960.

John F. Kennedy appears to have been every bit as sure as his
father was about the wisdom of the British government's policy of
appeasement. The younger Kennedy had spent much of the period
of his father's ambassadorship in London on leave from Harvard
University on a travel-study fellowship, which gave him the opportunity to observe at close hand the historic debates between British
leaders who sought to appease Hitler and those (like Churchill)
who thought it necessary to confront him. In late 1939, with the
war now on and events moving quickly, he returned to Harvard to
work on a senior thesis on the subject of British policy toward Germany from 1932 to the outbreak of war. His thesis, completed in
March 1940 under the title "Appeasement at Munich," was a

defense of appeasement (and of his father's views) on the grounds that the British public was strongly opposed to rearmament and, indeed, to any confrontational policy against Hitler that might make war more likely. Since (as he argued) it is unrealistic to ask political leaders to risk their offices by going against public opinion, Britain's leaders were bound by the canons of democratic politics to embrace any policy that might avert another war. The blame for Britain's failure to arm, he said, lay with the voters and the democratic system itself, not with Chamberlain or his predecessor, Stanley Baldwin.[16] This seemed such a transparent defense of his father's record that one of the Harvard professors who read the thesis said it should be titled "While Daddy Slept," a sarcastic take-off on a (then) recently published collection of Churchill's speeches titled *While England Slept*.[17]

Kennedy received encouragement from his father and a few of his father's associates, especially Arthur Krock of the *New York Times*, to publish the thesis as a book. Before doing so, however, he saw the necessity of adjusting the main argument in response to withering criticism it received from friendly reviewers who correctly pointed out that Kennedy's thesis was a counsel of cynicism to leaders to tell the voters whatever they want to hear.[18] From the vantage point of early 1940, of course, the policy of appeasement looked much different, and far more dangerous to the security of Britain, than it did two years earlier when Chamberlain ventured to Munich. Kennedy therefore recast his thesis to suggest that leaders should make the effort to educate the public and to shape public opinion when they believe the security of the nation is at stake—and then accept the consequences at the polls. This barb, however, was aimed more at Stanley Baldwin, Chamberlain's predecessor, than at Chamberlain himself, for Baldwin, by failing to prepare during his tenure in the mid-1930s, had limited Chamberlain's range of options in 1938. The revision nonetheless maintained the general theme that the democratic system itself, combined with the peace-loving character of democratic countries, was largely responsible for the failures of the 1930s. Though the revised version made a gesture in the direction of Churchill's position, which in any case was in the process of being vindicated by events, it also sought disingenuously to absolve Chamberlain (and Kennedy's father) of blame by suggesting that the appeasement of Hitler at Munich was made necessary by earlier decisions and, in any case, bought time for Britain to arm itself before war became unavoidable.[19]

Kennedy concluded his revised thesis with a coda directed to Americans, urging them to learn from the British the lesson that it is necessary to maintain military strength commensurate with the requirements of national security and threats from abroad—a conclusion that established the book's importance for the American reading public. Realizing that events in Europe were moving rapidly to make the book seem dated, Kennedy quickly found a publisher (with his father's help) who brought the book out in America in July 1940 under the title *Why England Slept*—another reference, and a somewhat audacious one, to Churchill's recently published collection of speeches. The book received generally favorable reviews and, aided by substantial purchases by Kennedy's father, even made a few bestseller lists.[20] More importantly for his future career, the book gave young Kennedy favorable publicity as an author and intellectual.

It is worth dwelling on this episode because of the formative role it played in Kennedy's political career and the influence this chapter in history had on postwar political debates. Chamberlain's appeasement at Munich, observed at close hand and ably defended by Kennedy, later became the central object lesson for American statesmanship during the Cold War. Liberals and conservatives alike, but especially liberals, took to heart the lessons taught by Britain's failure to maintain its strength in the face of Hitler's challenge. The episode demonstrated the futility of giving in to aggression; and it seemed to prove to democratic leaders that the best way to avoid war is to make preparations for it. "Appeasement" shortly became a term of contempt; "the Munich analogy" became a touchstone of foreign policy doctrine in the postwar period; and Churchill was held up as the very model of wise and courageous statesmanship. After the war, the lessons of Munich were redirected to the battle against communism, which had by then replaced fascism as the aggressive force in the world. Kennedy, who at the time was on the wrong side of the great controversy between Churchill and Chamberlain, absorbed these lessons just as deeply as did others in the postwar period, applying them to the threat from communism as his career advanced. After the war, moreover, Kennedy seized upon Churchill as his hero in politics, thus completely reversing the position he had earlier taken in his thesis and book.[21]

This episode, far from marking just a youthful chapter in the life of a statesman in training, was in many ways representative of Kennedy's later career—particularly as it brought into play his loyalty to his father, the prominent role played behind the scenes by the elder Kennedy in arranging for the publication and promotion of his son's book, and Kennedy's willingness later to reverse positions on Churchill and appeasement even as he continued to maintain the argument of his book. There was here even the question as to whether Kennedy actually wrote the book himself or relied on the writing skills of others in his father's circle to form the final product—a controversy that would arise again a few years later on the publication of Kennedy's second book, *Profiles in Courage*.[22] There can be little doubt that Kennedy's immersion in the appeasement controversy was invaluable preparation for a career in national office. Here, however, as at other critical points in his career, John F. Kennedy proceeded under the careful tutelage of his father.

Profiles in Courage, published in 1956, is a good illustration of Kennedy's penchant for defying political labels and adopting views that are difficult to pigeonhole as either liberal or conservative. The subject of political courage might seem a strange subject for Kennedy's second book, given the position he took before the war and his father's antagonism toward Churchill for doing precisely what Senator Kennedy would go on to praise in the book. It was also something of a risky topic for a book by a young politician, as it would naturally establish a standard by which the author's own record might be judged.

This volume, as Kennedy wrote in the first chapter, was dedicated to United States senators who over the course of our history have gone against the narrow interests of state or section or the views of their constituents to uphold the Constitution or the welfare of the nation as a whole. Risking one's political career or reputation for principle or the greater good was for Kennedy the definition of political courage. This was, as some said at the time, an expression of the Whig concept of representation under which the duty of the representative is to the public good as opposed to the narrower interests of his constituents. *Profiles in Courage* won the Pulitzer Prize for nonfiction in 1956, albeit with some help from Kennedy's father and the timely intervention once more of Arthur Krock, who happened to be a member of the Pulitzer committee.[23]

In this exercise, however, Kennedy managed to praise political figures on all sides of the vexing issues that have divided the nation in the past. Both Democrats and Republicans came in for praise in near equal measure. Kennedy paid homage to Senators Daniel Webster, Henry Clay, and even John C. Calhoun for the various and conflicting positions they took on secession, sectionalism, and the Compromise of 1850. He commended the Unionist senator Edmund Ross of Kansas for casting the decisive vote against the impeachment of Andrew Johnson, but also the secessionist and former Confederate military officer Lucius Cincinnatus Lamar for his sympathetic eulogy in 1874 for Senator Charles Sumner, who had been the most radical of antislavery Republicans, to the point at which (before the Civil War) he was beaten nearly to death on the Senate floor by a Southern congressman as a consequence of remarks he had made about slavery and slave owners. More importantly for contemporary politics, he devoted a chapter in praise of the late Senator Robert A. Taft of Ohio, the titular leader of the conservative wing of the Republican Party and briefly Kennedy's colleague in the Senate until he died of cancer in 1953. Taft was singled out for commendation because of his criticisms in 1946 of the Nuremburg war crimes tribunals. Taft characterized the verdicts at Nuremberg as a form of victor's justice. He further said that the trials violated our own Constitution's ban on *ex post facto* laws. Kennedy lauded Taft for speaking up for principle in defense of legal standards, unpopular though his position may have been at the time.

Kennedy thus touched nearly every political base during the course of his historical survey of political courage. As if to make his message more confusing still, he wrote also in support of moderation and compromise and against "fanatics and extremists" who think only of their own principles and points of view.[24] Though some might think of political courage as standing up for principle— and, indeed, this seemed to be the author's point in praising Taft —for Kennedy it also meant the courage to compromise in the fashion of Webster or Clay. By the time one finished the book, it was not clear if Kennedy meant to encourage principled leadership or compromise, or perhaps a little of both and each at the proper time. The book, moreover, totally divorced political courage from any cause it may have advanced. Webster's courageous defense of the Union was placed on the same footing as Calhoun's principled defense of slavery and secession. His book thus conveyed a mixed message as being for principled leadership but at the same time for moderation and compromise. From the standpoint of philosophy or consistent principle, *Profiles in Courage* was something of a muddled production.

Yet in important ways it reflected Kennedy's overall political strategy, for in each of his two major campaigns, in 1952 for the Senate and in 1960 for president, he sought to outflank his Republican opponents by adopting positions on their right. By this tactic he presented to the voters an ideologically ambiguous message of being neither liberal nor conservative—or perhaps something of both. Most importantly, Kennedy did not want anyone to tag him as a liberal, which he (along with his father) regarded as the kiss of death in electoral politics.

Kennedy's campaign for the Senate in 1952 pitted him against the popular Republican incumbent Henry Cabot Lodge, himself a member of an influential Massachusetts family, albeit one with Protestant roots in contrast to Kennedy's Irish Catholic background. It was a race that few thought Kennedy could win. Lodge, after all, had represented Massachusetts in the Senate since 1936, except for two years of military service during the war. Lodge, moreover, was an influential national figure who took the lead in convincing Eisenhower to run for president that year on the Republican ticket and in ensuring that he received the nomination against a strong challenge from Senator Taft.

During the campaign, Kennedy sought to win votes from conservatives by claiming that his positions on foreign policy were much more in keeping with Taft's positions than were Lodge's—even though Kennedy was a Democrat and Taft and Lodge Republicans. Kennedy claimed that between the two candidates he was the stronger critic of Truman's foreign policy, which he said was soft on communism. "In this respect," a campaign statement claimed, "he [Kennedy] is much closer to the position of Taft than Lodge."[25] Kennedy also sought to exploit the resentment of conservatives against Lodge for assisting Eisenhower in elbowing aside Taft for the Republican nomination. When the Republican National Convention was concluded with Eisenhower the nominee, Kennedy openly courted supporters of the Taft campaign in Massachusetts by setting up a group called "Independents for Kennedy" directed by one of the leaders of the Taft organization. In this way he gave disappointed Taft supporters a place to rally following the defeat of their candidate. It also gave them a means of getting even with Lodge—even though Taft himself would later endorse Lodge over Kennedy. Nevertheless, Kennedy's successful appeal to conservative Republicans played an important role in his narrow victory over Lodge in November.[26]

Kennedy replayed the same tactic in the 1960 presidential race against Richard Nixon when he accused the Eisenhower administration of jeopardizing the nation's security by allowing a "missile gap" to develop between the United States and the Soviet Union. Following the successful launch of the *Sputnik* satellite in 1957, Americans were panicked at the possibility that the Soviet Union had gained the upper hand in the space race and in science generally. Speaking in the Senate in 1958, Kennedy expressed concern that the Soviet Union was gaining an advantage in long-range missiles. This was a theme that he returned to frequently as he made preparations for a presidential race. Throughout the 1960 campaign, Kennedy stressed the idea that the Eisenhower administration had been asleep at the switch, thus allowing a communist tyranny to establish a base in Cuba and the Soviets to establish a dangerous advantage in offensive missiles that might leave the nation open to attack. Further emulating Churchill, Kennedy also called for a spirit of sacrifice among Americans so that they might begin to turn back the challenge of communism. Such charges and appeals were effective in placing Vice President Nixon on the defensive in the campaign. Both Eisenhower and Nixon, however, knew the "missile gap" to be a fabrication since they had secret intelligence from surveillance aircraft to show that the Soviets had no advantage of the kind Kennedy described. Yet they were unable publicly to reveal the sources of their information.[27]

Kennedy's charge was part of his overall campaign theme to "get the country moving again" following eight years of lethargic and unimaginative Republican leadership. It was also part of his design to run "on the Churchill ticket," as Harold MacMillan called Kennedy's tactic, meaning that Kennedy was now playing Churchill's role of bravely warning the people of dangers on the horizon. When the Soviet leader Nikita Khrushchev cancelled a planned summit meeting in May of 1960 after an American reconnaissance aircraft was downed over Soviet territory, Kennedy said that it marked the end of an era—"an era of illusion."[28] From this point forward, Kennedy's campaign emphasized the international weakness and passivity of the Eisenhower administration, along with his own pledge to restore the nation's security. His emphasis on national security was especially helpful in the South, where it neutralized doubts about his stand on civil rights.

But there was a great difference between Kennedy's use of the "missile gap" in the 1960 campaign and Churchill's warnings about Hitler in the 1930s—because while Churchill warned of a real danger to Great Britain, Kennedy exploited a nonexistent danger to the United States. The threat that Great Britain faced from Hitler in the 1930s was far different from the one that the United States faced from the Soviet Union in the 1950s. Americans were well aware of the dangers they faced from the Soviet Union; indeed, in the eyes of many liberals, they were all too aware of the threat. The "missile gap," moreover, never existed at all, a reality Kennedy was forced to acknowledge soon after he became president. It was, as he admitted to close associates, a fabrication designed for the immediate purposes of his campaign. Once he took office, Kennedy saw that it was dangerous to call attention to the issue because to do so might encourage Soviet leaders to act against the United States out of a false sense of advantage.[29]

The missile gap, like the appeal to Taft voters, was a shrewd effort on Kennedy's part to broaden his appeal to voters across the entire spectrum of opinion. Kennedy's narrow victory in 1960 proved both the wisdom and the necessity of that strategy.

Kennedy assumed the presidency as a moderate representative of the postwar consensus: tough and aggressive on communism and national defense; confident of America's crucial role in the world as champion of liberty and democracy; devoted to economic growth as the surest and most direct path to national progress; a prudent supporter of civil rights and the welfare state. When Daniel Bell spoke of the consensus among intellectuals around the welfare state, political pluralism, and a mixed economy, he might just as easily have been speaking of Kennedy along with the advisers and officials who formed his inner circle. Indeed, in the sorrowful days after Kennedy's death, Richard Rovere would comment on the president and his circle of associates in tones remindful of Bell's thesis on the end of ideology: "There was not a reformer among them as far as anyone could tell," he wrote. "Pragmatism was rampant. 'Facts' were often valued beyond their worth. 'Ideology' was held in contempt and was described as a prime source of mischief in the world."[30] Kennedy and his men were pragmatists, at least so they thought, because they had witnessed the consequences of ideology in politics.

In view of his posthumous reputation as a liberal, it is curious that Kennedy's brief presidency is notable in retrospect as a time when Cold War tensions reached their most dangerous point—and, indeed, during the Cuban missile crisis might easily have escalated into an all-out nuclear war. Kennedy meant it when he said that he would challenge Soviet ambitions in Europe, Latin America, and the developing world. Cuba, as things turned out, was the flashpoint of the conflict between Soviet expansion and the Kennedy administration's aggressive resistance to it. Kennedy tried to overthrow Castro by force in 1961, and then a year later threatened to use military power to remove Soviet-placed offensive missiles on the island. Throughout his tenure in office, Kennedy approved and encouraged assassination plots against the dictator, though these plans were not known to the public or to most officials in the government until more than a decade after his death.[31] These efforts eventually proved so dangerous and destabilizing that Lyndon Johnson and presidents who followed him decided that a better policy was simply to ignore and isolate Castro in the hope that his regime would collapse of its own ineffectiveness.

Looking back on Kennedy's actual record in office, one finds the same ideologically ambiguous mix of policies and appeals that was so evident in his major election campaigns. If in the field of foreign policy there were some progressive initiatives—such as the Alliance for Progress, which sought to promote development and democracy in Latin America, and the American University speech in 1963, where Kennedy proposed a nuclear test ban treaty with the Soviet Union (this following the dangerous confrontation over nuclear weapons in Cuba)—there were also counterbalancing initiatives of a more conservative nature, such as Kennedy's military buildup in Vietnam, his support for counterinsurgency efforts, his harsh approach toward Castro, and his vigorous anticommunist rhetoric. Over the decades since his death, Kennedy's policies have been emulated as much (or even more) by conservative Republicans as by liberal Democrats. Kennedy's anticommunism, for example, was shortly rejected and abandoned by liberal Democrats like George McGovern and Jimmy Carter, but was thereafter carried forward by conservative Republicans like Ronald Reagan, whose policies eventually brought the Cold War to an end. Kennedy's aim of spreading democracy abroad as an element of U.S. foreign policy was picked up in the 1980s by Reagan and later by George W. Bush, who made it a centerpiece of his foreign policy. Kennedy's efforts to assassinate Castro, when they were eventually revealed, scandalized liberals far more than conservatives.

Kennedy's bold and patriotic rhetoric provides a more vivid illustration of this point. To the extent that anyone today hears the kinds of themes and concepts deployed by Kennedy, it is usually in speeches given by conservatives. In a speech to the Massachusetts legislature a week before his inauguration, Kennedy said (quoting the Puritan John Winthrop) that America is like a "city on a hill," an example of liberty and democracy looked up to by people around the world. He used this image as an incentive, so to speak, to perfect our own democracy and to hold it up to others as an example to emulate. A few decades later this would also be a favored image of President Reagan, who used it as a central theme in his Farewell Address (for which he was derided by liberal Democrats). "Let every nation know," Kennedy declared in his Inaugural Address, "whether it wishes us well or ill, that we shall pay any price, bear any burden, meet any hardship, support any friend, and oppose any foe to assure the survival and success of liberty." With this statement he announced what was at stake in the Cold War, and his intention to contest it with both arms and ideals. This was perhaps the most sweeping and ambitious statement of American aspirations in the world until George W. Bush announced in his 2005 Inaugural Address that the objective of U.S. policy would be to end tyranny in the world. To meet the challenges of world leadership, Kennedy called for a new spirit of patriotism that would guide Americans to think more of what they can do for their country than of what their country can do for them. He embraced Churchill's strategy of arming for peace (later phrased by Reagan as "peace through strength") by asserting that "only when our arms are sufficient beyond doubt can we be certain beyond doubt that they will never be employed." He thus rejected the argument that armaments themselves are a cause of war.[32]

Kennedy's domestic agenda, though appropriately modest, was more consistently liberal in orientation than his foreign policy. He supported and favored labor unions in their conflicts with business and accepted the advice of Keynesian economists that the federal government could smooth out the business cycle with a carefully calibrated fiscal policy. He favored, but did not push hard for, a program of federally funded medical care for seniors. One of the major items on his agenda at the time of his death was a landmark civil rights bill, which (when it was passed in 1964) outlawed discrimination in interstate commerce, employment, and government operations. Another important item, however, was a major tax cut to stimulate the economy. "The lesson of the last decade," he said in 1962, "is that budget deficits are not caused by wild eyed spenders but by slow economic growth and periodic recessions. In short, it is a paradoxical truth that tax rates are too high today and tax revenues are too low and the soundest way to raise revenues in the long run is to cut rates now."[33] Kennedy proposed to cut marginal rates across the board by some 30 percent, with the highest rate to be reduced from 91 percent to 65 percent—the largest tax cut ever proposed. He pushed for this bill in the belief (later vindicated) that a cut in tax rates would stimulate economic activity to the point where tax revenues would actually increase. His tax bill, too, was passed in 1964 with modest adjustments, and it had impressively favorable results for the economy.

Kennedy's innovative tax policy was never again pursued by Democratic leaders or by post-Kennedy liberals, but was instead later picked up by Republicans who sought to cut the size of government. Ronald Reagan used Kennedy's tax cuts as political ammunition for his own proposals to cut taxes to reverse the "stagflation" of the Carter era. That policy had similarly favorable results in reversing an economic slide. Just as Kennedy's Cold War policies were later picked up by Republicans and conservatives, so also was his tax policy. From the late 1970s forward, tax cutting as a means of stimulating the economy has been orthodox Republican doctrine.

From the standpoint of consistent principle, Kennedy was thus

very much a protean figure with one foot each in the liberal and
the conservative camp, a characteristic that helps account for his
popularity with the public. Voters, before and after his death, never
saw him as an ideological figure. It is impossible to rank Kennedy
alongside figures like Woodrow Wilson or Franklin D. Roosevelt
as a path-breaking liberal leader. Kennedy broke little new ground
in the field of policy, perhaps because of his tragically abbreviated
tenure in office. His best speeches, while memorable, did not introduce anything new or important into liberal thought, as Wilson did
with his "Fourteen Points" or F D R with his "Four Freedoms." Kennedy's legacy is further complicated by the fact that, within a few
years of his death, liberals would repudiate many of his central ideas,
thereby paving the way for conservatives to claim them. The liberalism of 1970 had only a tenuous connection to the liberalism that
Kennedy stood for when he ran for president in 1960. Liberals
admired Kennedy after his death, and continue to do so, but their
admiration was but loosely related to his actual program. Kennedy
stood for something important in the evolution of American liberalism, but it is not to be found in anything so concrete as a program
or a speech.

Arthur Schlesinger Jr. tried to get at Kennedy's unique contribution by suggesting that he communicated change and progress
through the force of personality. Kennedy, he wrote, personified a
series of qualities that he transmitted to the liberal cause via his
presidential leadership. Such qualities were distinguishable from
actual positions he may have taken on civil rights, communism, or
taxes. In the first place, Kennedy encouraged a more critical and
detached attitude toward American society than was the norm in
the complacent 1950s. By his wit and good humor, Kennedy stood
in marked contrast to the humorless Republican figures (like Nixon
and Eisenhower) who dominated the decade. Kennedy appreciated ideas, artists, and intellectuals, and thus cultivated channels
of communication between the world of thought and the arena
of power. Indeed, as a prizewinning author, Kennedy could be

considered an intellectual himself. His appreciation for intellectuals and artists was reflected in Schlesinger's own presence on the White House staff, but even more powerfully so in the participation at Kennedy's inaugural ceremony of Robert Frost, who prepared a poem for the occasion declaring that Kennedy's election marked the arrival of a new Augustan age, "A golden age of poetry and power of which this noonday's the beginning hour." Such grandiose hopes could not be fulfilled, as most sensible people should have known. Yet it was still true that for many, Kennedy kindled the hopes. His wit and humor, his detachment and penchant for self-criticism, his appreciation for ideas and artists—these qualities (according to Schlesinger) brought a new and creative dimension to American liberalism. This was the key to Kennedy's influence and popularity—and to his posthumous appeal.[34]

Schlesinger was on to something here, especially in his suggestion that such stylistic qualities were now central to the advancement of liberalism. Kennedy had managed to enlarge the boundaries of liberalism. No longer a purely programmatic doctrine, liberalism would henceforth be a cultural creed as well and would have its own style, marked by elegance, wit, and intelligence. The only difficulty with this analysis is that none of the attributes that Schlesinger claimed for Kennedy was particularly characteristic of post-Kennedy liberalism. While it is true that after Kennedy's death liberal thinkers and activists began to focus on the cultural dimensions of political life, they did so in ways that contradicted Kennedy's approach. Indeed, liberal thought as it developed in the 1960s was notable for qualities directly opposite of those that Schlesinger admired in Kennedy. If post-Kennedy liberals and leftists were known for anything, it was for taking themselves and their causes far too seriously. Amid all their serious work, there was little place for wit and humor, even if Kennedy's death had not cast a pall over their political mood. Far from admiring detachment and self-criticism, they exalted unquestioning commitment to their cause. The work of artists and intellectuals came to be viewed as diversions from direct political action; in order to be worthwhile such work had to be politically "relevant." By the end of the 1960s, poets like Robert

Frost were viewed by liberals as hopeless reactionaries because their work (besides celebrating America) could not be enlisted in the cause of change, reform, or revolution. Liberalism, long the party of ideas in American politics, soon ceded that terrain to the conservatives in one of the more remarkable reversals in the history of American politics. The wonder is that all this was done while liberals embraced John F. Kennedy and grieved over his death.

Even while all this was so, Schlesinger still may not have gone far enough in identifying the source of Kennedy's appeal and influence. For all his conventional political positions, Kennedy added something strikingly novel to the legacy of American liberalism: that is, he skillfully managed to transcend his role as a politician to become a cultural figure or, indeed, a celebrity. The historian Daniel Boorstin drew a distinction between the hero and the celebrity: "The hero was distinguished by his achievement; the celebrity by his image or trademark. The hero created himself; the celebrity is created by the media. The hero was a big man; the celebrity is a big name."[35] In his style, Kennedy seemed most unlike other prominent political figures of his time—men like Truman, Eisenhower, Nixon, Johnson, or Humphrey. Eisenhower may have been a military hero, but even so he was regarded by Kennedy and his followers as a tired old man. Norman Mailer, in an adulatory article about Kennedy the candidate, went so far as to call Eisenhower an "antihero" because he failed to engage the imagination of the nation.[36] Kennedy, on the other hand, better fit the definition of a celebrity. He was young and articulate; he wore his hair long; he sailed and played touch football; he consorted with Hollywood stars and Harvard professors alike; he spoke beautifully and used inspirational words and phrases; he was rich; he was an accomplished author. His wife, moreover, was beautiful and glamorous; she wore French fashions and spoke French (and Spanish, too). The two Kennedy children were every bit as photogenic as their parents. The American people had never seen anything like the Kennedys, except perhaps in the movies. Kennedy saw that a president must not only lead but entertain as well.

President Kennedy was thus our first president—and the only

one so far—successfully to marry the role of politician to that of cultural celebrity. It would not have occurred to Harry Truman or
Franklin Roosevelt that he might burnish his political credentials
by seeking a Pulitzer Prize. Nor would either man have had much
interest in hanging about with Hollywood stars and starlets as
Kennedy did (following his father's example). Kennedy was quite
the opposite of Ronald Reagan, who moved into politics from the
world of celebrity, while Kennedy bridged that divide from the
other direction. Reagan may have represented Hollywood's past,
but Kennedy represented its future. His success in linking liberalism with celebrity was greatly responsible for turning Hollywood
into the liberal-left fortification that it later became.

Kennedy achieved this through what Schlesinger called his
"cool" style, which gave the appearance of a man at the cutting
edge of new cultural trends, in contrast to other politicians (like
Nixon or Eisenhower) who generally represented the established
patterns and morals of middle-class life. Sorensen acknowledged
that Kennedy at his inauguration deliberately played up the stylistic contrast between himself and his tired and aging predecessor.[37]
Schlesinger saw in Kennedy's style a substantive statement in and
of itself: "His coolness was itself a new frontier. It meant freedom
from the stereotyped responses of the past. . . . It offered hope for
spontaneity in a country drowning in its own passivity."[38] Mailer
saw Kennedy as an "existential hero," a man who would risk death
in quest of authentic experience. With Kennedy in the lead,
"America's politics would now be also America's favorite movie,
America's first soap opera, and America's best seller." Kennedy's
youth, good looks, and beautiful wife, according to Mailer, were not
merely accessories to the man but necessary instruments for in-
spiring new acts of national creativity.[39] Mailer was writing from the
standpoint of what we have called the "new" radicalism—the idea
that politics must involve the redefinition of culture in the direction
of liberation, experimentation, and the casting off of traditional
assumptions about family, sex, and education. He saw Kennedy
(correctly) as a potentially important cultural example.

The problem was that while Kennedy understood political

leadership to involve facing down communism or putting a man on the moon, Mailer and others were thinking in terms of "a revolution in the consciousness of our time." While it is true that Kennedy cultivated a style, it is also obvious that many read into it far more than was really there. In projecting their hopes onto Kennedy, liberals like Schlesinger and cultural radicals like Mailer were redefining liberalism more in terms of a style or a posture toward the world than as a coherent body of ideas about government and politics. Indeed, by investing so much in Kennedy's style they came dangerously close to creating a cult of personality around him, thereby linking liberal ideals too closely to Kennedy the man. Because Kennedy embodied sophistication, he was seen after his death as a more authentic liberal than figures like Johnson or Humphrey who labored for legislative victories, but appeared hopelessly old-fashioned in terms of their style and comportment.

Through this contrast with conventional figures, Kennedy augmented his own popularity by standing for a style of life to which many aspired, especially the college-educated young, who mistakenly thought his style was a rejection of the blandness and conformity of middle-class life, when in fact it reflected more the ways of the American aristocracy to which he and his wife belonged. In the new age of television, moreover, glamour and celebrity were suddenly assets to a political career as they had not been before. Television had created a vast audience of voters who judged political leaders by the way they appeared on the visual screen. Intellectuals, journalists, and commentators, along with their own audience on college campuses and elsewhere, had created a new constituency that was as attentive to matters of style as to policy. After his death, Kennedy was admired more for his attractive and sophisticated style than for any breakthroughs in policy.

Lasky, along with Kennedy critics from the left such as Garry Wills and Christopher Lasch, pointed out that this was a manufactured and manipulated image at odds with a darker reality.[40] This point is largely true, though perhaps it misses the point because all celebrity is based on the careful crafting and manipulation of images for wider consumption. This is to some extent true of political life itself, a fact which facilitates the merging of the world of politics with that of celebrity, particularly in the age of television and movies. This was something that Kennedy understood far better than any other politician of his time. Still, there were facts about Kennedy's "real" life (kept secret at the time) that would only have enhanced his reputation as a hip cultural figure—namely, his use of drugs and his reckless pursuit of sex, two activities that just a few years later would define the youth culture of the 1960s. Kennedy, however, was on to these amusements long before the youngsters discovered them. In this sense he anticipated these new directions in the culture. Here, too, Kennedy behaved far more like a Hollywood star than like a conventional politician.

It is Kennedy's status as a cultural figure that is responsible for the enduring interest in the man and his presidency and for his transfiguration in death into a liberal hero. Because of his premature death, Kennedy was not in office long enough for the wear and tear of politics to have stripped away his cultural luster. In this sense, his untimely death only magnified his posthumous cultural appeal. Kennedy, moreover, in seeming to stand above and apart from the conventions of middle-class life, opened up new possibilities for cultural politics and cultural criticism that were eventually absorbed into the mainstream of liberal reform, so much so that within a few years liberals seemed more preoccupied with cultural issues—feminism, sexual freedom, and gay rights—than with the traditional issues of economic security that had animated Roosevelt, Truman, and even Kennedy himself. It was thus through the opening that Kennedy provided that the ideas associated with cultural radicalism began to blend with the broader movement of liberal reform. Yet it was perhaps this immersion in cultural politics following Kennedy's death that as much as anything brought about the end of the liberal era. Liberals after Kennedy identified their doctrine with his style and his sophistication while, in many areas, abandoning the substance of his ideas. To them Kennedy represented more a cultural ideal than a political leader with a program.

Kennedy's unique contribution was to have maintained this cultural stance in combination with his ardent nationalism—

a balancing act that proved impossible for successors to sustain. Kennedy was a decorated war veteran and an outspoken nationalist, but at the same time a symbol of cultural sophistication, a combination that appealed to both traditional Americans and the new cultural reformers. After Kennedy's death, these two groups divided into conflicting camps, thereby establishing the terms for the long-running cultural war that continues today between cultural liberals and traditional middle-class Americans.

Kennedy was thus a bridge between the old liberalism and the new—between the programmatic liberals who followed FDR and the cultural liberals and radicals who gained influence following Kennedy's death. Daniel Bell and other liberal analysts of the post-war period turned out to have been correct when they suggested that "the end of ideology" in the 1950s might eventually lead to new forms of radicalism focused on issues of culture. Yet they could not have foreseen the surprising way by which this came about. Kennedy made politics seem interesting and exciting, albeit through the avenues of celebrity and glamour. His sudden death left a void that could not be filled by programmatic liberalism.

THREE · MARTYR: LINCOLN

K ENNEDY'S ELECTION to the presidency stimulated the energies of the far right after a period of
quiescence in the late 1950s. Senator McCarthy's censure in 1954
and his death in 1957 had deprived the right of its most popular
and effective spokesman. With a Republican administration in
power, far-right organizations found it difficult to gain any traction
on their core issues of anticommunism and domestic subversion.
The formation of the anticommunist John Birch Society in 1958
generated a brief flurry of public attention, particularly when its
founder accused President Eisenhower of being a conscious and
dedicated agent of the communist conspiracy. Yet that accusation,
which was difficult for anyone to believe, served to discredit the
Birch Society and to mark it as an extremist organization. Kennedy's election generated renewed activity from two separate
directions: from the anticommunists (including Birch Society leaders) who claimed that the Kennedy administration was about to
sell the nation out to the communists or to the United Nations; and
from southern segregationists who opposed Kennedy's civil rights
bill or feared that his administration would proceed to enforce the
integration orders of the Supreme Court.

This new activity encouraged Daniel Bell to come out with a revised and updated edition of his 1955 volume on political extremism, this one titled *The Radical Right*. Richard Hofstadter developed his theory of the "paranoid style" in 1963 in response to the rightist renewal. The Anti-Defamation League published a full-length book, *Danger on the Right*, which contained detailed chapters on all the influential groups operating on the far right.[1] This volume was widely assigned during the early and mid-1960s in college courses in American history and government. President Kennedy frequently spoke out against the irrationality and extremism of groups on the far right, though in doing so he may have given them more attention than their influence warranted. Indeed, he meant to address the subject in the speech he was scheduled to deliver in Dallas on the day he was assassinated. "There will always be dissident voices heard in the land," he was to say, "expressing opposition without alternative, finding fault but never favor, perceiving gloom on every side and seeking influence without responsibility. Those voices are inevitable. But today other voices are heard in the land—voices preaching doctrines wholly unrelated to reality, wholly unsuited to the sixties, doctrines which assume that words will suffice without weapons, that vituperation is as good as victory, and that peace is a sign of weakness."[2] Kennedy understood that these voices were influential in the city in which he was to speak. One of Dallas's more prominent citizens was retired Army general Edwin A. Walker, a nationally known anticommunist spokesman and head of the Birch Society chapter in the city.

In the months leading up to President Kennedy's trip to Dallas, violent acts committed by representatives of the radical right seemed to be escalating. In May of 1963, Americans were horrified to see photos in the newspaper of police in Birmingham, Alabama, turning fire hoses and police dogs against civil rights demonstrators. In June of 1963, the civil rights leader and NAACP official Medgar Evers was assassinated by gunfire outside his home in Jackson, Mississippi. A week later, in a demonstration of sympathy, Kennedy met with the Evers family in the White House. A few months after that, in September, a bomb was set off in the Sixteenth

Street Baptist Church in Birmingham, Alabama, killing four young black girls. The Ku Klux Klan was linked both to the Evers shooting and to the Birmingham bombing.

This latter attack occurred barely two weeks after the historic civil rights march in Washington, D.C., where, on the steps of the Lincoln Memorial, Martin Luther King delivered his historic "I Have a Dream" speech, and only a week after George Wallace, the segregationist governor of Alabama, openly defied a federal court order to integrate the public schools of Birmingham. President Kennedy expressed his "deep sense of grief and outrage" over the deaths of the young girls and, without naming him, implicitly blamed Governor Wallace for creating an atmosphere in which such an attack was made possible. "It is regrettable," the president said, "that public disparagement of law and order has encouraged violence which has fallen on the innocent." James Reston of the *New York Times* wrote that the conflict in Birmingham and across the South was not just between whites and blacks, "but between order and anarchy." Acts of this kind, he wrote, create a crisis of lawlessness, destroying "the confidence of the whole community in law and order." These violent events, combined with the historic (and peaceful) March on Washington in late August of that year, dramatized for the nation the whole issue of civil rights and the treatment of the Negro in the South, thereby driving the issue to the top of the national agenda.[3]

In short order, however, the focus of attention turned from the racial bigots to the anticommunist extremists. In late October, Adlai Stevenson, then the United States ambassador to the United Nations, ventured to Dallas for a speech to commemorate "United Nations Day." There he was met by chanting and placard-carrying demonstrators proclaiming "United States Day." The protests were organized by a rightist group, the National Indignation Committee, which sponsored a speech by General Walker attacking the United Nations the day before Stevenson arrived in the city. Stevenson was heckled during his formal remarks, jostled and spat upon by protesters as he tried to depart the auditorium where he spoke, and finally hit over the head with a cardboard placard as he made his way to his car. Municipal officials in Dallas apologized profusely to Stevenson for the reception he had received, declaring in a telegram to him that the city was "outraged and abjectly ashamed of the disgraceful discourtesies you suffered at the hands of a small group of extremists." Governor John Connally said the demonstration against Stevenson was "an affront to common courtesy and decency." Nevertheless, and not withstanding such apologies, the melee in Dallas gave White House aides pause about the wisdom of the president's scheduled trip to that city the next month. Stevenson described the mood of the city as one of "unpredictable madness." Dallas, Kennedy's aides feared, was a hotbed of right-wing extremism and a dangerous place for the president to visit. When the Dallas Police Department planned security operations for the presidential visit, they made it a point to keep an eye on known right-wing extremists of the type involved in the Stevenson disruption.[4]

These events seemed to fit into a pattern of violence from the far right, and were readily assimilated into the structure of liberal thought as it had developed over the previous decade. Those who had studied the writings of liberal analysts like Hofstadter and Bell could hardly have been surprised by these outbursts from the far right. Now, however, the foot soldiers of the far right, egged on by the irresponsible rhetoric of their leaders, had proceeded beyond talk to real acts of violence in which people were physically attacked and even killed. Largely because of these excesses, the far right in 1963 was in the process of losing the sympathy and indulgence of the American people.

Kennedy, for a mix of political reasons, would in the end overrule the concerns of his aides about the safety of the Dallas trip. It would have been difficult to back out of it in any case. The visit was scheduled as a favor to Vice President Johnson to assist him in patching up a rift in the state's Democratic Party in preparation for the 1964 election. Besides, a president could not acknowledge that there was a city in the nation that he was fearful of visiting. In addition, this would be the first trip Mrs. Kennedy was to make with her husband since the couple had lost an infant child the previous August. Nonetheless, as the president embarked on the trip he was heard to say, "We're headed into nut country now."[5]

When the word spread on the afternoon of November 22 that the president had been shot, the immediate and understandable reaction was that the assassin must be a right-wing extremist—an anticommunist, perhaps, or a white supremacist, but in any case "a right-wing nut." Such an assumption made perfect sense in view of the events of the previous months, the warnings the White House had received about extremists in Dallas, and, indeed, the political script that had been written over the previous decade. Speculation to this effect went out immediately over the national airwaves.[6] John Kenneth Galbraith was not alone in suggesting that the president had been a victim of hatred encouraged by the radical right. When they were informed that afternoon that President Kennedy had died, a colleague said to Robert Kennedy that he hoped the tragedy might somehow end the "hate."[7]

It therefore came as a shock when the police announced later that day that a communist had been arrested for the murder of President Kennedy, and when the television networks began to run tapes taken a few months earlier showing the suspected assassin passing out leaflets in New Orleans in support of Castro and in opposition to Kennedy administration policies. Lee Harvey Oswald was not just any communist or leftist playing games with radical ideas in order to shock relatives and associates, but a dyed-in-the-wool communist who had defected to the Soviet Union and married a Russian woman before returning to the United States the previous year. Those who had earlier come in contact with the suspect, particularly FBI agents who had been monitoring his activities in Dallas, agreed that Oswald was capable of committing an act as heinous as assassinating the president.[8] If Oswald was in fact the assassin, he had confounded every expectation about the likely source of political danger.

Many Americans had difficulty accepting the fact that the president might have been killed by a communist in such a conservative or reactionary city as Dallas. Some, including prominent political figures, refused to believe it at all. Others feared that Oswald's deed

might produce such a revulsion against communism as to undermine President Kennedy's efforts to improve relations with the
Soviet Union. (They feared no such overreaction against the right
should a right-winger have been tagged with the crime.)[9] In an
extreme case, the reaction might lead to another dangerous confrontation between the two superpowers. For their part, officials in
Dallas were relieved to learn of Oswald's arrest since it meant that
it would now be more difficult to blame Dallas and its anti-
Kennedy atmosphere for the assassination. As things turned out,
neither of these reasonable expectations—that there would be a
revulsion against communism or that Dallas would escape blame—
proved to be true.

Mrs. Kennedy, when informed that Oswald had been arrested
in connection with the assassination, lamented bitterly that her
husband may have been shot by a warped and misguided communist. "He didn't even have the satisfaction of being killed for civil
rights," she said. "It had to be some silly little communist. It even
robs his death of any meaning."[10] Mrs. Kennedy, too, like everyone
else, had simply assumed that the killing had been the work of
right-wingers. She was sure that her husband, like Lincoln one
hundred years before, had been killed because of his support for
racial justice and equal rights. Oswald, she seemed to understand,
had intervened in history against the expected flow of events. Mrs.
Kennedy also spoke instinctively for many liberal Americans for
whom civil rights at home was a far more urgent issue than the
Cold War, which (they felt) had been blown out of proportion by
the far right. There was also in her reaction the implication that
right-wingers are truly malevolent but communists merely "silly"
or misguided—another of those enduring liberal ideas that President Kennedy never accepted. The thought that Kennedy was a
martyr to the Cold War was never seriously considered, though it
fit the known facts better than any alternative interpretation. As
between these two causes—civil rights versus anticommunism—
there was little question in Mrs. Kennedy's mind as to which would
bear the more honorable legacy. Her remark suggested that she
was already thinking of how President Kennedy's legacy should be

framed and that she sensed the identity of the assassin might prove inconvenient in this regard. She would shortly instruct White House aides to plan President Kennedy's obsequies on the model of Abraham Lincoln's.

The assassination of President Kennedy was an overwhelming event for many reasons, not least because of the disquieting questions it posed to the established assumptions of liberal thought. If President Kennedy was killed by a communist, then was it the case that the conservatives and anticommunists had been correct all along in their warnings about domestic communism? Did it prove that the postwar liberals had misdiagnosed the threat to democratic institutions when they focused their attention exclusively on the "radical right?" Was it credible any longer to wail about the threat from the right after the president had been assassinated by a communist? Did Oswald's intervention imply that history, far from being a benign and progressive process as many assumed, was ultimately unpredictable, absurd, and meaningless? Was the assassination a potent reminder that history is a theater for tragedy more than for rational progress? Did the harsh facts of the case open up a divide between what we expect and hope to be true and what the evidence tells us is true? If something so cruel could happen here, did it hint at the possibility that America, rather than standing as a "city on a hill" as Kennedy had described it, was in fact something far different and perhaps even sinister in its deepest nature? If President Kennedy had been martyred, what was the cause for which he gave up his life? Such questions (and others) arising from the assassination would disturb and trouble liberal thought for a generation afterwards. The surprising answers that gradually emerged shaped the contours of liberalism over the last decades of the century.

It was natural for Mrs. Kennedy and the Kennedy family, along with television commentators and public officials, to associate the fallen president with Abraham Lincoln. Both, after all, had been assassinated at the height of their powers, Lincoln at the conclusion of a terrible civil war fought over the issue of slavery, and Kennedy in the midst of what some have called the Second Reconstruction, in which civil rights for American Negroes were finally guaranteed. Few compared Kennedy to Presidents Garfield or McKinley, both of whom were cut down in office by assassins acting out of extreme political motives. Neither man any longer stood for or symbolized anything of continuing interest or urgency. Lincoln, unlike these successors, was a national symbol, a martyr to the Union and the cause of racial justice. The effort to link the two men was based on the assumption that they had died in the same cause—an assumption that was far from being the case.

Mrs. Kennedy sought to establish that link by organizing President Kennedy's death rites in imitation of Lincoln's a century before and by using every opportunity to cement the association between the two assassinated leaders. She had decided within hours of the assassination that Lincoln's death would serve as the motif for the mourning and funeral rites for President Kennedy.[11] Yet the rites surrounding Lincoln's death were themselves politicized to an unusual degree, in part to suggest that harsh measures against the defeated South were more than justified.[12] It is far from clear that Lincoln himself would have approved of the way his death was mourned or the uses to which it was put. Lincoln, moreover, was assassinated at a time when the concepts of sacrifice and martyrdom were powerfully connected to Christian religious ideals. It was not a great leap for Americans at that time to see Lincoln as a martyr and to use his death constructively to advance the ideals for which he stood. Kennedy, however, was killed in a liberal age during which such religious ideals had been effectively debunked in the name of secular standards. The attempt to cast Kennedy as a martyr alongside Lincoln added even more confusion to an already confused event. It was not clear that the two cases were comparable in terms of the meaning that the public might take from them.

The Civil War was fought (and Lincoln was assassinated) near the tail end of a long-running Protestant revival that began in the 1820s.

The Second Great Awakening, as it was called, was a reprise of the original Great Awakening that brought a religious revival to the New England states from the 1730s to the 1760s. These two "awakenings" were driven forward by a personal vision of Christianity that emphasized the sinfulness of each person and a confession of faith in Jesus Christ as the one true path to redemption and eternal salvation. Sandwiched between these two evangelical revivals was the American Enlightenment, which provided the intellectual framework for the Revolution, the Declaration of Independence, and the Constitution. Its leading lights—Jefferson, Madison, Hamilton, Franklin, and John Adams—addressed their energies and attention to the great task of building a nation and establishing its political institutions. While not hostile to religion, the founding fathers emphasized the secular ideals of individual liberty, representative government, and the separation of church and state. To the extent they were religious, they followed the rational religion of Deism, which denied the role of a personal God, or, alternatively, one of the traditional Protestant denominations. The evangelical revival of the antebellum period began when, once the nation's political institutions were in place and the founding generation began to pass from the scene, religious leaders expressed worries about a decline in piety and churchgoing, which they attributed to the secular preoccupations of the era. No one understood better than Abraham Lincoln the tension between the secular ideals expressed in the Declaration of Independence and the Constitution, and the evangelical pietism that characterized the religious revival through which he lived.

The Second Great Awakening was one of those decisive developments, along with the rise of Jacksonian democracy, that shaped the political culture of the expanding nation. The historian Perry Miller wrote that "one can almost say that the steady burning of the Revival, sometimes smoldering, now blazing into flame, never quite extinguished until the Civil War had been fought, was a central mode of this culture's search for national identity."[13] The revivalist preachers of the Second Great Awakening reinforced the democratic and decentralizing trends of the antebellum era as they rode the circuits across the new settlements in the Midwest and border states preaching the Gospel to great numbers of unchurched and uneducated listeners. In this way the religious revival worked in tandem with the populist elements of Jacksonian democracy, though in terms of cultural influence the religious movement was the more important impulse. The First Great Awakening had been centered in New England, took place within the Methodist, Congregational, and Presbyterian churches, and preached a severe form of Calvinism and predestination. The Second Great Awakening, by contrast, had its largest influence on the developing frontier, where its preachers taught a far looser and less severe form of Protestantism that held out the promise of salvation to every sinner who would renounce his depraved conduct and open his heart to Jesus Christ. Their appeal was emotional and to the heart rather than to the mind and the intellect, an approach that scandalized leaders of traditional Protestant denominations.

The revivals of the period were generally mixed affairs from a theological or denominational standpoint, as ministers were brought in to preach the Gospel with little regard for denominational affiliations. The historian Russel Nye writes that "The main thrust of the movement was toward inter-denominationalism. The trend was to de-emphasize doctrinal differences, to consider the spirit of the faith more important than doctrine." Those who attended the revivals, after all, had little interest in the theological distinctions among the Methodist, Presbyterian, or Baptist churches. The Second Great Awakening was, finally, highly communal both in form and in its ambitions. Miller quotes a minister of the era who observed that just as the Gospel can save individuals, "it can also renew the face of communities and nations. The same heavenly influence which in revivals of religion descends on families and villages may in like manner descend to refresh and beautify a whole land."[14]

The Second Great Awakening brought important innovations to American religion and the nation's civic culture. Among these was the local religious revival itself, which was originally conceived by Charles Grandison Finney on the model of the communal camp meeting. Here preachers would descend on a local area for several days, during which they would preach the Gospel to hundreds and even thousands of listeners in order to impart to the community a renewed sense of piety and faith and to win converts to Jesus Christ. Denominations associated with these revivals—Methodists and Baptists primarily—flourished in the new settlements. New evangelical sects and denominations were created during this time, including the Disciples of Christ, the Church of Jesus Christ of Latter-Day Saints, and the Seventh-Day Adventists. Calls for moral reform spilled over into politics through the creation of temperance and abolitionist societies, since the former sinner, once saved, had an obligation to help others and to improve the wider society in which he lived. The language of evangelism—sin, redemption and salvation, reform—was deployed in political controversies. The political convention developed on the model of the revival meeting.

The revivalist leaders sought to shape the culture in a more pious and God-fearing direction, and at the same time to save the Union itself from threats arising from greed, lawlessness, intemperance, and (importantly) sectionalism. These threats hanging over the Union gave added urgency to evangelical appeals beyond those geared to personal salvation. Lyman Beecher, along with Finney one of the two great evangelical leaders of the time, argued that the revivalist movement might yet save the Union from destruction. In an article published in 1831 under the title "The Necessity of Revivals of Religion to the Perpetuity of Our Civil and Religious Institutions," Beecher argued that the great danger to the national union came "from our vast extent of territory, our numerous and increasing population, from diversity of local interests, and the fury of sectional jealousy and hate."[15] The same factors that Madison said (in The Federalist, Number 10) would preserve the Constitution against a tyranny of the majority were cited in this article as threats to the underlying unity of the Republic. The evangelical leaders, taking a different view from Madison and the founding fathers, did not believe that the Union could be held together over a large land area with diverse interests without a strong religious foundation. Neither the balance of interests in the Constitution nor education nor even patriotism could provide the basis for an enduring union. The centrifugal forces tearing the Union apart could be counteracted only by revivals of religion inspired by God, which might give the people a common sense of morality and faith. Here again the secular assumptions of the founding fathers came into conflict with the pietistic outlook that guided the evangelical awakening.

Abraham Lincoln, at barely thirty years of age, provided his own surprising answer to the question of how the Union might be preserved. In a speech titled "The Perpetuation of Our Political Institutions," delivered in 1838 to the Young Men's Lyceum of Springfield, the young Lincoln rejected the claims that it could be maintained either by a balance of interests or by universal conversion to Christian teaching. It was as plain to Lincoln as to everyone else that the greatest danger of disunion would arise from the sectional split over slavery. Later, during the Civil War, he would refer to the insufficiency of both Madison's and Beecher's solutions when he observed (in his Second Inaugural Address) that slavery constituted an interest for which its advocates would rend the Union but that it was far from clear whose side God had taken in the great contest. The startling thing about this early speech is that, as Edmund Wilson has observed, Lincoln as a young man was already projecting himself into the role that he would later fulfill as savior of the Union.[16]

In this early speech, Lincoln assumed that because of geographical factors the danger to the Union could never come from abroad. "If destruction be our lot," he said, "we must ourselves be its author and finisher. As a nation of free men, we must live through all time or die by suicide." An important source of danger, he argued, was the "increasing disregard for law that pervades the country and the disposition to substitute wild and furious passions in lieu of the sober judgment of courts"–this a reference to a rising tide of lynch law in the land, in particular to a recent case in which the editor of an abolitionist newspaper had been lynched near St. Louis and his printing press tossed into a river. Some abolitionists, on the other hand, while themselves the victims of lynch law, had also called the Constitution a "covenant with death" and an "agreement with hell" because of its protections for slavery. Some appealed to a "higher law" which justified civil disobedience in opposition to slavery. Mob rule and disregard for law, Lincoln argued, if permitted to continue, would eventually destroy the attachment of the people to their government. "Whenever the vicious portion of the population shall be permitted to gather in bands of hundreds and thousands, and burn churches, ravage and rob provision stores, throw printing presses into rivers, shoot editors, and hang and burn obnoxious persons at pleasure, and with impunity, depend on it, this Government cannot last." By such events, the feelings of loyal and law-abiding citizens will become alienated from the government, leaving it without the support needed to sustain it. Lincoln, as he did throughout his career, tried to chart a path between political extremes.

At this point Lincoln's speech takes a strange turn, for now he suggests that the alienation of the people from their government will provide an opportunity for a dictator on the model of a Caesar or a Napoleon to arise and "overturn that fair fabric, which for the last half century, has been the fondest hope of lovers of freedom throughout the world." Up to this point in the nation's history, Lincoln says, the passions of the people and the ambitions of their leaders worked in favor of liberty and self-government. At the time of the Revolution, the lovers of liberty sought fame and celebrity in making the nation's experiment in self-government a success. The destructive passions of hatred, jealousy, and resentment were not aimed at ourselves or our own institutions, but at the British, a foreign and now defeated adversary. "The experiment is now successful," Lincoln continues, "and thousands have won their deathless names in making it so. [But] this field of glory is harvested, and the crop is already appropriated." It is certain, he says, that in the future men of talents and ambitions will arise to seek gratification in new fields of fame and glory. The question for Lincoln, then, is this: "Can that gratification be found in supporting and maintaining an edifice that has been erected by others?" The answer is no. Ordinary men of high ambition would be satisfied to hold a seat in Congress or to win the presidential chair—"but such belong not to the family of the lion or the tribe of the eagle. Think you these places would satisfy an Alexander, a Caesar, or a Napoleon? Never! Towering genius disdains a beaten path. It seeks regions hitherto unexplored. . . . It thirsts and burns for distinction and, if possible, it will have it, whether at the expense of emancipating slaves or enslaving free men." When such a person of towering genius and lofty ambition should appear on the American scene, it will be necessary for the people, in order to counter his designs, to be attached firmly to one another and to their institutions.

Lincoln seems here to have looked into the future in the most striking and extraordinary way, describing this figure looming on the horizon with, as Edmund Wilson puts it, "a fire that seemed to derive as much from admiration as from apprehension." It was as if Lincoln "had not only foreseen the drama but had even seen all around it with a kind of poetic objectivity, aware of the various points of view that the world must take toward the protagonist."[17] It was as if he had also foreseen in an eerie way the violence and lawlessness that would tear the Union apart two decades later, from "Bloody Kansas," to Senator Sumner's beating in the Senate chamber, to the Dred Scott decision, to John Brown's raid, to the secession crisis and civil war, all the way down to his own assassination. Lincoln might well have seen himself in the role of the statesman who would stand up to his "towering genius" in defense of self-government and the Constitution. At the same time, he was perceptive enough (as the Lyceum speech demonstrates) to have foreseen also that opponents might view him in an entirely different light— that is, as the American Caesar against whom he has warned.[18]

His solution to the crisis he foresaw was to urge Americans to look upon the Revolution, the Constitution, and the laws of the nation with religious devotion. "Let every American," Lincoln said in the Lyceum speech, "every lover of liberty, every well wisher to his posterity, swear by the blood of the Revolution never to violate in the least particular the laws of the country; and never to tolerate their violation by others. As the patriots of seventy-six did to the support of the Declaration of Independence, so to the support of the Constitution and Laws, let every American pledge his life, his property, and his sacred honor." He urged Americans to cultivate a reverence for their laws and institutions to the point at which such reverence is turned into "the political religion of the nation" and people of all colors and conditions will "sacrifice unceasingly on its altars." In Lincoln's political theology, reverence for the nation's laws is the foundation of self-government, the "rock" upon which the nation (like the Church) is built.

In this early speech, Lincoln sought to establish a fusion between the secular ideals of the founding era and the evangelical teachings of the Second Great Awakening such that the Constitution and the laws would be revered and worshipped like the sacred symbols of a church. He thus conflated biblical images with the symbols and institutions of the nation—as when he said in the Lyceum speech that reverence for the laws is the rock upon which the nation is founded. He rather candidly acknowledged that the basis upon which the founding fathers had built the Constitution would be insufficient to sustain it over the long run. The largely rational and secular arguments of the Declaration of Independence and *The Federalist* seemed weak in relation to the powerful currents of religion and sectionalism that were then gathering force. Instead of arguing for a strict separation of religion and politics, as many do today, Lincoln sought to use religious devotion as a means of strengthening the institutions of self-government, thereby deflecting it from a religious to a secular purpose. Something outside the Constitution—a faith or a political theology—was required to maintain it. The great question was whether such a theology could be imparted by argument and appeals to reason, as Lincoln tried to do in his Lyceum speech, or if some overwhelming event was required to engrave it in the hearts and minds of the people.

Judged in retrospect, Lincoln's strange ability to look into the future is truly impressive, to put it mildly. With little in the way of formal education and instructed as a boy mainly by the Bible and the works of Shakespeare and the founders, Lincoln assessed the dangers to the nation, seeing how they might unfold and how the Union might finally be saved. He saw more deeply into the political challenges of the Union than anyone else of his time. Acting on the basis of this understanding, he played a decisive role in bringing his own prophecies to fulfillment. The young John F. Kennedy, by contrast, owning the best secular education that money could buy, with direct access through his father to leading statesmen, scholars, and journalists, ventured to England in 1938 to witness the historic debates between Churchill and the advocates of appeasement—and took (along with his father) the side of appeasement. It is no disparagement of John F. Kennedy to point out that he judged wrongly the great political crisis of his youth while Abraham Lincoln, facing a parallel challenge, judged it rightly. The wonder is not that Kennedy got it wrong but that Lincoln got it right—and in so many pertinent details.

The Civil War was a fulfillment of Lincoln's fearsome apprehensions but also the overwhelming event that, with his help, turned the Union into an object of reverence. This could not have been accomplished without Lincoln's inspired rhetoric, but perhaps also not without the pietistic feelings that had been aroused by the Second Great Awakening, the religious imagery it had imparted to the culture of the North, and the prominent persons whose ideals and ambitions had been shaped by it. The ethic of the Republican Party as it was formed in the 1850s borrowed heavily from revivalist imagery—for example, the immorality and sinfulness of slavery, the concept of an "irrepressible conflict" between freedom and slavery, an almost religious conception of the Union, and the idea that God had a special plan for the United States that the North in particular had a duty to fulfill.[19] Finney, one of the founders of the revivalist movement, was an ardent Republican, so much so that he was disappointed in Lincoln's lukewarm endorsement of the antislavery cause after he was given the party's presidential nomination in 1860.[20] Lyman Beecher's daughter, Harriet Beecher Stowe, was the author of the influential antislavery novel *Uncle Tom's Cabin*, published in 1852. Julia Ward Howe's "The Battle Hymn of the Republic" explicitly conflated the Christian and Union causes. It is hard to imagine the Civil War occurring at all—or at least in the way that it occurred—in the absence of the great evangelical awakening that preceded it.

Lincoln played the most significant role in advancing a religious understanding of the war, though his purpose was not to promote Christianity but rather to impart sacred meaning to the Union and the national experiment in self-government. He spoke deliberately in terms that were immediately understood by Christians well versed in the Bible. The general import of his speeches and statements was to suggest that God intervenes in human history and that the nations of the world stand under heavenly judgment.

Lincoln first came to national attention with his "house divided" speech in 1858, which employed as its main theme a metaphor ("A house divided against itself cannot stand") used by Jesus in a confrontation with the Pharisees. The Gettysburg Address was almost biblical both in its rhetoric ("Four score and seven years ago"; "this hallowed ground"; "a new birth of freedom") and in its theme that those who had perished in the war had done so for a sacred cause. The "new birth" of freedom was a well-understood reference to the evangelical concept of one being born again in Christian faith. The speech, which begins by pointing to the past in the founding of the nation in 1776, ends by looking to the future in the pledge that "government of the people, for the people, and by the people shall not perish from the earth."[21] His letter of condolence in 1864 to Lydia Bixby, who (Lincoln was told) had lost five sons in battle, ends with the consolatory sentence, "I pray that our Heavenly Father may assuage the anguish of your bereavement and leave you only the cherished memory of the loved and lost, and the solemn pride that must be yours to have laid so costly a sacrifice upon the altar of freedom."[22] The Second Inaugural Address, as many have observed, reads more like a sermon than a political address for a secular occasion. Some immediately called it Lincoln's "Sermon on the Mount." The central theme of the address was that the enormous suffering of the war must be understood as a punishment by God visited upon both North and South for the offense of slavery—and that with the offense now eradicated, the nation may begin its life anew in a rebirth of freedom. This speech was the culmination of Lincoln's lifelong aspiration (in Harry Jaffa's words) "to transform the American story into the moral elements of the Biblical story."[23]

Lincoln, however, far from being a devout Christian, had been known throughout his career as a freethinker, not unlike Jefferson, who did not attend services on a regular basis and did not belong to any denominational church. This had been something of an issue in one of Lincoln's earlier campaigns for Congress in the 1840s, when he was attacked by an opponent for his apparent lack of religious belief. When Lincoln was nominated for president in 1860, only three of the twenty-four ministers in his home city of Springfield could bring themselves to endorse him. His speeches are laced with moving references to God and the Almighty but few to Jesus Christ. While Lincoln never expressed an anti-Christian thought, never either, so far as the record shows, did he express an affirmative statement of Christian faith.[24] This later proved to be a slightly awkward matter for those who, after the assassination, brought forth comparisons between Lincoln and the martyred Savior. Yet never before did the nation have as a leader one who deployed biblical imagery and language with such power and effect. If Abraham Lincoln was not in fact a righteous man of God, he certainly spoke like one. Slavery, moreover, as Lincoln certainly recognized, had an ambiguous status in relation to the churches and Holy Scripture. It had been tolerated through the ages in all kinds of societies, ancient and modern, biblical and nonbiblical, and even had the support of many American churches in his time. The slave owners who broke up the Union claimed that the Bible sanctioned and even encouraged the institution of slavery. In his Second Inaugural Address, Lincoln concluded that the violently unpredictable course of the war was a sign that the Almighty in fact condemned slavery. Nonetheless, throughout his public career, he saw slavery as more of a sin against those other sacred institutions and ideals: the Declaration of Independence and the foundational assumptions of self-government.

Abraham Lincoln was shot by the itinerant actor and Southern partisan John Wilkes Booth on April 14, 1865, Good Friday on the Christian calendar, while he and Mrs. Lincoln were watching a play from the presidential box at Ford's Theater in Washington. Booth was immediately recognized by veteran theater-goers as he leaped to the stage from the president's box, shouting the Latin phrase *Sic Semper Tyrannis* ("Thus Always to Tyrants"), the motto of the Commonwealth of Virginia and an exclamation attributed to Brutus after the assassination of Caesar.

Booth did not view his deed as the killing of a beloved republican leader but rather as an act of tyrannicide, one of the great themes of classical drama in which he was well versed. Like Brutus in defense of the Roman Republic, Booth would kill Lincoln to preserve the honor of the Confederate republic. In keeping with that classical theme, he hoped to shoot Lincoln on April 13, the monthly day of reckoning (the "Ides") in the Roman calendar. A change of plans on Lincoln's part aborted Booth's plans on that evening. The next morning Booth learned quite accidentally while picking up his mail at Ford's Theater that Lincoln had decided on short notice to attend that evening's performance of *Our American Cousin*. Booth would yet have his opportunity to play the role of Brutus.

One of Booth's co-conspirators, Lewis Powell, attacked the secretary of state, William Seward, at his home the same evening, though Seward's attendants were able to fight off the would-be assassin before he could inflict fatal injuries. Booth had apparently viewed Seward as Lincoln's great ally, akin to Caesar's Marc Antony, who had to be eliminated as well if the overall plot was to succeed in destabilizing the Union and turning the tide in favor of the Confederacy. This was perhaps a miscalculation: The secretary of war, Edwin Stanton, turned out to be a more determined and ruthless foe of the conspirators than Seward might have been. Booth's co-conspirators were quickly captured. He was tracked down by Union troops to a Virginia farm where, nearly two weeks after the assassination, he was shot by a Union soldier while hiding out in a barn. Booth saw quickly, however, that his deed was not widely viewed in a heroic light. During his desperate flight from Washington, he wrote in his diary: "After being hunted like a dog through swamps, woods, and last night being chased by gun boats till I was forced to return wet, cold and starving with everyman's hand against me, I am here in despair. And why: For doing what Brutus was honored for, what made Tell a Hero. And yet I for striking down a greater tyrant than they ever knew am looked upon as a common cut-throat." Booth mistakenly thought that after assassinating Lincoln he would be welcomed as a hero in the dying Confederacy. As Michael W. Kaufmann writes in his fine study of Lincoln's assassin, "Booth had hoped to kill Lincoln on the Ides and highlight his resemblance to Caesar; but instead he shot him on Good Friday, and the world compared him to Christ."[25]

There was little question that Booth had acted to avenge the South and as a last-ditch attempt to save the Confederacy from final defeat. Many speculated that Booth, out of arrogance and a sense of self-importance, had assassinated Lincoln to assure himself a place in history. In the end, he achieved far less than he intended. Few saw him as a hero; his deed was repudiated in the South; Lincoln's death united the North; no one (at least after the assassination) voiced agreement with his portrait of Lincoln as a tyrant; indeed, Lincoln would soon be held up as a symbol of liberty.

Lincoln's assassination occurred just five days after the Civil War had ended with Lee's surrender to Grant at Appomattox. When Lincoln passed away early the next day, victory celebrations across the North were replaced by rituals of grief and mourning. "The Songs of Victory Drowned in Sorrow," ran a headline in the *New York Times* the day after Lincoln died.

One immediate reaction (also an enduring one) was to view Lincoln as a martyr for liberty and the Union. The fact that he was killed on Good Friday magnified the image and brought forth obvious comparisons between the assassinated president and Jesus Christ. As one correspondent said at the time, "The two events have been providentially associated and henceforth no human power can disassociate them."[26] The ground had also been well prepared for such comparisons by the long-running evangelical revival, the crusade against slavery, and Lincoln's own wartime rhetoric. Northerners understood what a martyr was in its deepest religious sense and they understood further why their assassinated leader qualified as such. A martyr is one who gives his life for a cause or an ideal in order to inspire others to renew their dedication to those ends. A martyr, or a hero, is therefore an inspirational example to others. Lincoln, in his Gettysburg Address, had already made this case eloquently on behalf of the soldiers who had died fighting for the Union.

The Sunday following the assassination was known in the North as "Black Easter" in mourning for the fallen president. In pulpits across the North, ministers preached sermons in churches draped in black praising Lincoln and trying to find meaning in his death. A minister in Hartford sounded one of the main themes: "Yes, it was meet that the martyrdom should occur on Good Friday. It is no blasphemy against the Son of God and the Savior of men that we declare the fitness of the slaying of the Second Father of our Republic on the anniversary of the day on which He was slain. Jesus Christ died for the world, Abraham Lincoln died for his country."[27] Henry Ward Beecher asked, from the pulpit of his church in New York City, "Who can recount our martyr's sufferings for his people?"[28] Another minister sermonized that "the crime committed last Friday night in Washington is the worst ever committed on any Good Friday since the crucifixion of Christ. It was not only assassination; it was parricide, for Abraham Lincoln was as a father to the whole nation." Lloyd Lewis writes, in *Myths after Lincoln*, that "Within a week after the assassination, the phrase 'savior of his country' was a slogan for orators, editorial writers and makers of funeral mottoes over the entire North."[29] When Lincoln was not being compared to Jesus Christ, he was compared to Moses, who, like the slain president, led his people through hardship to the Promised Land, but could not enter.

A second response to the assassination was to blame the South and its sympathizers in the North for the criminal deed. Some in the North whose expressions of grief were deemed insufficient and disrespectful were beaten and, in rare cases, even killed. No one doubted that John Wilkes Booth shot the president and was at the head of a conspiracy to kill other leaders of the government. Booth was a member of a prominent theatrical family and had even played Ford's Theater more than once; he was a well-known figure in Washington and in urban centers up and down the East Coast. He was immediately identified to authorities and then to Secretary of War Stanton, who set Union soldiers on his trail. Booth was known further as a friend to the South. There was little question that he committed the deed and why he did it. The next morning's edition of the *New York Times* ran a headline saying the assassination was "The Act of a Desperate Southerner" even before the editors knew that Booth had been identified as the assassin. Henry Ward Beecher, speaking from his pulpit in Brooklyn, said that Booth "was himself but the long sting with which slavery struck at liberty. . . . Never while time lasts will it be forgotten that slavery, by its minions, slew him and in slaying him, made manifest its whole nature and tendency." Another minister in New York City said, "The warfare which the southern rebellion has made on our government is really warfare against God. Not Israel was more truly a nation divinely collected, divinely governed, divinely commissioned, or divinely prospered than have been these United States of America." Ministers and politicians alike called for vengeance against the rebels. "Lincoln the man was never so dead as on 'Black Easter,' his policies drowned in his own blood," wrote Lloyd Lewis on the Northern reaction to Lincoln's murder.[30] Lincoln's hopes for reconciliation in a Union reborn were being cast aside amid calls for harsh punishments against the South.

In the hours immediately following Lincoln's death, it fell to Stanton as the effective head of government to dictate final arrangements, after consulting with members of the cabinet, for the president's funeral and burial.[31] Mrs. Lincoln was far too distraught to attend to practical matters of any kind. It was quickly decided that a funeral would be held in the White House, the late president's body would lie in state in the Rotunda of the Capitol, and burial would follow in Springfield. Stanton, one of the radical Republicans who wished for harsh measures against the South, "decided to make the corpse of the martyr an exhibit to the North of Southern perfidy," according to Lloyd Lewis.[32] Whether or not this was true, Lincoln's funeral was an event of the like the American people had never before seen—and have not seen since, with the possible exception of the funeral proceedings for John F. Kennedy.

Lincoln's funeral was held in the East Room of the White House on Wednesday, April 19, five days after he was shot. The day before, mourners thronged the White House to file through the East Room, where the flag-draped coffin rested on a catafalque constructed for the occasion. The large crowd was an early sign of things to come. The funeral ceremony itself was attended by dignitaries only—the new president, the cabinet, members of Congress, governors, foreign ministers, Grant and his generals, along with Lincoln's two sons, Robert and Tad. Mrs. Lincoln was too upset to attend. The brief ceremony was presided over by four clergymen representing the Episcopal, Presbyterian, Methodist, and Baptist churches, each of whom prayed and spoke briefly. Then, with the services over, the coffin was taken out of the White House for the final time for a sorrowful procession down Pennsylvania Avenue to the Capitol, where the president's body would lie in state. From this moment until it was interred in Springfield more than two weeks later, Lincoln's casket was in nearly continuous public view, attracting during its mournful journey some of the largest crowds ever assembled in the United States or anywhere else for that matter.[33]

Church bells rang throughout Washington as the glass-encased hearse moved slowly along Pennsylvania Avenue toward the Capitol, accompanied also by the sound of muffled drums. The route was lined with people, many having come long distances to view the historic event. The windows and rooftops along the way were filled with silent mourners. Officials were stunned at the enormous size of the crowds. The next day, hour by hour mourners filed through the Capitol Rotunda to view the coffin. By the time the doors to the Capitol were closed that evening, more than 25,000 people had paid their respects to their late president.

On Friday, April 21, the coffin was taken to Union Station, where it was placed on a nine-car train for the long trip back to Springfield. It was decided by Stanton and others, following entreaties from congressmen and governors, that the train should retrace the route Lincoln had taken from Springfield when he came to Washington in 1861, thus allowing various cities along the way to hold their own ceremonies of mourning. At Baltimore, the first stop in the extended procession and a city now known for its warm feelings toward Lincoln, 10,000 mourners filed past the open casket in the Exchange Building in a matter of three hours. Dense crowds lined the tracks as the train moved through the Pennsylvania countryside on its way to Harrisburg, where thousands awaited its arrival. In Philadelphia, some 300,000 mourners passed by the open casket in Independence Hall. Surging and sometimes disorderly crowds lined the streets to watch the casket pass by. In New York City, where just two years before there were tumultuous riots against Lincoln's war policy, more than 160,000 people marched in a procession through the streets by which the casket was borne to City Hall. Many thousands more lined the streets in quiet observance. At one point, some 500,000 people waited in line to view the open casket in the rotunda of City Hall. The next day, the funeral train made its way to Albany, where the casket was taken to the state house for viewing. There some 4,000 mourners per hour filed past the casket, all day and all night, since now (given the huge crowds assembling) the doors were no longer being closed at midnight.

The funereal journey back to Springfield was turning into an extravaganza of mourning that was beyond the thoughts of any of its planners. As news circulated across the nation, cities along the future route determined that they should not be outdone by Philadelphia, New York, or Albany. "Each must now be outdoing anything that any other city had done," as Lloyd Lewis wrote. "Decorations must be larger, crowds bigger, ceremonies finer, and orations more idolatrous." The procession was in danger of getting out of hand, so extravagant and delirious were the expressions of grief across the North. "The thing had become half circus, half heartbreak."[34]

Great crowds gathered along the tracks as the train moved westward from Albany toward Buffalo, past the small and medium-sized towns of northern New York. In Buffalo, the casket was viewed by more than 100,000 mourners, including past and future presidents Millard Fillmore and Grover Cleveland. In the city of Cleveland, the casket was placed in a pagoda in a public park where huge crowds assembled for viewing. The crowds thickened along the tracks when the train moved into the Midwest, Lincoln's home territory. Towns along the path covered the tracks with arches of evergreen boughs and American flags. From Cleveland the procession went to Columbus, then to Indianapolis, then northward to Chicago, where the streets were clogged with mourners from around the region who had begun to converge on the city days before as news spread westward of the outpouring of grief for the native son of Illinois in the great cities of the East. More than 125,000 persons viewed Lincoln's casket in the Chicago Courthouse. Speaker of the House Schuyler Colfax addressed a large crowd in a speech that praised Lincoln as the most forgiving of men, while denouncing the South for countless acts of wickedness committed during the war.

From Chicago, the procession moved at last toward Springfield, Lincoln's home and final burial place. All day on May 3, mourners filed past the casket in the state house of representatives, where Lincoln first served in public office and in 1858 delivered his "House Divided" speech. The next day a long procession led by General Joseph Hooker marched slowly through Springfield, past Lincoln's home, toward Oak Ridge Cemetery, where his body was to be interred with that of his young son Willie, who had died of typhoid fever three years earlier in Washington. Lincoln's horse, "Old Bob," marched riderless behind the hearse wearing a mourning blanket, the riding stirrups turned backwards in remembrance of the fallen soldier whom he once carried. The ceremony concluded with the singing of a funeral hymn, "Rest, Noble Martyr," that had been composed by a clergyman for the occasion.

Lincoln was finally buried in Springfield three weeks after he was shot in Ford's Theater. The procession across the country had lasted two weeks, during which time Lincoln's open casket was displayed in eleven different cities and viewed by more than one and a half million Americans. Lincoln's hearse or coffin had been looked upon by at least seven million mourners, counting those gathered in parades and city streets or alongside railroad tracks, a number representing more than a third of the population of the entire North.

The event was immortalized in Walt Whitman's elegiac tribute to Lincoln:

> Coffin that passes through lanes and streets,
> Through day and night, with great cloud darkening
>   the land,
> With the pomp of inlooped flags, with the cities draped
>   in black,
> With the show of the states themselves as of the crepe-
>   veiled women standing,
> With processions long and winding, and the flambeaus
>   of the night,
> With the countless torches lit—with the silent sea of faces
>   and the unbared heads,
> With the waiting depot, the arriving coffin, and the
>   somber faces,
> With the dirges through the night, with the thousand voices
>   rising strong and solemn,
> With all the mournful voices of the dirges, poured round
>   the coffin,
> The dim lit churches and the shuddering organs—Where
>   amid these you journey,
> With the tolling, tolling bells' perpetual clang,
> Here, coffin that slowly passes,
> I give you my sprig of lilac.

Lincoln had turned out to be the "redeemer president" that Whitman had written about some years earlier, a rough-hewn leader out of the West who would purge national politics of its petty corruptions and the rascality of politicians. Whitman saw that Lincoln by his life and death had given the Union a strength and solidity it had previously lacked:

The final use of the greatest men of a Nation is, after all, not with reference to their deeds in themselves, or their direct bearing on their times or lands. The final use of a heroic-eminent life—especially a heroic-eminent death—is its indirect filtering into the nation and the race, and to give, often at many removes, but unerringly age after age, color and fiber to the personalism of the youth and maturity of that age and of mankind. Then there is a cement to the whole people, subtler, more underlying than anything written in the constitution, or courts or armies—namely the cement of a death identified thoroughly with that people, at its head, and for its sake. Strange—is it not?—that battles, martyrs, agonies, blood, even assassination, should so condense a Nationality.[35]

The solemn and profoundly moving proceedings of Lincoln's funeral resembled nothing so much as an extended revival, mixing political with religious themes in the manner of Lincoln's political religion, and encompassing not just a locality but the entire nation. During these protracted rituals of grief, Abraham Lincoln's reputation as savior of the Union was cemented in the minds of Northerners and in the history of the nation. It was an event that bound the nation together—or at least it bound the North together—in a ritual of grief and dedication. The long process of mourning demonstrated to the North what it had lost with the assassination of Lincoln (and also what acts of perfidy the rebellious Southerners were capable of committing). G. K. Chesterton once wrote that "The United States is a nation with the soul of a church." If this is true, or if it was once true, it was Lincoln who was instrumental in making it so.

In the context of his time, Abraham Lincoln must be judged as a liberal, though that term was not used in American political controversies until several decades after his death. Like John F. Kennedy, Lincoln was flanked on all sides by opponents who said he was doing either too little or too much to address the problems at hand. Nevertheless, Lincoln stood for popular government and the nobility of the common man, his rights rooted in the Declaration of Independence, the "sheet anchor" of American freedom. He looked to an unfolding future in which the ideals of the Declaration might be progressively realized such that the United States would continue to serve as a standard bearer in the world for the democratic ideal. Lincoln's career was based on a conviction that the experiment in self-government could not succeed unless the people looked upon their institutions with religious-like devotion.

Some of Lincoln's core convictions, however, stand in contrast to the assumptions of modern liberalism as they began to take shape in the United States after 1900. The reform tradition, as it was called by Hofstadter and others, sought to undo that connection between religion and politics that Lincoln had labored so hard and creatively to establish. It has been an article of faith among modern liberals that the Constitution, with its dispersed powers and numerous veto points, is the greatest of all institutional impediments to political reform. Behind this obstacle lies another—namely, the sense of reverence with which the American people view the Constitution and the founding fathers. It was plain to Progressives, and to later generations of liberals, that to advance the cause of reform it would be necessary to shake off such reverent attitudes—in other words, to undo and to overcome Lincoln's political theology, which they argued was based on a series of "myths" about the founders and the Constitution.

One of the landmarks of Progressive history was Charles Beard's *An Economic Interpretation of the Constitution*, published in 1913, which tried to prove that the founding fathers wrote the Constitution as an instrument to defend their economic interests in manufacturing, slaves, and government debt. Beard's purpose was to show that the framers of the Constitution did not act mainly from patriotic motives or to secure a national government on the basis of enduring principles, but rather to protect property interests that had been made insecure under the weak national system created by the Articles of Confederation. It followed that, if the Constitution had not in fact been the creation of inspired and patriotic men, and if it was not built on the basis of permanently valid principles, then succeeding generations could adjust it according to their own needs and interests without fear that they were tampering with something sacred. From Beard's point of view and from the standpoint of reformist liberalism in general, Lincoln's political theology was backward-looking because it exalted the past at the expense of the present and the future. Moreover, by elevating the Constitution into a symbol for the nation, it permanently forced a dynamic society into a straitjacket of institutions created for a pre-industrial situation. Beard did not mean to disparage the founders but only to suggest that they were little different from the political actors of any other time. The Progressives wished to remake the Constitution so it would be more amenable to reform and modernization.[36] Beard suggested that this is exactly what the founders did in their own time and would not hesitate to do again if they were to come back to life.

Carl Becker, another prominent historian of that period, also sought to delimit the influence of the founders to their own period of history. His landmark book, *The Declaration of Independence: A Study in the History of Political Ideas*, published in 1922, argued that the ideals of the Declaration of Independence had but little relevance to the modern age.[37] Becker, as a historian, viewed the political thought of the past as taking place within a "climate of opinion" that changes like fashion with the generations. All of us, historians and statesmen alike, are more or less prisoners of the climate of opinion within which we live and think. There can be no permanent truths in politics or history, only claims that have the appearance of truth within the historical contexts in which they are made. The assertions in the Declaration of Independence cannot be said to be true or, indeed, even to be false, Becker argued, but only to be convenient or functional assertions for people of Jefferson's time and circumstances. Indeed, Becker wrote that the philosophy announced in the Declaration is "naïve" and "superficial"; it is a faith "that could not survive the harsh realities of the modern world."³⁸ The contemporary age, shaped by industry, science, and militarism, has brought forth an entirely new climate of opinion, Becker wrote, one that has rendered antique and out of date the ideas of Jefferson and the founders.

While Beard and Becker have hardly had the last word among scholars on the Declaration of Independence and the Constitution, their general outlook on the past and on the founders survived over the decades as important features of American liberalism. The rub, from the liberal point of view, is that these two founding documents enshrined liberty as the highest political principle and sought to protect it by creating a government of limited scope, while the general goal of modern liberalism has been to promote equality through the agency of a much expanded national government. Given this clash of ideals, liberals wished not to be overly tied down by the past—especially by commitments the founders had made in circumstances far different from our own. The ideal of limited government may have been appropriate for a small agricultural society in the 1770s and 1780s but not for a complex industrial society of the twentieth century. During the 1950s, historians and political scientists were preoccupied with finding ways around the restrictions of the eighteenth-century Constitution. Many criticized the Constitution for some of its less than democratic features, such as judicial review, the apportionment of seats in the Senate, and the Electoral College. Some argued for loose construction of the Constitution as a means of giving the Supreme Court needed latitude to bring the document up to date; others placed hope in the political parties as institutions that might overcome the inertia built into the constitutional system.³⁹ From a liberal point of view, Lincoln's political theology was part of the problem that reformers had to overcome.

As heirs to the Progressive tradition, John F. Kennedy and his supporters had far more in common with thinkers like Beard and Becker than with Abraham Lincoln. The attempt by Mrs. Kennedy and others to link the two assassinated presidents was largely symbolic rather than substantive, done mainly to contribute meaning to a painful event that otherwise appeared senseless. For the reasons discussed above, the association was unlikely to stick once the initial shock of the assassination had passed.

Lincoln was assassinated in the midst of a culture that had carefully nurtured the ideals of sacrifice and martyrdom for a cause. The Protestant revival of that time encouraged the belief that the history of the American nation was a reprise of the biblical story of ancient Israel. Lincoln's own thought and rhetoric further encouraged such an understanding. The Civil War, concluding with Lincoln's own assassination, was readily assimilated into this cultural framework within which religious and political ideals were intimately intertwined. It made perfect sense, given such deeply held assumptions, to see Lincoln as a martyr for emancipation and Union, and to look to the South as the party responsible for his death. The extravagant and long-running funeral held for the fallen hero finally cemented these ideas in the collective mind of the North.

We can only imagine what cultural confusion would have been visited upon the supporters of Lincoln and the Union across the North if, instead of being killed as he was through a conspiracy of Southern partisans, Lincoln had been assassinated by an abolitionist. Such an act would have been nearly impossible for Northerners to assimilate within the cultural framework of the Civil War era. For one thing, it would have rendered somewhat illogical the assertions of martyrdom on behalf of the slain president. The Christian pastors who on "Black Easter" portrayed Lincoln as a martyr would have had to wrestle with the discordant reality of his death. How, after all, could Lincoln be deemed a martyr for emancipation and Union if he had been killed by a partisan of that very cause? The Southern rebels, meanwhile, who had brought about the conflict by trying to break up the Union, would have to be held blameless in his death. In such a case, the outpouring of grief following the president's assassination would have been mixed with confusion as to the moral meaning of the event. The anger across the North that was in fact directed against the South would in this case have had no rational outlet in relation to the great conflict that had just been waged. There must have been in that case a strong temptation to disregard the facts by blaming the South anyway as a means of restoring moral cohesion to the situation. It would have been said by many that the abolitionist assassin was in fact an agent of the slave power or perhaps was not really an abolitionist at all.

Something bizarrely similar to this happened with the assassination of John F. Kennedy, which is one reason why the aftermath of that event was so confusing to many Americans—and especially to liberal Americans. Kennedy being killed by a communist was more or less the historical equivalent of Lincoln being killed by an abolitionist—though in one case it actually happened and in the other it did not. The attempt to square this brutal fact with the received assumptions of the era proved a most difficult challenge for liberal doctrine from 1963 forward. The challenge was rendered even more imposing by the posthumous elevation of Kennedy's reputation. If Kennedy was in fact a leader dedicated to peace, equality, and racial justice, why should a leftist wish to kill him? It made much more sense, given the premise (which was itself highly exaggerated) to think that he must have been killed by a racist or a bigot—or at any rate by someone acting on behalf of the far right. Liberal thinkers took pride in the claim that their ideas, unlike the delusional theories of the radical right, were grounded in fact and reason. After World War II, the far right in America was challenged to come to terms with the reality of communist power in the world. Instead of doing so, its leaders attributed this power to treason and conspiracies. Now, following Kennedy's assassination, liberals were faced with a parallel challenge of making sense of an event that contradicted their deepest beliefs. As events would show, the liberals performed no better in facing their challenge than the rightists had earlier fared in facing theirs.

Liberals in particular struggled to find meaning in Kennedy's death in the midst of a political culture that, by their own actions, had more or less been stripped of religious themes and images. The crusade begun in the Progressive era to unwind Lincoln's political theology had largely succeeded by the time Kennedy came to the presidency—or it had largely succeeded among those who called themselves liberals. Religious symbols and images, as they might be applied to politics, had been more or less washed out of the culture by the time Kennedy came to office and no longer carried the depth of meaning that they carried in Lincoln's time. One no longer thought of the United States as a biblical nation nor as a "Christian nation," but rather as a secular nation in which religion was increasingly a matter of private conscience. The feeling once prevalent that the history of the United States was a modern re-enactment of the biblical story had by now largely disappeared, certainly so among liberals. The reverent feelings for the founders and, indeed, for Lincoln had been greatly attenuated. One might invoke the term "martyr," but it no longer carried much cultural meaning. People might hear the word as applied to an important leader but it contributed little in the way of comfort or understanding. Thus it was that John F. Kennedy was called a martyr after he was assassinated —even though in the secular culture of the 1960s the concept did not bear much in the way of spiritual meaning, particularly among liberals reared in the reformist tradition. Besides, even if one granted the concept, it was not all that easy to figure out what Kennedy stood for, why he was a martyr, and what the connection was between his assassination and his supposed martyrdom. A martyr's death should inspire acts of emulation. In the wake of Kennedy's death, one saw precious little of this. Indeed, the event as it penetrated through the culture seemed more to encourage acts of negation on the parts of those who said they admired him.

There was (as we have implied) a factual syllogism that might have rendered Kennedy's death as intelligible as Lincoln's—though its acceptance would have raised other challenges to liberal convictions. If Oswald shot Kennedy and if Oswald was a communist and an admirer of Castro and the Soviet Union, then it followed that communism was the large cause behind the assassination and, further, that Kennedy was a martyr to the ideals at stake in the Cold War. Such a logical and factual account of Kennedy's assassination was rarely attempted, even though most thoughtful people had to acknowledge at some level that it was true. Such an analysis, however, did not comport with what many felt must be true or hoped was true. For many, such a thought was no more intelligible than the idea that Lincoln might have been assassinated by an abolitionist. Given the known facts surrounding the Kennedy assassination, the immediate response to it was unexpected and not entirely reasonable.

FOUR · MARTYR: KENNEDY

IF LEE HARVEY OSWALD had indeed shot President Kennedy, as the immediately known facts seemed to say, then it would be difficult to escape the logical implications of that premise: President Kennedy was a victim of the Cold War. If this conclusion was unacceptable, however, one might try to wave aside the premise. One might conjure up reasons to believe that Oswald was really a right-wing extremist. If he was not, he might easily have been one in the political atmosphere of Dallas in 1963. Perhaps, in addition, some wider cause beyond the actions of a warped individual might be assigned ultimate blame for the tragic event. This latter explanation made far more sense to rational people than an outright denial of the obvious facts. After all, in many circumstances, interpretations are far more compelling than mere facts since they can prescribe what meanings we should attach to those facts.

Once again, Mrs. Kennedy instinctively hinted at such a cause in the grief-filled hours following the assassination, even before she knew that Oswald had been arrested in connection with the crime. On the trip back from Dallas to Washington aboard Air Force One on the afternoon of the assassination, various people, including

Lady Bird Johnson, urged Mrs. Kennedy to change out of the blood-spattered clothes she was still wearing. These were compassionate gestures, made on the assumption that Mrs. Kennedy did not wish to appear in those clothes in front of the television cameras that would be waiting at the airport when the plane landed. Such an assumption, however, was mistaken, perhaps because she was still in a state of shock following the sudden and shattering events of that day. "No," she replied more than once, "I want them to see what they have done."[1]

Who, exactly, were "they"? And what did "they" do?

James Reston supplied an answer of sorts in an article that appeared the next day in the *New York Times* under the title "Why America Weeps: Kennedy Victim of Violent Streak He Sought to Curb in Nation." Reston wrote that "America wept tonight, not alone for its dead young president, but for itself. The grief was general, for somehow the worst in the nation had prevailed over the best. The indictment extended beyond the assassin, for something in the nation itself, some strain of madness and violence, had destroyed the highest symbol of law and order." Reston, among the nation's most distinguished political reporters, was searching for an explanation that went beyond the identity of a lone assassin. "The irony of the president's death," he continued, "is that his short administration was devoted almost entirely to various attempts to curb this very streak of violence in the American character. When historians get around to assessing his three years in office, it is very likely that they will be impressed with just this: his efforts to restrain those who wanted to be more violent in the cold war overseas and those who wanted to be more violent in the racial war at home." Reston went on to observe that "from the beginning to the end of his administration, he was trying to tamp down the violence of the extremists from the right."[2]

Reston seemed to be suggesting that the nation itself, in combination with violent tendencies of the radical right, was somehow responsible for the death of the president. He had pointed implicitly to the malignant influence of the anticommunists who had mugged Ambassador Stevenson in Dallas and the racists who had assassinated Medgar Evers and bombed the Negro church in Birmingham. The fact that the assassin was actually a communist did not enter the equation or alter Reston's judgments as to who was ultimately responsible for the crime, even though an extensive report on Oswald and his communist affiliations appeared in Reston's own newspaper adjacent to his article. He seems to have reached an instinctive conclusion about the cause of the event without any reference to the actual identity of the assassin.

Reston returned to this theme two days later in an article suggestively titled "A Portion of Guilt for All," in which he wrote that there was "a rebellion in the land against law and good faith, and that private anger and sorrow are not enough to redeem the events of the last few days."[3] He was writing now not just about the assassination of President Kennedy but also about the shooting of Oswald, which had occurred the previous day. He went on to mention a climate of violence and lawlessness in the nation, and cited a sermon delivered on November 24 by a Washington clergyman who, linking President Kennedy with Jesus, told his congregation, "We have been present at a new crucifixion. All of us had a part in the slaying of the President." The pastor continued: "It was the good people who crucified our Lord, not merely those who acted as executioners. By our silence; by our inaction; by our readiness to allow evil to be called good and good evil; by our toleration of ancient injustices, we have all had a part in the assassination." President Kennedy was a martyr, like Lincoln, or so the pastor suggested by using the term "crucifixion." The nation itself, he seemed to say, was an accessory to the crime by its toleration of injustice or by its unwillingness to end it. Napoleon said that "it is the cause and not the death that makes the martyr." But what was the cause for which President Kennedy gave up his life? And what was the connection between this cause and the identity of the assassin? Neither Reston nor the pastor he cited bothered to address such pertinent questions.

This idea, that the nation itself was finally to blame for the assassination, was repeated widely in the days following the event. It was the dominant theme in commentaries about the assassination and in eulogies for the late president. Northerners had not blamed themselves for the murder of Lincoln, but here prominent Americans were blaming the nation at large for the act of a single man who, as the facts would show, was hardly representative of the American people. Martin Luther King observed that President Kennedy's death had to be seen against the background of growing violence in the South in reaction to the civil rights movement. Liberals in particular tended to see Kennedy's death in this light—that is, as an outgrowth of a violent or extremist streak in the nation at large.

The *New York Times*, in an editorial three days after the assassination (and after Oswald's killing), took up Reston's theme. Under the title "The Spiral of Hate," the editorial begins thus: "The shame all Americans must bear for the spirit of madness and hate that struck down President John F. Kennedy is multiplied by the monstrous murder of his accused assassin while being transferred from one jail in Dallas to another."[4] The editorial develops the theme further: "None of us can escape a share of the fault for the spiral of unreason and violence that has now found expression in the death by gunfire of our martyred president and the man being held for trial as his killer." The editorial concludes by quoting President Kennedy himself, who rightly said (echoing Lincoln in the Lyceum speech), in remarks made in connection with civil rights and violence against Negroes in the South, that "Our nation is founded on the principle that observance of the law is the eternal safeguard of liberty and defiance of the law is the surest road to tyranny."

The implicit message of the editorial, however, was somewhat misleading, for it connected President Kennedy's death to the violence and violations of law committed by opponents of civil rights. The editorial again deployed the term "martyr" to describe the fallen president and suggested that he was a victim of the "spirit of madness and hate" that he had fought to suppress in American life. Yet it appeared that the assassin had struck from another direction altogether. The same newspaper had already carried several factual stories describing the evidence against Oswald and his extensive communist connections. The previous day, the *Times* had published a long article on Oswald under the title "Marxism Called Oswald's

Religion." The subsequent editorial proceeded as if such facts could be safely disregarded.

The New York Times was not alone in setting forth this interpretation of the assassination; or perhaps, as in other situations, it was influential in establishing a framework within which others began to interpret the event. Earl Warren, chief justice of the Supreme Court, observed in a written statement on the afternoon of the assassination that "A great and good President has suffered martyrdom as a result of the hatred and bitterness that has been injected into the life of our nation by bigots." In a eulogy for President Kennedy delivered at the Capitol two days later (on invitation from Mrs. Kennedy), he said that such acts "are commonly stimulated by forces of hatred and violence such as today are eating their way into the bloodstream of American life." Pursuing this thought, he said further that "If we really love this country, if we truly love justice and mercy, if we fervently want to make this nation better for those who are to follow us, we can at least abjure the hatred that consumes people, the false accusations that divide us and the bitterness that begets violence." He concluded by suggesting that President Kennedy was a martyr, albeit for a somewhat ambiguous cause: "It is not too much to hope that the martyrdom of our beloved president might even soften the hearts of those who would themselves recoil from assassination, but who do not shrink from spreading the venom which kindles thoughts of it in others."[5] Warren, like Reston and others commenting on the event, was not exactly precise as to the cause for which Kennedy gave his life, though there was the thought that he had been a victim of hate and unreason that had insinuated themselves into the nation's culture. One did not have to reach very far after hearing Warren's remarks to think of the radical right as the source of these poisonous influences. It was as if the chief justice were reading from a script prepared for the event in advance, even though the actual facts contradicted the story line.

Senator Mike Mansfield, Democrat from Montana and majority leader of the Senate, delivered another eulogy the same day making a nearly identical point: "He [President Kennedy] gave us his love that we, too, in turn, might give. He gave that we might give of our-selves, that we might give to one another until there would be no room for the bigotry, the hatred, prejudice and the arrogance which converged in that moment of horror to strike him down." Such words, crafted in the midst of grief, are emotional indeed, perhaps excessively so for a public occasion. The implicit compari-son between Kennedy and Jesus Christ ("He gave us his love that we, too, in turn, might give") is striking—and in somewhat question-able taste. Whatever John F. Kennedy was in life, this was most def-initely not him. One might also have wondered what connection Mansfield's words had to the facts of the assassination. Oswald, so far as we knew then, was not a bigot at all but something quite the opposite. Like many communists, Oswald saw the unjust treatment of Negroes in the United States as a further indictment of the nation and its institutions—and, indeed, perhaps as further justifica-tion for striking out against the nation's elected leader. The record suggests that Oswald was a staunch foe of racial segregation and an advocate of equal rights for Negroes. He even wrote that racial seg-regation should be abolished. Oswald may not have been inspired by "hate" at all but by cold-blooded dislike for everything American, including John F. Kennedy. Mansfield, like Reston and Warren, suggested a narrative of the assassination that was more than a little misleading.[6]

President Lyndon Johnson, in a message to Congress two days after the funeral, announced that "No memorial oration or eulogy could more eloquently honor President Kennedy's memory than the earliest possible passage of the civil rights bill for which he fought so long." The next day, in a Thanksgiving Day message to the nation, President Johnson advanced this theme further and perhaps finally established it as the official interpretation of the assassination, at least among liberals. The new president reflected on the tragedy while praying that profound lessons might be learned from it. "Let us pray," he said, "for His divine wisdom in banishing from our land any injustice or intolerance or oppression to any of our fellow Americans, whatever their opinion, whatever the color of their skins, for God made all of us . . . in His image." He

continued: "It is this work that I most want us to do—to banish ran-
cor from our words and malice from our hearts—to close down the
poison springs of hatred and intolerance and fanaticism."[7] While
the reference to fanaticism might have been read as a reference to
Oswald's communist faith, it might also have been seen as another
indictment of the far right as complicit in the assassination. Certainly
that notion was reinforced by his pointed references to bigotry and
intolerance. It appeared that Kennedy's assassination was being
used to promote an agenda that was disconnected from the actual
facts of the case.

Leaders in other walks of life repeated this theme at every
opportunity in the days after the assassination. Even as President
Kennedy was eulogized on the national day of mourning in his
honor, there was a note of anger, even of warning, in the voices of
ministers and laymen alike. "Speakers said that discord and violence must not be allowed to infect the political and civil life of the
republic any longer," wrote McCandlish Phillips in the *New York
Times*, thus suggesting a degree of continuity between the assassination of the president and some of the violent acts that preceded
it. The Reverend Adam Clayton Powell (also a congressman) cautioned his congregation in New York: "Weep not for Jack Kennedy,
but weep for America. Weep for a land that does things to people
because they are black. Weep for a state [sic] that can bomb seven
churches in one day." Powell, like others, was determined to place
the assassination in the context of the civil rights struggle.

Drew Pearson, the influential syndicated columnist, may have
outdone his colleagues at the *New York Times* in attributing the
assassination to hatred and intolerance emanating from the far
right. In a column titled "Kennedy a Victim of Hate Drive," he
wrote, "If you study the history of American presidents who have
been assassinated, you find that most of these tragedies did not
come about through the fanaticism of one man. They came about
because powerful influence molders in the nation had preached
disrespect for the authority of the government and the man in the
White House who symbolized government." This generalization,
which was false as it may have applied to other assassinations and

assassination attempts in American history, was the premise for Pearson's conclusion that President Kennedy was felled by a climate of hate especially in Texas but also in the nation at large. Pearson speculated, citing statements by others, that the shooting was carefully planned and carried out by at least three gunmen. When his column appeared on November 29, Oswald had been arrested and charged with the assassination, and the director of the FBI along with the chief prosecutor in Dallas had stated that he had probably acted alone. Pearson called attention to a plan initiated by Pat Brown (governor of California) and Charles Taft (former mayor of Cincinnati and son of President William Howard Taft) to organize a series of candlelight processions in cities across the nation "to pledge the end of intolerance and to affirm that such tragedy shall not happen in America again." In a statement about the proposed vigil, the two men said that "The demented mind of the assassin who took the life of John F. Kennedy in Dallas is no different from the mind of the murderers who snuffed out the lives of the four little girls in Birmingham. These shameful blots on America's conscience will continue until America's conscience speaks out." The statements cited by Pearson presumed that the conscience of the assassin might have been reached by such appeals.

The rector of St. Bartholomew's Episcopal Church in Manhattan said that the assassination was a consequence of a "sin in the hearts of man not only in this country but the world over. That is, the sin of prejudice." Grayson Kirk, president of Columbia University, urged the government to apply "more energy against extremists and their poison." It seems unlikely that he was urging more energetic actions against communists because liberals like Kirk had for years been criticizing such crackdowns as inconsistent with civil liberties. This was, after all, what the hated Senator McCarthy had called for. Kirk seemed to be asking (illogically) for a crackdown against the radical right in consequence of the assassination of the president. A rabbi in New York, after hearing the eulogies to the president, said that Kennedy's death was the result of an "insane hatred that poisoned the hearts of otherwise decent and respectable citizens." Yet "decent and respectable citizens" had nothing to do with the assassination. Neither had the radical right, nor conservatives, nor bigots, nor anticommunists, nor any such group of Americans.[8]

The cultural and political understanding of the assassination had become detached from the details of the event itself. It appeared that the liberal leadership of the country–the *New York Times* editorial board, James Reston, Earl Warren, Mike Mansfield, President Johnson, religious leaders, the president of Columbia University, and even Mrs. Kennedy–had come together in a campaign to blame the assassination of the president on hatred and intolerance which (they said) had engulfed the country. It was but a short step from this to the conclusion that the nation itself had to bear the guilt for the president's death.

Castro and Soviet leaders were gravely concerned–unnecessarily, as things soon turned out–that communism or Cuba or the Soviet Union might be blamed for Kennedy's assassination, and they prepared themselves for a powerful reaction against communism in the United States. From their point of view, a repetition of the extreme anticommunism of the McCarthy period seemed possible or even likely. This was not an unreasonable fear given that the likely assassin was a communist who had just a few years earlier defected from the United States to the Soviet Union (and then back again) and had recently made an attempt to travel to Cuba.

Within hours of Kennedy's death, the Soviet press put out a report that "rightists" were responsible for the assassination and that plots were being hatched to blame the crime on a communist. Oswald was compared to Marinus van der Lubbe, the Dutch communist who was accused by the Nazis of having set fire to the Reichstag building in 1933–thus providing Hitler with an excuse to dissolve the parliament and to claim extraordinary powers for himself. Oswald, the Soviets suggested, was merely a patsy, a scapegoat set up to take the blame for a crime committed by sinister elements on the right. *Pravda*, the official Communist Party newspaper in the Soviet Union, claimed that American "reactionaries" were attempting to use President Kennedy's death "to fan anti-Soviet and anti-Cuban hysteria." The Soviet news agency Tass said that the Dallas Police Department was falsely trying to implicate the Communist Party in the assassination, and insisted that the crime was committed by "racists, the Ku Klux Klan, and Birchists." One Soviet spokesman said that "Senator Barry Gold-water and other extremists on the right could not escape moral responsibility for the president's death." Castro also insisted that Oswald was a reactionary anticommunist who was part of a "Machiavellian plan" to pin the blame for Kennedy's death on Cuba.[9]

Little did Castro and these Soviet figures know that this was the rough conclusion that many American leaders were already circulating (though without explicitly blaming Senator Goldwater). Indeed, Lyndon Johnson among others was entirely sympathetic to their fear. According to Reston, writing in the *New York Times*, "One of the things President Johnson is said to be concerned about is that the pro-Communist background of Lee Harvey Oswald . . . may lead in some places to another Communist hunt that will divide the country and complicate the new President's relations with Moscow."[10] Johnson felt that it would complicate matters politically to lay too much stress on the accused assassin's communist background, affiliations, or motives. Yet someone or some group had to be blamed for this most consequential of events. If not communism or communists, then who should take the blame?

A few influential figures tried to speak out against this interpretation of the assassination that deflected blame from the communist who actually shot the president and directed it toward conservatives and the far right who were in no way connected to the crime. Arthur Krock, writing in the *New York Times*, gently pointed out that the effort to pin the blame on Dallas's conservative political atmosphere made little sense because Oswald's personal history did not fit the dossier of a right-wing extremist.[11] Senator Milward Simpson, Republican from Wyoming, speaking in the Senate chamber two weeks after the assassination, denied that "hate was the assassin that struck down the president" but rather the teachings of communism. Senator Simpson criticized those who sought political advantage by blaming "rightists and conservatives," since the actual murderer "was a single kill-crazy communist." Republicans in general deplored the concerted effort to blame Americans as a whole for Oswald's deed.[12] Such observations, however, though entirely accurate, were regarded as somewhat impertinent objections to the hallowed consensus that had formed in the days following the assassination. As a result, they were not incorporated into the broader cultural interpretation of the Kennedy assassination. Dallas, the radical right, the coarseness of American society, a flaw in the national soul, a failure properly to regulate guns—all were assigned the burden of guilt for Kennedy's death.

William Manchester, in his authoritative history of the assassination published more than three years after the event, relegated Simpson's objections to a footnote while highlighting and emphasizing the remarks of Warren, Mansfield, and others who attributed the assassination to a climate of hate and bigotry. Arthur Schlesinger, in his thousand-page history of the Kennedy administration, could not bring himself to mention Oswald at all in connection with the assassination but allocated several paragraphs to a description of Dallas's hate-filled atmosphere. For all one might discern after reading his long volume, Dallas and right-wingers were responsible for the death of President Kennedy. Schlesinger's young daughter, no doubt repeating something she had heard from adults, said tearfully to him on the evening of the assassination, "Daddy, what has happened to our country? If this is the kind of country we have, I don't want to live here anymore."[13] Schlesinger quoted this comment with approval. Like many at that time, the youngster blamed the assassination not on Oswald the communist, but on the nation and its illiberal culture. The idea took hold that Kennedy was a victim of a violent streak in the national culture or of a climate of bigotry and intolerance cultivated by the radical right. It was this interpretation that would lay claim (irrationally) to the liberal mind in the years after the assassination.

President Kennedy's funeral was organized so as to reinforce the imagery of the brave leader slain for his support of racial justice and equal rights. Many elements of the three-day ceremony were produced on the example of Lincoln's extended funeral. President Kennedy's coffin was brought back from Dallas to the White House and placed for private viewing in the East Room, where Lincoln's coffin had rested. On Sunday, two days after the assassination, it was taken in a procession down Pennsylvania Avenue to the Capitol Rotunda, where it was placed for public viewing on a catafalque originally constructed for Lincoln's funeral. Russell Baker, covering the events for the *New York Times*, wrote that "the analogy to Lincoln's death must have been poignantly apparent to most of those who passed the flag-draped coffin."

Mourners lined up for miles outside the Capitol to pay their respects to the late president. Capitol police estimated that more than 250,000 mourners made their way past the coffin before the doors of the Capitol were closed Sunday evening.[14] Many of these were young people who admired Kennedy's combination of style and idealism. On Monday the funeral procession made its way from the Capitol to the Cathedral of St. Matthew, where the funeral mass would be said. A riderless horse followed the caisson carrying the coffin, much as "Old Bob" had followed Lincoln's coffin out to Oak Ridge Cemetery for burial. Family members and world leaders followed on foot. One million people lined the streets of Washington to watch the solemn procession. After the religious ceremony, three-year-old John Kennedy saluted his father's coffin on the steps of the cathedral in the most memorable and touching moment in the entire proceeding. Mrs. Kennedy, now having regained her composure after the horrifying events of the previous Friday, was the very model of bravery and dignity throughout.

The funeral procession then made its mournful march to Arlington National Cemetery accompanied by muffled drums and cannon salutes, very much in the style of Lincoln's funeral. Following the brief ceremony, Mrs. Kennedy lit the eternal flame that would mark President Kennedy's gravesite and symbolize the ideals for which he stood. (A week later, two Kennedy children who had died in infancy were reinterred next to their father, in another parallel to Lincoln's burial.) There had been no need to display the slain president's coffin in cities around the country because in 1963 (unlike 1865) all Americans could watch the somber pageant on television. Kennedy's funeral was the most dramatic and one of the most widely viewed political events to occur in the United States since Lincoln's funeral. In all its sorrowful elements, Kennedy's funeral augmented feelings of grief and loss felt by most Americans on the death of their young president.

According to the journalist Theodore H. White, the four-day process of mourning transformed the late president into a figure of myth and legend. "There was in the drama of four days," he wrote, "all things to bind all men: a hero, slain; a villain; a sorrowing wife; a stricken mother and family; and two enchanting children. So broad was the emotional span, embracing every member of every family from child to grandparent, that it made the grief of the Kennedys a common grief."[15] While but one in three Americans were able to witness Lincoln's procession, the omnipresent television cameras carried the Kennedy funeral into homes all across the nation. The constant references to Lincoln and to the similarities between the two funerals strengthened the association between the two men. Some foreign leaders, and not a few Americans, found the funeral somewhat more mournful than was necessary to pay appropriate respects to the fallen president. Charles de Gaulle, for example, found it an "over-produced and over-dramatized spectacle." On his return to France he drew up instructions for his own funeral, which prescribed the simplest of ceremonies.[16] Yet, notwithstanding such reactions, there was little question that White was correct in saying that the grand funeral was a critical element in transforming the man into the stuff of legend.

Stanley Levison, a close associate and advisor to Martin Luther King, was astounded at the hushed and somber atmosphere surrounding the proceedings. In the midst of grief, he saw a hopeful sign for the civil rights movement. The news commentators spoke earnestly about the climate of hate that had taken over the country and contributed to the assassination. "A feeling like that covering a whole country can be more important than anything else," Levison told an associate. He immediately understood that such a mood, surprising though it was because Kennedy had not been a strong advocate of civil rights and had been shot after all by a communist, could go a long way toward advancing the cause of equal rights.[17]

Taylor Branch, in his history of Martin Luther King and the civil rights movement, described Kennedy's surprising legacy as it was crafted from the public ceremonies surrounding his untimely death:

> In death, the late president gained credit for much of the purpose that King's movement had forced upon him in life. No death had ever been like his—Niebuhr called him "an elected monarch." In a mass purgative of hatred, bigotry, and violence, the martyred president became a symbol of the healing opposites. . . . President Johnson told the nation that the most fitting eulogy would be swift passage of his civil rights bill. By this and other effects of mourning, Kennedy acquired the Lincolnesque mantle of a unifying crusader who had bled against the thorn of race.[18]

Branch seemed to understand that the anomalous facts surrounding Kennedy's death had been redirected by the culture along more familiar and established paths. There was an irony in this, for (as Branch wrote) Kennedy had come slowly and reluctantly to the support of the movement King led. It was not even the case that the slain president had "bled against the thorn of race." Yet this is what was believed, and this surprising response to the assassination had profound consequences. "The reaction to Kennedy's assassination pushed deep enough and wide enough in the high ground of political emotion to allow the (civil rights) movement to institutionalize its major gains before receding."[19] Kennedy had somehow come to be seen as a martyr for civil rights and the heir to the legacy of Abraham Lincoln. Within months of his death, a landmark Civil Rights Act was passed through the Congress; the next year a similarly historic Voting Rights Act was approved. Following these legislative victories, the influence of the civil rights movement began to recede.

It was true, as Branch suggested, that Kennedy by his martyr's

death had usurped King's title as the inspirational symbol of the civil
rights movement. This, however, proved to be so only in the short
run. King would justly earn that title back posthumously following
his own assassination five years later. The civil rights movement
represented the one great exception to the secular emphasis of
modern reformism, led as it was by a Protestant minister who
framed the struggle in biblical terms. Thus, as between these two
assassinated leaders, King was by far the more legitimate heir to
Abraham Lincoln. Kennedy represented the secular tradition of
progressive liberalism; Lincoln and King the biblical or prophetic
strain in American history. King's rhetorical imagery was biblical,
Kennedy's entirely secular. Kennedy, looking to the past, saw an
unfolding tale of secular progress through political reform. King
told the story of his people—and of their struggle for freedom—as a
reprise of the biblical epic of the ancient Israelites who found their
way to freedom in the Promised Land, even going so far as to imply
a role for himself as a modern-day prophet. He further challenged
Americans (just as Lincoln did) to live up to the sacred creed of
equal rights expressed in the Declaration of Independence. Branch
appropriately assigned biblical titles to his three-volume biography
of Martin Luther King: *Parting the Waters*, *Pillar of Fire*, and *At
Canaan's Edge*. The peroration to King's "I Have a Dream" speech,
fittingly delivered on the steps of the Lincoln Memorial, was taken
from the Negro spiritual "Free at Last." Just as Lincoln had seemed
to foretell his own death in the days before Booth shot him, King's
final speech in 1968 contained an ominous prophecy of his own
death. He had been to "the mountaintop," he said, and had looked
into the Promised Land, but cautioned his listeners that he might
not get there himself. The next day he was assassinated. King was
thereby turned into a martyr for civil rights, albeit a more compelling symbol for that cause than was John F. Kennedy. The historic success of the civil rights movement in a short span of ten
years from 1955 to 1965 was due greatly to the imaginative way by
which King, like Lincoln before him, linked the biblical story to the
American promise of democracy and equal rights.

The reaction in liberal circles to Kennedy's assassination brings to mind the well-known theory of "cognitive dissonance" that was developed in the 1950s by Leon Festinger and his colleagues at Stanford University. The theory was devised to account for the ways in which people reconcile deeply held beliefs with evidence that clearly contradicts those beliefs. "Cognitive dissonance" is simply an academic way of describing an intense conflict among beliefs that generates psychological tension. In order to eliminate the tension, or the dissonance, people search for ways of making their beliefs consistent, either by denying or ignoring key facts or by reinterpreting facts in such a way as to make them consistent with deeply held convictions. Festinger cited numerous examples of such stratagems, though he found the most powerful illustrations in millenarian religious movements whose leaders have identified a particular date for the destruction of the world or the second coming of Jesus Christ.

Such prophecies, some inspired by the end-of-days themes in the book of Revelation, are not all that uncommon in the history of religious movements. The intriguing question is: What is the reaction of cult followers to the inevitable failure of those prophecies in which they have placed such faith and confidence? Believers must in this circumstance find some way to reconcile their religious beliefs with the reality of a world that continues on as before. Festinger observed that they are likely to do so in various ways, some acting more or less rationally by renouncing the cults, others denying or ignoring the plain evidence before them, and still others reinterpreting the facts such that they are made compatible with the prophecies. In the latter case, followers will often recast the prophecy to some future date or suggest that God or some other force has intervened to save the world or to postpone its destruction. It seems ever to be true that people are prepared to go to great lengths to preserve deeply held convictions despite their being contradicted by obvious facts.[20]

The liberal leaders cited above—Chief Justice Warren, James Reston, Senator Mansfield, Lyndon Johnson—dismissed as irrelevant the fact that President Kennedy was shot by a communist.

They, like many Americans, reinterpreted the event so that it was made consistent with liberal assumptions, which held that threats to the nation were most likely to come from the irrational conduct of the radical right. Thus President Kennedy was said to be a victim of intolerance and bigotry which had infected the bloodstream of the nation (as the chief justice had put it). In many quarters, it was said that President Kennedy was a victim of the nation itself, with its violent culture where people are allowed to buy and carry firearms as if they were toys. This perverse conviction filtered into the popular culture in the 1960s, so much so that it was expressed in songs by famous rock-and-roll groups (the analog in the 1960s to Walt Whitman in Lincoln's time). "Sympathy for the Devil," a popular song written in 1968 by the Rolling Stones following the assassination of Robert Kennedy, contains the verse: "I shouted out, 'Who killed the Kennedys?' When after all, it was you and me." Another popular song from the same year, titled "Abraham, Martin, and John," was crafted to link the three men (Lincoln, King, and Kennedy) together as martyrs to the cause of civil rights.

The public did not hear in that dark time the explanation that President Kennedy had been killed for his advocacy of liberty in the face of communist tyranny in Cuba and elsewhere, or that he was a casualty of "the long twilight struggle" to defend and promote freedom in the world. Few linked his death with the bold themes articulated in his Inaugural Address that "we shall pay any price, bear any burden, meet any hardship, support any friend, oppose any foe in order to assure the survival and success of liberty." No one linked the fallen president to others who had died in the battle against communist tyranny. Few suggested that there may have been a connection between the assassination and the tense confrontation the year before over nuclear missiles in Cuba. Such accounts of the assassination would have been consistent with the facts and entirely compatible with Kennedy's forceful and idealistic leadership. It was true, as will be acknowledged later, that pertinent information that would shed light on the assassination was not known either to the public or to some (not all) leaders at the time. Still, enough information was available in 1963 and 1964 to suggest that Kennedy's assassination was more a consequence of the Cold War than of the civil rights crusade. Such an account might have been advanced in a responsible way without inciting calls for war against the Soviet Union or Cuba.

Instead, prominent figures advanced a different interpretation of the assassination, one that required for its acceptance the denial or disregard of some obvious facts. Such a distortion of the record might have been defended on the grounds that it helped advance the all-important cause of civil rights. This being so, the misinterpretation of the Kennedy assassination brought about great good but caused little in the way of offsetting harm. If the official interpretation of the assassination was a lie, at least it was a noble lie. This is a point that bears some examination.

By the time of Martin Luther King's assassination in 1968, the country was far along in a process of unraveling that had begun shortly after Kennedy's death. The violence and disorder that Americans witnessed on college campuses and in major urban centers made the earlier antics of the radical right seem like child's play. No serious person could say any longer that the main threat to public order and democratic civility came from the far right, as it was obvious that it came from the far left—in particular from the protest movement against the war in Vietnam and from riots in the cities that developed after the legislative successes of the civil rights movement. These protest movements—and the violence accompanying them—came from different sociological sources: the protests against the Vietnam War were a phenomenon of the educated classes; the urban riots a product of the black underclass that had moved to the northern cities from the South. These movements shared, however, some common ideological themes—most importantly the idea that America was a nation deeply corrupted by the evils of racism and militarism. A few days after President Kennedy was assassinated, James Reston wrote, in an article titled "A Time to Heal," that "The death of President Kennedy and the shock of the brutality that caused his death have changed the direction of American politics from extreme conflict toward moderation."[21] It would be hard to find a well-intentioned political prediction that turned out to be more profoundly mistaken. Kennedy's death led to a period of intensifying political conflict that originated in attacks from the far left against liberals and moderates. Some of these attacks originated in differences in policy, as in the protests against the war in Vietnam; others were cultural in character, as in the far left's attack on American capitalism, on greed and selfishness, on the boredom of suburban life, on racism and sexism, and so on. In the 1960s, following Kennedy's death and partly as a consequence of it, the radicals began to overtake the liberals as spokesmen for the American left.

Lincoln had said that the Civil War was divine punishment for the sin of slavery; now the American left said that civil disorder was a secular punishment for the sins of racism, militarism, and mindless anticommunism. The idea of national guilt, which surfaced in more innocent form following Kennedy's assassination, had now spread through the institutions of politics, academe, and journalism that shaped liberal culture. The reformist emphasis of American liberalism, which had been pragmatic and forward-looking, was overtaken by a spirit of national self-condemnation. The biblical element that King and others had brought to the civil rights movement was similarly pushed aside by the strength of this new current in American political thought. Both movements—liberal reformism and civil rights—receded in political strength as they were overtaken by this new and surprising mood.

In a few short years, from late 1963 to 1968, the liberal movement absorbed a disposition that can only be described as antiAmerican. As it did so, many began to reject liberalism altogether in favor of more radical alternatives, such as one or another variant of Marxism or Leninism, which expressed this disposition in far more systematic and compelling ways than liberalism ever could. Among those who tried to maintain a foothold in the liberal camp, there was a strong tendency to accept the left-wing critique of American society as crass, violent, racist, and militarist. Thus both the leftists and the liberals, despite disagreements on doctrine, agreed that real change must come about, not through programmatic reforms, but through cultural criticism that leads to a revolution in thought and conduct.

There is little question that the animus that pushed liberalism and the left onto this politically dubious path had its origins in the aftermath of the Kennedy assassination. Once having accepted the claim that Kennedy was a victim of the national culture, many found it all too easy to extend the metaphor into other areas of American life, from race and poverty to the treatment of women to the struggle against communism. These were no longer seen as challenges to be overcome but as indictments of the nation. None of this expressed the genuine convictions of John F. Kennedy; nor did the new mood promise a more constructive approach to national problems than did the tradition of reform liberalism that Kennedy represented. In a bizarre paradox, Kennedy's arch-enemy, Fidel Castro, was turned into a hero in the late 1960s by many of those young people who had mourned Kennedy's death in 1963.

The intense radicalism of the 1960s, mixed as it was with anti-Americanism and romantic conceptions of socialism and third-world dictators like Castro, may not have developed as it did if blame for the Kennedy assassination had been properly assigned to a communist acting out of ideological motives. In that case, the admiration that many felt for John F. Kennedy would have been in conflict with the radical doctrines that were responsible for his death. As things turned out, the tactic of interpreting Kennedy's death as a landmark in the history of civil rights served mainly to introduce confusion on top of tragedy. The sequence of the Cold War president being shot by a communist but then held up as a martyr for civil rights made little sense to those who thought about it for very long. The confusion was compounded when the official government report on the assassination was released nine months later under the name of Earl Warren himself. That report—in contradiction to the statements Warren had made—identified a communist as the lone assassin.

FIVE · CONSPIRACY

THE LIBERAL WRITERS of the postwar era saw the conspiratorial accusations coming from the far right as expressions of the irrational in politics, an attempt to fix moral blame on persons or political movements for developments beyond the control of any individual, group, or party. Richard Hofstadter, Daniel Bell, and others wrote that people turn to conspiracy theories in reaction to their loss of status in a changing society; as they lose power and influence over politics and culture, they look for conspiracies as explanations for their distress and as targets for moral outrage. A conspiracy theory is a moral explanation of things gone wrong, at once an account of how things happened and also an assignment of blame against those responsible. Because such accounts, being either false or greatly exaggerated, cannot restore anyone's declining status in society, they are fundamentally irrational in nature, expressing more anger and distress than a wish to accomplish anything practical or concrete. Conspiratorial thinking is thus intimately connected to reactionary politics and for this reason is more closely associated with the political right than with the left—or at least so it was said by the liberal historians of that era.

The historians of the 1950s and 1960s portrayed the followers of the radical right in unmistakably negative terms: they were paranoid, delusional, frustrated about their social status, out of touch with reality, irresponsible, irrational, reactionary, a threat to democratic norms of civility and tolerance, potentially violent and dangerous, yet surprisingly influential out of all proportion to the actual merits of their case. Their obsession with conspiracies arose from deeper mental and social disorders. No reasonable person could possibly believe that communists had infiltrated the United States government to any significant degree or that communism posed a domestic threat to the nation. It was rather the overreaction to communism that most threatened the institutions of a free and democratic society.

Liberalism represented a diametrically different philosophy of politics and history: it was rational in approach, optimistic about the future, democratic in spirit, perhaps even somewhat egalitarian in outlook, realistic about threats to democracy and what can be accomplished through government action, determined to deploy American power to promote democracy and freedom in the world, more concerned with meeting challenges and overcoming problems than with ruminating over past mistakes or injustices. Liberals were as critical of conspiratorial thought as the radical right was obsessed by it.

John F. Kennedy's assassination posed a challenge to the self-assurance of liberal thinkers and liberal thought. The liberal leaders of the nation had more or less acknowledged in November of 1963 that Kennedy had been shot by a communist, but said at the same time that he was a victim of bigotry and intolerance, or of the radical right, or (more broadly) of a deep violent streak in the nation itself. Oswald shot the president but was not ultimately responsible for it. Prominent liberal figures said this openly and repeatedly with the entire nation listening in. Liberals were supposed to ground their conclusions in facts and reality rather than in preconceptions and ideology. Yet here were the liberal leaders of the nation, backed by intellectuals and academic leaders like Arthur Schlesinger Jr. and Grayson Kirk, saying and doing something quite different—

ignoring the facts and jumping to highly tenuous conclusions in exactly the manner of the radical rightists whom they had relentlessly criticized. It began to dawn on some, in the months and years following the assassination, that such an open contradiction required a resolution. Perhaps it was true after all that Oswald was a patsy or a front man for agents of the radical right. Perhaps, alternatively, if the nation was in fact responsible for Kennedy's death, a connection could be drawn between the assassination and an agency of the government, like the CIA or the FBI. The intensifying anti-Americanism of the liberal left in the 1960s seemed to require an explanation of this kind. Charges of conspiracies and plots were shortly circulating in books and articles written by liberals and leftists. Conspiratorial thinking, recently believed to be the exclusive property of the far right, was now overtaking the liberal community in America, reinforcing their sense that there was something deeply wrong with a nation whose government might go so far as to assassinate a president.

Lincoln's assassination also produced speculation about conspiracies, though most of this reinforced the conclusion that Southern rebels were responsible for his murder. Newspapers at the time reported that Booth had earlier met in Canada with representatives of the Confederate government, thus sparking speculation that the assassination plot had been hatched at the highest levels of the Confederacy.[1] There was little question that Booth was the key figure in the plot, since he had shot Lincoln in front of a live theater audience—much as Jack Ruby would a century later assassinate Oswald before a live television audience. The main question at issue was whether Lincoln had been killed by a narrow conspiracy organized by Booth or by a broader conspiracy that involved the Confederate government, a controversy that involved matters of degree rather than of kind and did not fundamentally call into question the political meaning of the event. There was indeed some evidence to suggest that Booth had been working in league with agents of the Confederacy, particularly some months before the assassination when Booth was laying plans to kidnap Lincoln and spirit him southward behind Confederate lines.[2] The military tribunal that tried the surviving conspirators in May and June of 1865 heard much testimony along these lines, but could not in the end demonstrate a wider conspiracy involving Confederate officials. Much of the speculation about conspiracies faded away after the nine accused conspirators were convicted of involvement in the assassination, and four were executed in early July 1865, barely three months after Lincoln had been shot. These proceedings brought a spirit of closure to the event, a spirit that was reinforced by the end of the war itself and the redirection of the nation's attention and energies to issues of reconstruction and reunion.

There were, however, numerous books and articles published in the decades following Lincoln's death that sought to document one or another conspiracy in connection with the assassination.[3] Mrs. Lincoln was convinced that Vice President Andrew Johnson must have played some part in the conspiracy because Booth was seen at Johnson's hotel on the day of the assassination. Others later suggested that Secretary of War Stanton was the ringleader of a conspiracy because of his disagreements with Lincoln over reconstruction policy. Stanton, it was alleged, failed to arrange proper security for Lincoln at Ford's Theater, thus facilitating the assassination, then gave orders to Union troops to kill Booth when he was found so he could not testify at a trial. The killing of Booth, like Ruby's shooting of Oswald, promoted speculation about conspiracies. There was also a vividly drawn theory asserting that Booth carried out the assassination as part of a Jesuit plot to suppress Lincoln's doctrine of liberty, which the Vatican in Rome associated with radical Protestantism. Evidence for this theory was found in the fact that some of the conspirators were Roman Catholics or had attended Jesuit-founded Georgetown University. John Surratt, a Catholic who was involved in the plot, escaped to Canada afterwards, later being captured (subsequently escaping again) while a member of the Papal army in Rome. He was brought back to the United States in 1867 and held for trial (civil rather than military), which ended in a hung jury. In a reflection of the changed mood of the country, federal courts rejected efforts by the government to try him again on charges of espionage.

Though both the Stanton and the Jesuit conspiracies were logically plausible—as conspiracy theories often are—neither gained any wide currency among Americans in the years following Lincoln's death and neither made any impact on the public's interpretation of the assassination. The official explanation fit the facts far better than any alternative explanation. Moreover, it made perfect sense morally and politically, which is a critical factor not to be overlooked. Conspiracy theories are most likely to be propagated and believed in connection with events that confound expectations and contradict widely accepted assumptions. The search for conspiracies is thus not an entirely irrational act but in some ways is an understandable attempt to impose order and meaning on a confused and perplexing situation.

Conspiracies have existed throughout history, as Hofstadter emphasized, but systematic political doctrines incorporating conspiracies are modern phenomena associated with the rise of secular politics. Daniel Pipes coined the term "conspiracism" to describe an outlook that sees conspiracies operating everywhere as the moving forces behind great events.[4] Hofstadter formulated the concept of the "paranoid style" to describe the same phenomenon. Both terms suggest a mental outlook that is partial to "the plot theory of history." Such an outlook typically begins with a belief in conspiracy and then searches out the facts that tend to confirm it. Conspiracy theories are attractive to some because they identify ultimate causes for important events, thereby denying that such events might be caused by chance or coincidence. Conspiratorial doctrines also carry with them an aspect of secret knowledge that is denied to those of conventional beliefs. Such doctrines seem most alluring when they point to some fundamental betrayal on the part of those in positions of trust and authority. A plot set in motion by an enemy seems nowhere near as interesting as one concocted by an ostensible ally or friend. An undertone of betrayal or broken trust frequently gives emotional power to charges of conspiracy. Liberals of the postwar era were correct to associate the paranoid style with ideological or sectarian politics and to highlight its incompatibility with the open-minded and skeptical spirit of modern liberalism. Yet they may have been too hopeful in their assumption that liberals, because of their commitment to rationality, are immune to conspiratorial fantasies. The fascinations of conspiracy theory attract adherents all the way across the political spectrum.

Both Hofstadter and Pipes traced the modern origins of conspiracism to the aftermath of the French Revolution, when conservatives blamed secret societies–the Illuminati and Freemasons–for the unprecedented attack on the institutions of civilization.[5] According to these influential theories, the secret societies did not simply play a role in supporting the revolution or in expressing some of its central ideals, but actually directed and plotted the course of the whole event. More worrisome still, the Masons and the Illuminati (according to the charges) continued to be active in the political affairs of France and other countries, undermining established political and religious institutions through their clandestine influence. John Robison, a Scottish author, first advanced this case in 1797 in a volume with the suggestive title *Proofs of a Conspiracy Against All Religions and Governments of Europe, Carried On in the Secret Meetings of Freemasons, Illuminati, and Reading Societies.* Around the same time, Augustus Barruel, a Jesuit priest who fled from France to England, published his own history of the revolution in which he indicted the Illuminati and the Masons for the parts they played in bringing about the upheaval: "Everything in the French Revolution, even the most dreadful of crimes, was foreseen, contemplated, contrived, resolved upon, decreed; everything was the consequence of the most profound villainy, and was prepared and produced by those men who alone held the leading threads of conspiracies long before woven in the secret societies, and who knew how to choose and to hasten the favorable moments for their schemes."[6] Sometime later the Jews were added to this conspiratorial mix on the grounds that they, too, promoted revolution in order to undermine Christianity. Some imaginatively suggested that the Jews had infiltrated or taken over the Masonic and Illuminist orders, thereafter taking charge of the revolutionary plots.

By the time of the French Revolution, the Freemasons had existed as an organized movement for well over a century, beginning as a craftsmen's guild and evolving over the generations into a secret society for the propagation of Enlightenment ideals. The Order of the Illuminati, on the other hand, was of more recent origin, having been established as a secret order in 1776 in Bavaria as an instrument for advancing the ideals of reason and equality, but also to counter the clandestine influence of the Jesuits in that region. The battle against Jesuit influence, however, seemed to require the adoption of the organizational techniques that had made the religious order so influential. As a consequence, Adam Weishaupt, the founder of Illuminism, built his order on the secretive organizational model of the Jesuits, thereby establishing (or continuing) a pattern by which the extremes of the political spectrum mimic the strategy and tactics of their adversaries.[7] Through this process of action and reaction, and through the epic upheaval of the French Revolution, the modern conception of conspiracy was linked to the activities of secret societies.

The claim that the French Revolution arose out of a conspiracy organized by secret societies proved so compelling that the charge was shortly broadened to other events and adopted by influential advocates in other countries. Metternich wrote about the threat to the established order posed by secret societies. Disraeli expressed many of those same fears both in speeches and in some of his novels.[8] The publication of the Robison and Barruel volumes provoked popular fears in the United States about the political influence of the secret societies, concerns which were allied with broader fears about the widening consequences of the French Revolution. Later, in the 1820s and in conjunction with the Protestant revivals of that period, an Anti-Masonic party was formed on the basis of claims that Masons were infiltrating the government and using their powers to reward fellow members and generally to subvert the Constitution, even though prominent figures like Washington, Franklin, and Adams had been members of the secret order. Leading evangelical ministers, like Charles Grandison Finney, viewed the secret orders as purveyors of a secular religion and thus a threat to genuine religious faith. Evangelical preachers used their revivals to urge Masons to renounce their membership and commit their lives to Jesus Christ. In short order, apprehensions about Masonic plots began to subside, but fears about conspiracies remained a more or less permanent part of the political fabric in the United States.

In Europe, meanwhile, activists on the left took to heart the claim that the old regime in France had been taken down by the machinery of secret societies. Liberal reformers identified the rise of secret societies and political clubs with the advancement of liberty. After all, such societies operated underground and in secret only because their activities were illegal in the anti-republican polities of the time. The development of secret societies, from this point of view, went hand in hand with the advancing strength of republicanism. Radicals and revolutionaries took this analysis a step or two further. They did not condemn the secret societies but embraced them as models for revolutionary change. Thus the radicals set about creating their own secret societies across Europe with the intent to overthrow established governments. The right had embraced conspiracy theory as an explanation for radicalism and revolution, but the left embraced it as a *modus operandi*, thereby perversely validating conspiratorial ideas of the far right. During the nineteenth and into the twentieth century, important figures across the political spectrum were keenly interested in the role played by secret societies and underground organizations in directing political events.

A fascination with conspiracies and their political possibilities was thus absorbed into the thought of radical movements as a reflection of their own tactics. As conspirators themselves, the revolutionaries began to view their adversaries in conspiratorial terms as well. Radicals even began to understand the core activities of government in terms of the machinations of bankers, spies, and the secret police. As Pipes writes, Marxism and Leninism are based on a conspiracy theory: "financiers and manufacturers group together to extract riches not rightfully due them by keeping down workers' wages and controlling the government."[9] Interestingly enough, Leninism also teaches that communism comes to power through a conspiracy led by a small group of dedicated revolutionaries.

Given such conspiratorial assumptions, it was but a small step to the idea that their adversaries operated in a like fashion. From here it was another short step to the idea that governmental intelligence agencies like the CIA or MI5 operate like powerful secret societies, manipulating or overthrowing governments, assassinating opponents, and generally sowing confusion in the ranks of radicals. For the radical left, such organizations have inherited the role of conspiratorial secret societies determined to undermine popular movements.[10] From the other end of the political spectrum, when conservatives later spoke about the "communist conspiracy" they were not indulging in a fantasy of their own creation but rather pointing to a concept that had a genuine historical background and even some grounding in reality. Conspiratorial doctrines, far from being a mode of thought adopted by the mentally or socially unstable, played an interesting part in the historical conflict between right and left as it developed after the French Revolution.

The preoccupation with conspiracies and secret societies culminated in the twentieth century with the rise to power of Nazism and communism, two revolutionary movements animated by conspiratorial doctrines and directed by tyrants obsessed with conspiracies. In Hitler's case, the conspiratorial enemies were Jews and communists; in Stalin's case, the enemies were all manner of internal opponents, both real and imagined. It was hardly a cause of wonder that movements driven by conspiratorial fantasies should have yielded up leaders whose political outlooks were distorted by the same fantasies. The rise of the totalitarian dictatorships combined with the catastrophic consequences of World War II provided a clear lesson to liberals in Europe and America that conspiratorial doctrines can bring about the most destructive consequences. It was against this background that the postwar liberals, adopting a moderate and rational position between the far right and the far left, denounced the conspiracy theories of the radical right as incompatible with democratic life.

It was a mistake, however, for these thinkers to have suggested that conspiratorial thought is an exclusive property of the political right. The postwar liberals wrote at a particular moment in history

when the conspiratorial impulses of the left, at least in the United
States and Europe, were relatively quiescent compared with the
activities of the right. This was, after all, a time when the left was
ascendant in light of the strides taken in the United States during
the 1930s in the direction of the welfare state and the socialist
measures adopted in Great Britain and elsewhere after the war.
Despite short-term reverses, progressives and socialists generally
believed that history was on their side and that events were moving
inexorably in the direction of planned economies and welfare
states across Europe and North America. If conspiratorial thought
is sometimes a reaction to distress and to the sense that history is
moving in the wrong direction, the left at that time had less reason
to resort to it than the right. Given the history of conspiratorial
thought, however, there was no reason to think that this would be a
permanent state of affairs. If the trajectory of history should
be altered, if the relative fortunes of the left and the right should be
changed, if some disruptive and unforeseen event should occur—in
those circumstances the older patterns might readily reappear.

Lee Harvey Oswald, just twenty-four years of age, was arrested by
Dallas police within two hours of the assassination of President
Kennedy. By the end of that eventful day, sufficient evidence had
been accumulated in the case to justify formal charges against
Oswald for the murders of both President Kennedy and Dallas
police officer J. D. Tippit. Oswald was arrested and then charged
on the basis of compelling evidence: he worked in the Texas School
Book Depository, from which location the shots were fired on the
presidential motorcade; he was placed by witnesses at the scene of
the shooting; workers on the fifth floor of the building heard shots
being fired from above and even heard the sounds of empty shells
dropping to the floor above them; the rifle and empty shells found
near the sniper's nest on the sixth floor were traced back to him;
the bullets that struck the president were fired from that weapon.
Witnesses on the street saw the gunman firing from a window
on the sixth floor of the building. One witness gave the police a

description of the man he saw in the window. On the basis of this description, which was immediately broadcast over police radios, Officer Tippit, who was patrolling in his car in another part of the city, stopped a man walking on the sidewalk approximately forty-five minutes after the shooting. As Tippit stepped out of his car, the suspect without any warning fired several shots, killing the officer, then fled on foot. Several people witnessed the slaying; one of them quickly called in a report from the radio in Tippit's police car. The gunman was soon traced to a movie theater a few blocks away, where, after a brief struggle with police during which he tried to fire his gun, he was taken into custody. As he was led out of the theater by police, the suspect shouted to an assembling crowd of onlookers that he was a victim of "police brutality." He was still carrying the .38 caliber revolver that had fired the shots that mortally wounded the police officer. He could not have gotten far after his crime, however, as he was carrying just thirteen dollars when he was arrested. The suspect in the Tippit slaying was none other than Lee Harvey Oswald.

Oswald had been identified as a possible suspect in the assassination because he was reported missing from duty by his supervisor at work after police had asked him (the supervisor) to make a roll call of his employees in the School Book Depository. Oswald had left the building within minutes of the shooting and before police had the opportunity to seal it off. Once on the street, amid the panic and confusion, he headed, first by bus and then by taxi, toward a house in the Oak Cliff section of the city, where he kept a room under a false name. After retrieving a jacket and a pistol, he made a quick exit from the room and headed out to the street. There he would shortly have the fatal encounter with Officer Tippit, who was checking out an independent lead based on a description of the gunman.

At police headquarters, Oswald denied involvement in either killing, claiming to reporters that he was a "patsy," a fall guy who had been set up to take the blame for the assassination of the president. Yet he made no effort to hide his communist loyalties, offering to reporters at one point the clenched-fist salute favored by radicals and later calling on a Communist Party lawyer in New York to defend him. Oswald, it may be surmised, was already looking forward to a sensational "show trial" in which he would portray himself as a revolutionary hero by exploiting the proceedings to indict the capitalist system and the policies of the Kennedy administration. This would explain why he would admit nothing in connection with the assassination or the murder of the police officer but was more than willing to announce his communist loyalties for all to see and hear. Indeed, during his interrogation at police headquarters, Oswald systematically lied about key pieces of evidence, denying for example that he owned a rifle or that he used an alias. Will Fritz, chief of the homicide bureau, who directed the questioning, felt that Oswald may have been trained to resist interrogation.[11] Notwithstanding Oswald's denials, however, the physical evidence against him was rapidly accumulating.

Henry Wade, the Dallas district attorney, announced the next day that enough evidence was already in hand to convict Oswald of the assassination of President Kennedy. "I think we have enough evidence to convict him now," Wade told the press, "but we anticipate a lot more evidence in the next few days."[12] He cited as key evidence the rifle found on the sixth floor of the School Book Depository that was traced to Oswald through the mail-order letter used to purchase it, the spent shells that matched the rifle, and Oswald's palm print that was found on a carton by the window from which vantage point the shots were fired. Witnesses to the shooting from the street also identified Oswald from a police line-up. Already the authorities were aware of Oswald's subversive past—the fact that he had defected to the Soviet Union, that he set up a front organization the previous summer in support of Castro, and that he referred to himself as a "Marxist." More evidence along these lines would soon be found. The Dallas police chief, trying to shift responsibility for the assassination from his own police department to the FBI, noted that the Dallas police had no record on Oswald but that the FBI had a long subversive record on him.[13]

The official police investigation of the assassination and of Oswald's role in it was aborted when Oswald himself was assassinated on November 24 by Jack Ruby while being transferred from one Dallas jail to another. The Dallas Police Department had been irresponsibly careless in allowing reporters and other hangers-on to mill about police headquarters in hopes of catching a view of the accused assassin. Ruby, taking advantage of such lax security, slipped in among the crowd of reporters gathered in wait for Oswald's transfer and, when he appeared in handcuffs escorted by two officers, seized the opportunity to shoot him. A national television audience witnessed the shooting and the melee that followed. Oswald's murder, following so closely on Kennedy's assassination, reinforced the sense across the nation that events were spinning out of control and accelerated rumors that the two murders were tied together by a conspiracy of some kind. With the formal police investigation prematurely closed, many feared that a final answer to Kennedy's assassination would now never be forthcoming.

The assassination of Oswald, combined with the rumors of conspiracy that it provoked and the prospect of various overlapping and conflicting state and federal investigations, led President Johnson to appoint a special seven-member panel, chaired by Chief Justice Earl Warren, to investigate the assassination of President Kennedy and "to report its findings and conclusions to the American people and to the world." Johnson was greatly concerned that rumors of conspiracy and of Oswald's possible connections to foreign governments could lead to an international crisis or even war, a concern that he raised in persuading the initially reluctant chief justice to sign on. Other members of the bipartisan panel were Senators John Sherman Cooper and Richard Russell, Representatives Hale Boggs and Gerald Ford, former CIA head Allan Dulles, and former diplomat and presidential advisor John J. McCloy, the latter two men appointed on the recommendation of Robert Kennedy. Except for Warren, a well-known liberal, the members of the panel were moderates and conservatives. The Warren Commission, as it came to be called, was granted all judicial powers needed to conduct an independent investigation, including the power to subpoena witnesses. Before the commission had an opportunity to begin its work, however, the FBI announced that it was satisfied on the basis of its preliminary investigation that Oswald was the assassin and that he acted on his own. This announcement was made in an attempt to foreclose speculation about conspiracies—particularly as such conspiracies might point toward possible Soviet or Cuban involvement.[14]

After ten months of hearings and investigation, the Warren Commission issued its final report on September 27, 1964, in the midst of a presidential election campaign and barely five weeks before the election itself. Lyndon Johnson had earlier expressed his view that the commission should release its findings well in advance of the election so that any lingering confusion about the assassination would be cleared up before voters went to the polls in November. The commission's report did not contain any great surprises. It concluded (as had the FBI ten months earlier) that Lee Harvey Oswald was the lone assassin and there had been no conspiracy involving any foreign government or domestic group. Citing the official autopsy reports, the commission said that President Kennedy had been hit by two shots fired from above and behind the presidential motorcade—that is, from the direction of the sixth-floor window of the School Book Depository. The bullets that killed President Kennedy were shown to have been fired from the rifle found at that location. The rifle had been ordered through the mail by Oswald the previous March. Oswald used the same rifle to fire a shot at General Edwin Walker (head of the John Birch Society in Dallas) the previous April while Walker sat near a window in his home. The shot missed, though the attempt on Walker's life was reported at the time in the Dallas press and investigated by the police. Oswald, the report said, had also shot Officer Tippit in his attempt to flee, a conclusion that was based on eyewitness reports and the fact that the bullets that killed the officer came from the gun Oswald was carrying when he was captured. The commission did not find any connection between Oswald and Ruby to suggest that Oswald was killed to keep him quiet. If Oswald was not connected to a conspiracy, it more or less followed that Ruby could not be connected to one either (since presumably both would have to be connected to a common conspiracy).[15]

The most controversial claim in the Warren Report was the so-called "single bullet" theory, according to which the first shot that hit Kennedy passed through his back and neck, then hit Governor John Connally (seated in front of him), passing through his shoulder and ribs, then through his wrist, before finally lodging in his thigh. Critics doubted that such a sequence was probable and asserted that Kennedy and Connally must have been hit by separate shots. If this was so, the critics reasoned, a second gunman had to be involved, since Oswald could not have fired off two separate shots quickly enough to cause the wounds to both Kennedy and Connally.

The analysis contained in the report, on the other hand, which was based on a frame-by-frame analysis of the Zapruder tape, suggested that such a sequence was likely and, indeed, was the only one consistent with other available evidence.[16] Nevertheless, this was one of the aspects of the report that encouraged speculation about a conspiracy, even though the existence of a second gunman would not by itself prove a wider conspiracy involving foreign governments, intelligence agencies, the Mafia, or other domestic groups. It would merely prove that Oswald had an accomplice.

One key question unanswered by the Warren Report revolved around Oswald's motive for carrying out the assassination. Oswald, the commission said (in a section titled "Unanswered Questions"), was driven to commit the act by several factors, including especially "a hostility to his environment," alienation from other people, a failure to establish meaningful relationships with others, problems in his marital relationship, and discontent with the world around him. The assassination was the product of a life "characterized by isolation, frustration, and failure." Seeking to redeem his failed life, Oswald tried to establish for himself a prominent place in history by killing the president. While the Warren Report took full note of Oswald's communist sympathies and activities, along with his hatred for the United States, it played these factors down as motivations for killing President Kennedy.[17] Some readers were plainly dissatisfied with this attempted explanation. James Reston, writing in the *New York Times*, concluded that "Oswald's motive for murdering the President remains obscure. The distinguished members

of the Commission and their staff obviously gave up on it." The far-
rago of causes cited by the commission implied that Oswald was
more a confused and frustrated loner than a motivated ideologue.
Reflecting on the assassination of President Kennedy following the
shooting of Robert Kennedy in 1968, Tom Wicker wrote that "An
authorized commission decided that John F. Kennedy was killed
by a mental misfit with a grim personal history."[18] For those who
could not accept the idea that a man might assassinate the president
for such flimsy reasons, it made sense to look for the real cause of
the assassination in some kind of conspiracy.

The Warren Report received something of a mixed reception
when it was published. Many were relieved to hear that there was
no wider conspiracy behind the assassination. The commission did
not find that any extremist group either of the left or of the right
had any connection to the assassination. The commission even
rejected Warren's earlier suggestion (made during the funeral proceedings) that the assassination had been caused by the reactionary climate in Dallas and a climate of bigotry and intolerance
in the nation as a whole. Importantly, the commission also rejected
claims that Oswald had received assistance from either the Cuban
or the Soviet governments. "This conclusion is primordial," wrote
C. L. Sulzberger in the *New York Times*. "It was essential in these
restless days to remove the unfounded suspicions that could excite
any latent jingo spirit."[19] American leaders were determined that no
accusing fingers should be pointed at either of these governments.

The Soviet press, on the other hand, and the left-wing press
around the world denounced the Warren Report as a shameful
cover-up and rejected the claim that a communist could have
killed President Kennedy.[20] Even before the report was issued,
Thomas Buchanan, an American communist, published a book
asserting that the fatal shots were fired from the area of the grassy
knoll, that Oswald was framed, and that he had been trained as an
intelligence agent by the CIA. Joachim Joesten, a German writer
with communist sympathies, published a similar volume in 1964
(*Oswald: Assassin or Fall Guy?*), claiming that Kennedy had been
killed by a conspiracy of right-wingers led by the oil magnate

H. L. Hunt. In this scenario, Oswald was connected both to the CIA and to the FBI.[21] The head of a leading Marxist-Leninist organization in the United States called the Warren Report "the clumsiest cover-up since the Reichstag fire." He said that the assassination had been "an attempted coup d'état by the forces of political reaction, racism, and unbridled militarism," suggesting thereby that the assassination was carried out by right-wing groups or officials associated with the U.S. military.[22] Mark Lane, a radical lawyer who had sought to defend Oswald before the commission, asserted (wrongly) that Oswald could never have been convicted in a court of law on the basis of the evidence presented in the report. American officials were eager to absolve the left from complicity in the assassination, but leftists were far from willing to reciprocate. They recognized the damage that could be done to their cause if it was widely acknowledged that President Kennedy had been shot by a communist.

In the years immediately following its publication, the Warren Report, though almost certainly accurate in its key conclusion that Oswald fired the fatal shots and that he probably acted alone, was hammered by critics along the lines prefigured by these early reactions from the far left. Several influential books sought to cast doubt on the conclusions of the Warren Commission, including *Rush to Judgment* (1966) by Mark Lane, *The Second Oswald* (1966) by Richard H. Popkin, *Six Seconds in Dallas* (1967) by Josiah Thompson, and *Accessories after the Fact* (1967) by Sylvia Meagher.[23] These books, which were widely read and discussed, suggested in one way or another that Kennedy was killed in a crossfire of shots on Dealey Plaza, that Oswald was probably innocent just as he said he was, and that a conspiracy of right-wing groups was behind the assassination. Prodded by these speculations, the New Orleans district attorney, Jim Garrison, indicted a prominent businessman from that city as the head of a conspiracy that assassinated Kennedy. In a 1968 press release, Garrison announced, "The federal government is a party with a special interest in this case. Our investigation has shown that the federal investigation was faked and the Warren Commission inquiry was faked to conceal the fact that

President Kennedy was killed in a professionally executed ambush." When Garrison brought his case into court, it was quickly dismissed by a jury.[24]

This, however, did not blunt the suspicions coming from the left about right-wing conspiracies. By the end of the 1960s, the American left in general, but also a large fraction of the American people, was convinced that the Warren Commission had covered up some dark truth about the assassination. As Edward Jay Epstein wrote in *Esquire*, "The distinguished members of the Commission never intended that their Report should become the basis for an amateur detective game. Yet this is precisely what is happening. A growing number of people are spending their leisure hours scouring the Commission's Report and the twenty-six volumes of testimony and exhibits for possible clues to a conspiracy. Others, using high powered magnifying glasses and infrared lights, are scrutinizing photographs of the assassination scene, hoping to find snipers concealed in the shrubbery."[25] At the same time that it was denounced as a fabrication, the Warren Report remained the key source of raw information about the tragedy in Dallas. The Kennedy assassination had become a national obsession for those who could not believe that an event as important as this could have been caused by a man as seemingly small and insignificant as Oswald. Far from settling the issue as President Johnson hoped it would, the Warren Report provoked as many questions as it answered.

That the Warren Report was a giant cover-up was more or less the standard view among members of the emerging New Left in the 1960s. Todd Gitlin, the radical author and historian of the 1960s, wrote that leaders of the New Left "were fascinated by the conspiracy theories, impressed by their critiques of the Warren Commission, doubtful of the single-assassin idea though unconvinced of any specific conspiracy."[26] It was an article of faith among members of the youthful New Left that Kennedy was the victim of a conspiracy. Indeed, belief in a conspiracy theory was one of the factors that attracted young people to the radical left. It proved difficult to maintain one's faith in American institutions while simultaneously believing that Kennedy had been eliminated by a right-wing conspiracy which was then covered up by a commission of distinguished national leaders. Here the old liberalism collided head-on with the new radicalism. It was ironic that the idealism encouraged by Kennedy's leadership was killed off by the cynicism arising from his assassination. The conspiracy theories, though probably false, dovetailed with the emerging radical critique of American society as violent, racist, and corrupt. Indeed, the conspiracy theories were taken as the strongest evidence for that very critique.

Support for conspiracy theories, however, did not fade away with the retreat of the New Left. The flow of books and even movies making the case for plots and conspiracies has continued more or less unabated since the publication of those early volumes in the mid-1960s. Many continued to argue that the plot was carried out by rogue elements of the CIA; in a new twist, a few researchers began to argue in the 1970s that elements of organized crime planned the assassination and then arranged for Jack Ruby to eliminate Oswald.[27] Mark Lane served as consultant to *Executive Action*, a popular film produced in 1973, starring Burt Lancaster and Robert Ryan, that pointed to a conspiracy organized by right-wing businessmen. The Watergate scandals of the mid-1970s reinforced suspicions that the government cannot be trusted. Those scandals, and the revelations of lying and corruption at the highest levels of government, also reminded the public that national leaders are capable of organizing illegal conspiracies. The House of Representatives, responding to this mood, created a select committee in 1976 to re-examine the assassinations of the 1960s, including the assassination of President Kennedy. The rejection of the major claims of the Warren Commission had spread from a small collection of conspiracy theorists into the mainstream of American opinion. By the mid-1970s, according to a Gallup Poll taken in 1976, some 80 percent of Americans were convinced that Kennedy was a victim of a conspiracy, a figure that has not wavered much since that time.[28] In the eyes of popular opinion, the Warren Report was largely discredited—and remains so today.

Such a situation is testimony to the power of repetition and the attractions of conspiracy theories as explanations for far-reaching events. The advocates of conspiracy theory have been numerous, the defenders of the Warren Commission very few. Nevertheless, several independent investigations, including those conducted by CBS in 1967 and by the House Select Committee on Assassinations in 1979, concluded that Oswald was the likely assassin. The House committee, which reviewed all of the old and some new evidence relating to the assassination, concluded (like the Warren Commission) that President Kennedy was hit by two shots fired from the rear, that the bullets were fired by the gun found on the sixth floor of the School Book Depository, that the gun belonged to Oswald, that he was seen in the area of the sixth floor just prior to the assassination, and that he was the likely assassin. The House committee found no evidence to link organized crime, the CIA, or the FBI to the assassination. The committee, before reaching its conclusions, commissioned a new analysis of the autopsy photographs and X-rays to address doubts that had been raised about the original autopsy conducted on the evening of the assassination. That analysis reconfirmed the Warren Commission's conclusion that both Kennedy and Connally were struck by bullets fired from behind and above them.[29]

Gerald Posner, in a careful study of the assassination, reached the same conclusion after reviewing the evidence, and after rejecting various conspiracy theories on the basis of that evidence.[30] Norman Mailer, a writer sympathetic to the political left, began his extensive study of Oswald with a prejudice in favor of a conspiracy but concluded "that Lee had the character to kill Kennedy, and that he probably did it alone." Like Earl Warren, who had every reason (in view of his comments after the assassination) to find a right-wing conspiracy if one existed, Mailer in the end came to terms with the painful reality. The intriguing question about the assassination, as Mailer concluded, is not if Oswald did it but rather why he did it. For Mailer, the question of Oswald's motives remained elusive.[31]

Yet Mailer, even as he finally rejected a conspiratorial explanation, touched on a reason why so many people are drawn to such accounts of Kennedy's death. Oswald sought to achieve historical notoriety (or infamy) for himself when he assassinated President Kennedy but ended up producing a far wider and more significant consequence. "It may never have occurred to Oswald," Mailer wrote, "that the obfuscation and paranoia which followed the assassination of Kennedy would contribute immensely to the sludge and smog of the world's spirit."[32] Oswald, by killing Kennedy, also killed the spirit of hope, progress, and sophistication that Kennedy embodied or represented—which is to say that Oswald compromised the animating emotions of American liberalism. It seemed to Mailer when he began his inquiry that something of this spirit might be redeemed if some rational account of Kennedy's death could be found. A conspiracy, particularly one engineered from the right, would supply an escape from political absurdity. Mailer, notwithstanding the frequently bizarre conduct that marked his career, was far too committed to rationality to convince himself of a conspiracy against the weight of the evidence. His study ends in a spirit of resignation that no such escape is available.

From the standpoint of the actual evidence, then, it is a near certainty that Oswald alone fired the shots that killed President Kennedy. It is possible, but not very likely, that he planned the assassination in concert with other persons still unknown. There is no solid evidence to suggest that Oswald worked with others in the weeks and months leading up to the assassination, but the possibility cannot be rejected out of hand. Nor is there any solid evidence to suggest that he was working in formal cooperation with any foreign government. At this late date, it seems unlikely that any such evidence will ever be produced.

To this day the Warren Commission Report remains a veritable treasure trove of raw information about the Kennedy assassination. Even the conspiracy buffs, as Epstein noted, sift through the report and the twenty-six volumes of accompanying evidence and testimony for clues that might suggest a different interpretation. It is also true that the report was poorly organized, such that the great volume of information gathered was never pieced together in the form of a narrative that was understandable to the American people. Oswald's activities on behalf of Cuba, for example, are discussed in differing levels of detail in at least four different sections of the report. The detailed factual report reads like an encyclopedia on the assassination rather than an interpretation of what happened in Dallas and how it should be understood from a political point of view.

Whatever difficulties or inconsistencies attend the Warren Report, however, they pale in comparison with those that confront the various conspiracy theories founded on assertions that are nearly impossible to accept. Oliver Stone, for example, in his movie *JFK* (1991), which was based on Jim Garrison's investigations in New Orleans, suggests that Kennedy was hit from the front (rather than from the rear) by shots fired from the infamous grassy knoll near the overpass toward which Kennedy's limousine was heading, a favored scenario of many conspiracy theorists because of the way Kennedy's head snaps backward in the Zapruder film when he is hit by the second (and fatal) bullet. (The public release of the Zapruder film in the mid-1970s provided abundant new opportunities for analysis and speculation by those amateur sleuths mentioned by Edward Jay Epstein.) Yet the autopsy conducted by doctors at Bethesda Naval Hospital on the evening of the assassination revealed that Kennedy had been hit by two shots that entered his body from the rear—that is, from the direction of the School Book Depository. Stone's theory, in order to deal with these facts, must suggest that the doctors who performed the autopsy were somehow involved in the conspiracy (or that the autopsy records were doctored). Others, taking a different tack, have argued that Kennedy's body was somehow switched or tampered with during the trip from Dallas to Washington to create false entry wounds from the rear.[33] Needless to say, both claims are far more difficult to believe than the much maligned single-bullet theory of the Warren Commission Report.

Most conspiracy theories of the Kennedy assassination are based on some claimed weakness or inconsistency in the Warren Report, which are in turn taken to imply that Oswald was framed or at least did not act alone. Alternative explanations are then concocted which have little or no evidentiary support. No conspiracy theorist, for example, has ever come up with any firm evidence to prove a link to the CIA, the FBI, or any conservative or right-wing group—that is, evidence comparable to Oswald's rifle and fingerprints, ballistic tests, autopsy reports, or eyewitness accounts. In order to do away with inconvenient evidence, it is sometimes asserted that the autopsy reports or photographs were tampered with, at other times that the Zapruder film was doctored, on still other occasions that Kennedy's wounds were altered. The authors of conspiracy theories do not subject their own accounts to anywhere near the kind of rigorous scrutiny to which they subject the Warren Report. Such theories—that the CIA or FBI or right-wing businessmen had President Kennedy killed—seem compelling because they make logical or ideological sense, not because they are backed up by real evidence.

Yet it is a mistake to discount the importance of the ideological factor and the power of a compelling and deeply held narrative to overwhelm factual objections to it. The violent history of the modern age provides abundant documentation for that observation. Conspiracy theories are produced not because they are true but because some people have a strong need to believe in them. On this point, Hofstadter, Bell, and the postwar liberals were certainly correct. It is sad to say, yet true, that there never would have been any serious speculation about conspiracies in the Kennedy assassination if the president had been killed by a right-winger whose guilt was confirmed by the same evidence as condemned Lee Harvey Oswald.

A serious weakness of the Warren Report, as has been noted, was that it never came to grips with Oswald's political motives in assassinating President Kennedy. An assassination is, almost by definition, a political act, yet the Warren Commission suggested a potpourri of personal motives in an attempt to account for Oswald's actions. In fairness to the commissioners, however, they saw as their main purpose the documentation of the key facts regarding the assassination. In their view, the whole mystery of Oswald's motives took them into the area of speculation rather than fact.

Nevertheless, there were powerful factors in operation to encourage the commissioners to downplay Oswald's possible political motives, which would have been rooted in his communist or Marxist loyalties. President Johnson did not wish to incite hostility against the Soviet Union or Cuba as a consequence of the role those governments might have played in the assassination. If there was evidence of a conspiracy involving either or both of those governments, Johnson preferred not to hear about it; indeed, he did everything he could to squelch speculation that Kennedy was killed as a consequence of a communist conspiracy. Nor did he, or liberals in general, wish to encourage a replay of the anticommunist politics of the 1950s that had done so much political damage to the Democrats. Robert Kennedy had other reasons to deflect attention away from Oswald's ideological motives. Mrs. Kennedy, aided by friends and allies sympathetic to her manifest suffering, wished to interpret President Kennedy's life and death within the context of the civil rights struggle rather than within the framework of the Cold War. Such an interpretation demanded that the assassin's communist sympathies be pushed into the background lest the public see how little logical sense it made.

Strangely enough, J. Edgar Hoover, the quintessential anticommunist and communist hunter, also encouraged such a view because it tended (as he thought) to mitigate the damage done to the FBI's reputation by Kennedy's assassination. FBI agents in Dallas had been watching Oswald but concluded that by the nature of his employment he posed no security or espionage risk. They had no idea in the fall of 1963 that it was Oswald who had taken a shot at General Walker the previous April. The FBI therefore saw Oswald a just another communist who had to be kept away from security-sensitive employment but beyond that posed no serious security risk. In October of 1963, however, the FBI learned, via an intercepted letter from Oswald to the Soviet embassy in Mexico City, and through telephone taps on the Cuban and Soviet embassies in that city, that Oswald was then seeking permission to travel to Cuba through Mexico City (it was illegal for American citizens to travel to Cuba). This, as Hoover understood, should have set off alarm bells in the FBI about the possibilities of defection, espionage, or worse. With this information in hand, the FBI agents in Dallas should have placed Oswald on a watch list or security index, perhaps then monitoring his whereabouts during the presidential visit. To make matters worse, FBI agents knew three weeks before Kennedy was shot that Oswald worked in a building overlooking the motorcade route.

After the assassination, when he learned the full scope of Oswald's activities, Hoover saw that the FBI would be liable for criticism for the way it handled Oswald's case. Hoover strongly opposed the idea of creating an independent commission to investigate the assassination in the belief that such an inquiry would reveal gaps in the FBI's investigation. When Johnson established the Warren Commission, Hoover viewed it as an adversary and tracked its investigation with great care, fearing that in its final report the commission would embarrass his agency by criticizing its handling of the Oswald affair. Hoover instinctively saw that an overtly political interpretation of Oswald's deed would raise immediate questions as to why the FBI had not placed him under closer scrutiny, especially following Oswald's suspicious trip to Mexico City. On the other hand, if Oswald could be passed off as a "crackpot" or a "lone nut," as an isolated figure lacking any suspicious subversive trail, the FBI might escape the crisis with only minimal damage done to its reputation.

This was more or less the official explanation of the assassination given by the FBI—at least to the public. Hoover knew better, for barely a week after the assassination he disciplined seventeen agents for their handling of the Oswald case, including James Hosty, the agent in Dallas who had been loosely shadowing Oswald since late 1962, when he inherited Oswald's file from another agent. (The Warren Commission was not informed of these disciplinary actions.) Hoover privately stated, in justifying these actions, that he would not "palliate actions which have resulted in forever destroying the Bureau as the top level investigative organization." The Warren Commission would indeed score the FBI for failing to see that Oswald posed a serious security threat. This criticism was directed at the failures of the FBI in the area of domestic intelligence—in other words, in its mission to gather information in order to prevent crimes from happening. The FBI, however, specialized more in the area of criminal investigation—that is, in solving crimes after they have occurred. The U.S. Senate would hit upon a related theme in its investigations in the mid-1970s, when it criticized the FBI for conducting its inquiry into the assassination as a traditional criminal investigation that did not explore broader questions, such as possible foreign involvement in the crime.[34]

Hoover publicly endorsed the "lone nut" theory of the assassination in order to protect his agency from public criticism in the wake of the most sensational failure in its history. The FBI released its preliminary report on the assassination just three weeks after the event, and long before the Warren Commission had an opportunity to review the case, in an effort to preempt the commission's work and to foreclose speculation about a conspiracy. The FBI's investigation was narrowly tailored to focus on evidence of Oswald's guilt and to avoid wider questions about his motives or possible contacts with foreign governments. At this time, Hoover was thinking in terms of a left-wing conspiracy; it did not occur to him that the predominant interpretive motif in the Kennedy assassination would eventually involve right-wing conspiracies.

The problem with the "lone nut" theory was that (as Norman Mailer saw) it tended to render Kennedy's assassination absurd, senseless, and impossible to decipher. On this telling, it seemed to be a random event, an act committed by a fanatic for his own reasons, a political calamity that had no wider meaning, notwithstanding the concerted effort made to cast Kennedy as a martyr for civil rights. No matter what the politicians said, most people understood that there was something more than a little odd about the assassination that was not satisfactorily explained either by the "lone nut" theory or by the "climate of hate" theory. If Hoover and others thought they were closing down speculation about conspiracies, they were badly mistaken. The vacuum of meaning created by their account merely accelerated the search for conspiracies, albeit of the wrong kind.

There was, in addition, a key fact that was unknown to the Warren Commission in 1964 which, if known, might have shed important light on Oswald's motives. In the mid-1970s, as a consequence of the scandals that engulfed the Nixon administration, the Senate established a select committee headed by Frank Church, Democrat of Idaho, to investigate U.S. intelligence agencies and the nature of their covert activities at home and abroad. In the course of that inquiry, the committee learned that the CIA had engaged over the years in secret operations to assassinate foreign leaders. Among these secret operations was a prolonged campaign during the Eisenhower and Kennedy administrations to topple Castro's regime by assassination, sabotage, or an American-sponsored invasion carried out by Cuban exiles. The committee, however, did not find conclusive evidence that either Eisenhower or Kennedy authorized or had direct knowledge of assassination plots, though both were fully aware that other measures were planned to eliminate Castro's regime.[35]

Yet it seems clear from the testimony of officials who worked on these projects that President Kennedy (along with Attorney General Robert Kennedy) was aware of the CIA's efforts to eliminate Castro by assassination, though he may not have known of the specific details of these plans. Shortly after he entered office in 1961, Kennedy authorized the continuation of operations to overthrow Castro that had begun under the Eisenhower administration. These operations mostly involved support for actions to be carried out by Cuban exiles. One plan called for an exile-led invasion of Cuba, with air cover supplied by the United States—an operation which, when set in motion shortly after Kennedy took office in 1961, led to an embarrassing defeat at the hands of Castro's army in the so-called Bay of Pigs invasion. Following this debacle, the Kennedy administration centralized control over covert operations in the White House, with Robert Kennedy taking an active interest in the whole area. The efforts moved along two fronts under the rubric of Operation Mongoose: support for Cuban exiles who hoped to launch a second invasion of Cuba, and promotion of various schemes to eliminate Castro through assassination. This effort continued with the implied support of the president—though perhaps without his direct knowledge—until the day Kennedy was assassinated in 1963. Robert Kennedy closely monitored these operations, even going so far as to complain to intelligence officials when they did not bear fruit. From the standpoint of the CIA, these operations were carried forward because of intense pressure from the White House to do something about Castro.[36]

The Warren Commission was never told of these operations, even though they may have shed some light on Oswald's motives, particularly as they may have been connected to his desperate efforts to travel to Cuba in September and October of 1963. Allan Dulles, a member of the commission, knew about the assassination plans because he had served as director of the CIA during the period in which they were set in motion. Others were aware of them as well, including J. Edgar Hoover, Robert Kennedy, McGeorge Bundy, Kennedy's national security advisor, and various officials at the CIA. Kennedy kept silent because he did not want the public to know about the administration's plots against Castro, no doubt out of concern for his brother's reputation. The CIA kept silent because the Warren Commission never directly inquired about the plots. Officials at the agency took the position that they would only respond to specific inquiries from the commission; if an inquiry was not made, relevant information would not be forthcoming. But, as a Senate report on the assassination later said, it was not possible to inquire about such plots unless one was already aware of them. In addition, the plots against Castro were not thought to have any relevance to the commission's main task, which was to investigate the assassination of President Kennedy and to tell the public by whose hands he was killed. Oswald was dead and the evidence against him was overwhelming. Revealing such explosive knowledge to the commission would have added an unnecessary complication to its investigation, since any public airing of these covert operations might have further aggravated tensions with Cuba and the Soviet Union and thrown the American public into an uproar over a possible link between Kennedy's assassination and the covert operations against Castro.

The Warren Commission, with such information in hand, might have filled in some of the missing pieces of the Oswald puzzle; on the other hand, the commissioners may have found such information far too hot to handle at that sensitive time. So it was that the Warren Commission proceeded in its investigation with the FBI already committed to a conclusion and the CIA (with the support of Kennedy loyalists) withholding highly sensitive information bearing on the assassination.[37]

SIX · ASSASSIN

THERE WAS LITTLE DOUBT in the minds of those in the know at the FBI and the CIA that Lee Harvey Oswald was somehow involved in the assassination and that he probably acted out of motives linked to his communist ideology. They were never deluded by the thought that President Kennedy might have been killed as a consequence of his civil rights policies or that he had been brought down by a climate of hate and intolerance. They knew that the assassination was rooted in the Cold War, whether Oswald had acted on his own or in concert with foreign agents or other domestic conspirators. Yet, for reasons mentioned above, they were reluctant to press this explanation to the public.

Oswald, they knew, was a strange and unconventional figure, even for a communist. As a southerner with little formal education, he was atypical of communists and socialists in the United States, who are mostly northern, urban, college-educated, and frequently from ethnic backgrounds. Many people refused to accept the fact that Oswald was a communist simply because he did not look like any other communist or socialist they knew. Oswald looked like an ill-educated roughneck, "a hick from the boondocks" as one reporter commented when she saw him in Moscow after his defection. He

did not possess the "style" that was popularly associated with political radicalism. As an assassin, he lacked the flash and the flair of a
John Wilkes Booth.

To be sure, there could not have been many people like Oswald
running around free in the United States in 1963. To confuse matters further, he spent two years in the Marines, hardly a training
ground for radicals. Unlike arm-chair or academic radicals, he had
a violent streak linked with a propensity to act on his beliefs.

In Oswald's mind, Marxism was not merely a theory but a
weapon for attacking ideological foes. His powerful sense of resentment coupled with his devotion to communist ideology made for a
highly charged political personality. Far from being a confused
loner in search of meaning, Oswald was politicized to a lethal
degree and certainly politically advanced for a man of his tender
age. No one who knew him in Dallas in the period leading up to the
assassination thought of him as a "nut," if by that term we mean a
person who is mentally or emotionally unstable. Oswald, they said,
was logical and cold-blooded to a fault. If he had trouble getting
along with others, it was because he saw a wide gulf between his
political outlook and the conventional views of those with whom
he came into contact. A communist revolutionary, after all, is
bound to have some difficulty in carrying on a conventional social
life and in getting along with others, particularly in a city like Dallas. The Warren Commission suggested that Oswald's failures in
employment caused him to seek outlets in radical political activity,
when in fact the causality worked in the other direction: his radical
political activity, and his preoccupation with politics, led to difficulties with supervisors and fellow employees. The same logic applied
to Oswald's difficulties with his wife and her frustrations with his
employment failures and inattention to family life. If President
Kennedy had not visited Dallas, Oswald would eventually have
struck out violently in another direction—as, indeed, he already
had done several months before.[1]

Who was Oswald? And why did he shoot President Kennedy?
The Warren Commission Report, though still the main source of
basic information on the assassination, did not answer these ques-

tions to the satisfaction of skeptical readers at the time. The later investigations (referred to above) carried out by the U.S. Senate in the mid-1970s and by the House of Representatives a few years later revealed important information about the assassination that was not previously known to the public, while at the same time confirming some basic conclusions reached by the Warren Commission. Several independent writers, adding information gleaned through their own researches, have published books and articles that, when taken together, go a long way toward answering these questions. Among these works are: *Legend: The Secret World of Lee Harvey Oswald* (1978) by Edward Jay Epstein, *Oswald's Game* (1983) by Jean Davison, *Oswald's Tale* (1997) by Norman Mailer, and *Live by the Sword* (1998) by Gus Russo—all of which piece together revealing clues to the assassination from Oswald's life and character and from his movements in the months leading up to November 22, 1963. These works by and large accept the evidence pointing to Oswald as the assassin but proceed from there to consider why he may have acted as he did.

Oswald's youthful years, which were reviewed in the Warren Commission Report, were notable for the frequency with which the family moved from place to place.[2] Oswald was born and spent his early years in New Orleans. His father died of a heart attack two months before he was born. He had an older brother, Robert, born in 1934, and a half-brother, John Pic, born in 1932 from his mother's first marriage. At the age of five, his mother (Marguerite) relocated the family to the Dallas-Fort Worth area and married for a third time, now to a salesman whose earnings gave Lee and his two brothers a more prosperous life. That marriage, however, fell apart within a few years, forcing the family to live once more on his mother's meager earnings. Owing to the divorce, financial circumstances, and employment opportunities, Oswald's family rarely stayed in one location for very long. Before Lee was ten years old, he had lived at more than ten different addresses and had attended six elementary schools.

In 1952, after her older son Robert enlisted in the Marines, Mrs. Oswald took Lee to New York City with a plan of settling near her oldest son, John, who was now married and living in Manhattan with his wife and infant child. While living in New York City, Lee received little supervision from his mother, who was preoccupied with her job and other concerns. He thus stopped going to school, spending his time watching television in their apartment or riding around the city on the subway, visiting parks, museums, and other interesting places. At length he came to the attention of authorities for his truancy and in the spring of 1953 was remanded by a family court judge to a youth home for counseling and evaluation. A battery of tests administered there suggested that Lee (now thirteen years old) was "a withdrawn, socially maladjusted boy, whose mother did not interest herself sufficiently in his welfare and had failed to establish a close relationship with him."[3] This evaluation made during Oswald's adolescence was a foundation for the Warren Commission's conclusion that Oswald was a socially maladjusted individual.

At about the same time, in May of 1953, Oswald in the course of his wanderings about Manhattan was handed a leaflet demanding clemency for the Rosenbergs, who at that time were awaiting execution for espionage committed in service to the Soviet Union. The leaflet, which was passed out throughout New York City by volunteers canvassing for subscriptions for a Communist Party newspaper, claimed that the Rosenbergs had been unjustly framed for crimes they did not commit and were in fact "martyrs" for democracy and workers' rights. This leaflet made an immediate and lasting impression on the boy, who later referred to it when he defected to the Soviet Union as the greatest cause of his conversion to communism. Jean Davison suggests that this was so, not because he empathized with the Rosenbergs, but because he saw himself as occupying a similar position as a victim of "the system"—in his case, of the juvenile court system.[4] From this time forward, Oswald saw himself as a communist, an unusual one perhaps because of the tender age at which he was converted, but a dedicated and hardheaded partisan nevertheless. Thus, as things developed, Oswald did not pick up his radicalism in New Orleans or Dallas after all, but rather in New York City, the intellectual capital of American leftism.

Mrs. Oswald soon took Lee back to New Orleans to escape the supervision of New York City's family court system, which she feared might order him into a juvenile treatment program to address his truancy and disruptive conduct in school. In New Orleans he attended public schools, earning indifferent grades but occasionally causing friction with friends and classmates when he declared his allegiance to communism and revolution. He even tried to convince one young associate to join him in seeking membership in the Communist Party. As he later said to a reporter in Moscow, he began at this time to read Marx's writings in a serious way, taking a special liking to *The Communist Manifesto* and *Capital*. Somewhat inconsistently with his developing leftist beliefs, he liked to watch *I Led Three Lives*, a popular television show of the era that portrayed the work of Herbert Philbrick as an anticommunist counterspy for the FBI. Oswald was heard in these years to make threats against national leaders, like President Eisenhower, on the basis of his feelings that they trampled on the rights of workers.[5] Oswald's ideological conversion now seemed to provide an outlet for his generally resentful disposition by supplying a motive to engage others in debate and to seek membership in political organizations. Once Oswald embraced communism, he could no longer be called a "loner" in the conventional sense of that term. His youthful conversion to communism, moreover, contradicted later accusations that he was recruited by the CIA or the FBI to pose as a communist. Unlike the character in *I Led Three Lives* who was a poseur and a double agent, Oswald saw himself as the genuine article—though perhaps the television program introduced him to the world of double- and triple-agentry.

Oswald dropped out of school altogether when he turned sixteen in 1955 in the hopes of enlisting in the Marine Corps on the basis of a false affidavit from his mother declaring that he was seventeen. When he was turned down, Oswald spent the next year working odd jobs in the New Orleans area while he waited for his seventeenth birthday, when he could legally enlist in the Marines. Meanwhile, his mother moved back to Fort Worth to be near her son Robert, who had left the Corps and was living in the area.[6]

Oswald spent nearly three years on active duty in the Marine Corps, from October 1956 to September 1959—that is, from the ages of seventeen to twenty. During basic training exercises, he learned to fire an M-1 rifle, earning a passing grade as a marksman. Later, while assigned to Air Force, Naval, and Marine air stations, he received training in aircraft maintenance, radar theory, map reading, air traffic control procedures, aircraft surveillance, and the use of radar. He was taught, among other things, to identify whether incoming aircraft were friend or foe, techniques for overcoming radar-jamming equipment, how to plot the path of aircraft on radar screens, and how to measure the altitude of aircraft. Oswald became highly skilled in his field of specialty, scoring seventh in proficiency exams in an overall class of thirty. After completing his training, he shipped out with his classmates for Japan, where he was assigned a tour of duty at the U.S. air base in Atsugi, some thirty miles distant from Tokyo.[7]

At that time, before the era of satellite photography, Atsugi was a base of departure for U-2 reconnaissance flights over the Soviet Union, which yielded important photographic information about Soviet military capabilities. The U-2 flights were part of a highly classified and top secret program. There was a significant danger that the Soviet Union might gain access to sensitive information about the U-2 that would enable them to shoot one down and thereby create an international incident of great propaganda value. The flights were so sensitive that they required presidential authorization before take-off. The U-2 was effective because, despite its unusual appearance, it could fly at altitudes of up to 90,000 feet, beyond reach of most surface-to-air missiles and high enough to elude tracking by radar. The Marines on the base saw the aircraft take off and land when it was called into action; the radar crews could monitor the U-2's rate of ascent. Since Oswald worked on those crews, he had many opportunities to track the secret aircraft. The hangar in which the U-2 was kept was off-limits to the Marines in Oswald's unit. The men were not supposed to know anything about the U-2's missions other than that they involved secret reconnaissance flights. Yet it was not too difficult to figure out that the aircraft must be flying missions over the Soviet Union.[8]

Oswald was stationed at Atsugi for a little more than a year, from August 1957 until September 1958. During his tenure there, he was subject twice to courts martial, the first time for possessing an unregistered privately owned firearm in violation of general orders, and the second for insulting an officer at a nightclub. Such infractions were clear signs of a reckless and defiant character. In both cases he was sentenced to periods of confinement at hard labor. When he was not confined, Oswald spent a good deal of his free time in Tokyo but would not reveal what he did there either to his fellow Marines or even to relatives. Lawyers for the Warren Commission later surmised that Oswald might have established contacts with communists in the area who sought military information and possibly coached him on the strategy and tactics of defection. Oswald subsequently revealed that he laid his plans to defect to the Soviet Union while stationed in Japan.[9]

By the time Oswald was shipped back to the United States near the end of 1958 he had lost his enthusiasm for the Marines, at least to the extent he ever had any. He was assigned to the Marine Air Control Squadron at the Marine Corps Air Station at El Toro, California, where he served on a radar crew engaged mainly in aircraft surveillance, an assignment which would have given him access to some classified material. During this time Oswald began to make plans for a course of action he would follow when his tour of duty ended several months hence. In March of 1959, he applied to Albert Schweitzer College in Switzerland for admission in the spring term of 1960, claiming that while there he would study philosophy, meet Europeans, and "live in a healthy climate and a good moral atmosphere." He also said on the application that he would enroll in a summer course at the University of Turku in Finland. This was a ruse designed to obtain a passport without raising questions about how he planned to meet his remaining obligation to the Marine Corps Reserve and to establish a legitimate reason to travel to a point near the Soviet border.[10] In the summer of 1959, Oswald applied for and was granted a hardship discharge that allowed him to leave the Marine Corps before his tour of duty was up in order to take care of his mother, who had been injured at her place of employment and could no longer support herself. This, too, was a ruse. A year later, after his defection to the Soviet Union, Oswald was given an undesirable discharge from the Marine Corps Reserve.[11]

On October 31, 1959, six weeks after his discharge from the Marine Corps, the *Washington Post* carried a story off the United Press wire under the headline "Ex Marine Asks Soviet Citizenship." The opening paragraph read, "Lee Harvey Oswald, 20, a recently discharged Marine from Fort Worth, Texas, disclosed today that he had taken steps to renounce his American citizenship and become a Soviet citizen. He said the reasons for his move were 'purely political.'" He was quoted by the reporter in Moscow as saying, "I will never return to the United States for any reason." Oswald said in another interview that he "could not be happy living under capitalism." Reporters in the United States interviewed Oswald's sister-in-law in Fort Worth, who said that "he wanted to travel a lot and talked about going to Cuba."[12] Oswald's appearance in Moscow occurred less than a year after Castro's successful revolution in Cuba and some months after Castro revealed that he was a communist revolutionary. Another article on Oswald's intended defection reported that an official at the American embassy encouraged him to hold off on signing any papers renouncing his citizenship until he was certain the Soviet Union would accept him.[13] In the end, Oswald did not give up his U.S. citizenship and was permitted to remain in the USSR as a resident alien—a decision which left the door open for his eventual return to the United States.

Oswald had arrived in the Soviet Union via Finland two weeks earlier, on October 15, with a tourist visa good for no more than six days inside the Soviet Union. He shortly made application to the Ministry of Internal Affairs for Soviet citizenship. On October 20, he was told that his application had been denied and that his visa had expired. Oswald was asked to leave the Soviet Union immediately. Always the man of decisive action, he responded to this rejection by slashing his wrists in his hotel room. He was found semiconscious in the bathroom and taken to a hospital, where he soon recovered (the wounds were not serious), and then was placed in a psychiatric ward for several days. The apparent suicidal act had bought him some valuable time.[14] When he was released from the psychiatric ward, Oswald raised the stakes by marching into the American embassy and declaring to consular officials that he wished to renounce his U.S. citizenship. There he presented to a senior official a note that read, "I, Lee Harvey Oswald, do hereby request that my present citizenship in the United States of America be revoked." In the same note he also wrote, "I affirm my allegiance to the Union of Soviet Socialist Republics," and declared, "I am a Marxist." Oswald went still further, threatening to turn over to the Soviets classified information he had acquired through his radar training in the Marines. This latter statement "raised hackles," as one embassy official recalled.[15] The official also had a sense that Oswald had been "tutored" in the rules and regulations pertaining to the renunciation of citizenship. It was later learned that the embassy offices had been bugged, so that Soviet officials probably heard everything Oswald said.

Oswald was asked to return the following Monday with the promise that his application would be acted upon at this time. The American officials in Moscow were giving him a few days to "cool off" and to reconsider a decision that would have permanent consequences. In the meantime, two American reporters, tipped off by the embassy, approached Oswald in his hotel for interviews to allow him to explain the reasons behind his defection. These interviews revealed little beyond Oswald's cardboard depictions of American capitalism. He did tell one of the reporters, however, that he had been working on his plan to defect for at least two years, thus locating the origins of his scheme in his tour of duty in Japan. He also referred to the Soviet government as "my government." In the end, Oswald did not return to the American embassy, despite the best efforts of consular officials and his own family to contact him. Soviet authorities had reversed their earlier decision and now decided that Oswald could stay in the Soviet Union (perhaps they overheard his threat to turn over secret military information). Thus Oswald never returned to the American embassy to execute the renunciation of his U.S. citizenship. A few weeks later, he disappeared into the Soviet Union and was not heard from again by his family in the United States for more than a year.[16]

On May 1, 1960, less than six months after Oswald's defection, a U.S. reconnaissance aircraft flying at high altitude was brought down by surface-to-air missiles over the Soviet Union after taking off from a U.S. air base in Pakistan. The pilot, Francis Gary Powers, was captured after he came down safely by parachute and was later put on public trial in the Soviet Union. The aircraft, a U-2, was likewise captured and placed on public display. The U.S. government used as its cover story the claim that the aircraft was gathering weather data and the pilot inadvertently flew off course over Soviet territory—claims that few believed. The downing of a U.S. military aircraft over the Soviet Union was a significant international incident that was most embarrassing to the United States and to President Eisenhower. In response to the incident, Premier Khrushchev walked out of a summit meeting with Eisenhower in Paris and appeared at the United Nations in New York to protest the violation of Soviet air space. This debacle ended the U-2 reconnaissance flights over Soviet territory.

Some years later, Powers (who had been brought home in exchange for a Soviet spy) wrote in his memoirs that the downing of his aircraft just a few months after Oswald's defection was not an accident. During his tour of duty at Atsugi, Powers wrote, Oswald had gained access through his radar work to critical information about the flying altitude of the U-2s. When Oswald defected, he told American officials that he would divulge to the Soviets critical information gained through his radar operations. Powers strongly suspected that Oswald had given the Soviets information that was used to shoot down his aircraft.[17] It turned out that during the deliberations of the Warren Commission, the CIA prepared a secret memorandum addressing the subject of "Lee Harvey Oswald's Access to Classified Information about the U-2." The commission did not release the classified memo, nor did it address this highly sensitive question in its final report.

The CIA memorandum was eventually released to the historian Stephen Ambrose in 1979 in response to a request made under the Freedom of Information Act. According to Ambrose, who discussed it in *Ike's Spies: Eisenhower and the Espionage Establishment*, the memorandum concluded that Oswald had no access to the highly restricted U-2 program at Atsugi and that, moreover, he did not have the knowledge or training required to distinguish the U-2 from other aircraft flying secret missions. The Russians, in addition, were already tracking the U-2 flights and thus knew how high the aircraft could fly.[18] The memorandum, however, seems unconvincing. For one thing, it suggests that it was just a matter of time until the Soviets shot down one of the overflights—which raises the question of why, if this was so, they were allowed to continue. In addition, Oswald and his fellow Marines watched the U-2 take off and land, commented on its unique characteristics, monitored its flight path by radar, and speculated on the nature of its missions. It was perhaps true that the Soviets already had the information needed to shoot one down, though this raises the question as to why this had not been done before Oswald appeared in Moscow. The question remains intriguing to this day and still has no clear answer.[19]

There was, however, another reason why in the wake of Kennedy's assassination the CIA may have wished to play down the damage Oswald had done to U.S. intelligence interests. If the agency acknowledged Oswald's possible role in the downing of the U-2, it would also implicitly acknowledge that he must have had strong ideological motives (linked to the Soviet Union) in acting to assassinate President Kennedy. In that case, the conclusion would be inescapable that Oswald had been the central figure in two of the most spectacular intelligence failures of the Cold War—the crash of the U-2 and the assassination of President Kennedy three years later. The implications for American intelligence and for the Cold War would have been profound if it had been acknowledged that the same man had engineered both events and that he had done so while in contact with the Soviet government. Such an admission, in turn, would have raised a whole series of potentially explosive questions about the competence of U.S. intelligence. Why did U.S. intelligence officials allow the U-2 flights to continue after Oswald's defection? Were they suspicious of Oswald's possible role in bringing down the U-2? If they were, why was Oswald allowed to return to the United States and, once there, why was he not placed under closer watch? For all of these reasons (and more), neither the intelligence establishment nor the Warren Commission wished to call attention to the potential linkage between the two events.

On June 9, 1962, the *Washington Post* carried a United Press dispatch from Moscow under the title "Third American in Two Months Leaves Soviet 'Home.'" The article informed American readers that "a former U.S. Marine who came here to live three years ago saying he would never return to America is homeward bound with his wife and child." The dispatch did not quote Oswald on the reasons for his change of heart, though it did say he stressed that he had retained his American citizenship during his stay in the Soviet Union. It was no longer in his interest to recall the determination he had expressed in 1959 to renounce his citizenship. A dispatch from the Associated Press noted that Oswald's wife was Russian and that he had "worked in a factory in Minsk until he got fed up."[20]

Oswald took the position on his return that the Soviet Union and the United States were equally corrupt and bureaucratic. He had not given up his Marxist ideals, he said, but did acknowledge that he had grown disillusioned with life in the Soviet Union. He resented the power exercised over him by Communist Party officials. Oswald was drawn to "revolutionary" politics, which is what he sought but did not find in the Soviet Union. He was searching for a "third way" between the bureaucratic communism of the Soviet Union and the harsh competition of American capitalism— hence his attraction to Castro and third-world revolutionaries. There was an element of naïve idealism in Oswald's political ideas —for example, in his rejection of the centralized state in favor of an informal style of local government and the elimination of economic competition from all aspects of life. There was in fact a strong resemblance between Oswald's ill-formulated ideas concerning socialism and revolution, and the loose theories about liberation and revolution that were popularized by the New Left later in the 1960s. Indeed, Oswald's ruminations on politics sound more than a little like the theories outlined in the Port Huron Statement, the New Left manifesto written in 1962 that denounced U.S. preoccupations with communism, criticized the Soviet Union as a status quo power, and exalted an alternative system based on a concept of participatory socialism. Apart from his less than hip style, Oswald might have been right at home among the cultural revolutionaries of the 1960s. Very few of those radicals understood, however, that they advanced their cause in close ideological kinship with the assassin of John F. Kennedy.

While in Minsk, Oswald wrote two accounts of his life under Soviet communism: the "Historic Diary," recounting his day-by-day experience in the Soviet Union, and "The Collective," which centered about the radio and television factory where he worked. The latter, he hoped, might be published in the United States, making him an authority on Soviet communism. Both titles pointed to his continued infatuation with Marxist language. Neither work, however, implicated Oswald in any illegal activities under American law that might have barred his return. Oswald was keenly aware of the kinds of acts and statements that might complicate the legal status of his return to the United States.

During his return trip back to the United States, Oswald composed a mock interview with American reporters in which he wrote down his true feelings alongside more prudent answers to questions that were likely to be posed to him. He intended to provide only those answers that would cast him in the most favorable light to Americans.

Question: Why did you go to the USSR?
Real answer: "I went as a mark of disgust and protest against

American political policies in foreign countries, my personal sign of discontent and horror at the misguided line
of reasoning in the U.S. government and people."
Prudent answer: "I went as a citizen of the U.S., as a tourist,
residing in a foreign country which I have a perfect right
to do. I went there to see the land, the people, and how
their system works."

Question: Are you a communist?
Real answer: "Yes, basically."
Prudent answer: "No, of course not."

Question: Did you make statements against the USA while
there?
Real answer: "Yes."
Prudent answer: "No."

Newspapers: "Thank you sir, you are a real patriot."

Oswald took satisfaction in his plan to conceal his real views in
front of the gullible Americans. He was eager to appear to American reporters as an idealistic tourist rather than as a determined
communist, since in that light he might be viewed in the United
States as more of a "crackpot" than a dangerous subversive.[21]

Oswald was returning to the United States in mid-1962, just as
the Cold War was about to arrive at a perilous intersection. It may
have occurred to Oswald that relations between the superpowers
had grown increasingly tense over the previous few years, beginning with Castro's revolution in Cuba in late 1958, followed by the
U-2 incident in 1960, the Bay of Pigs invasion in 1961, and continued efforts by the Kennedy administration to overthrow Castro
and blunt revolutionary movements in the third world. Oswald
may have concluded that if there was some role for him to play in
this conflict, he could not do it from his position as a factory worker
in Minsk. The Soviet system provided no constructive outlet for a
person with his political disposition. There, political activities were

monopolized by trusted members of the Communist Party. Oswald had little chance of being selected as a member of this elite group. The United States, on the other hand, provided a fair amount of freedom of movement—provided that the FBI could be kept at bay. Cuba was close by, and one might find a means to travel from the United States. The Americas represented an emerging and highly interesting theater of ideological conflict. Oswald may have sensed that Cuba would be the flashpoint for the next showdown between the superpowers. For all these reasons it made sense for a dedicated Marxist like Oswald to swallow his pride and head back to the United States.

Shortly after he returned to the Dallas area with his wife and child, Oswald was interviewed by FBI agents concerning his activities in the Soviet Union. The counterespionage section of the FBI was understandably concerned that Oswald might pose a security risk to the United States or that he (along with his wife) might have returned to the United States with some kind of intelligence assignment from the Soviet government. In the latter case, however, it was foolhardy for anyone to think that Oswald would openly confess to such an assignment. The agents who conducted the interview reported that Oswald was impatient and arrogant in their meeting and revealed no more about his background and future plans than was absolutely necessary. In answer to direct questions, however, he denied that he ever had any contact with Soviet intelligence during his stay in the Soviet Union. The FBI agents asked Oswald if he would take a lie detector test regarding these points, but Oswald refused. The agents did not like Oswald nor did they trust him, but they found little basis for concluding that he was a security risk. Oswald's case was given a "closed" status, which meant that no further action with regard to it was scheduled. With this routine debriefing out of the way, Oswald was more or less free to pursue his political interests and avocations in the United States without overbearing surveillance or supervision from the FBI.[22]

The possibility that Oswald had cooperated in some way with Soviet intelligence during his stay remains one of the more troubling questions about his life and character. It also goes to the heart

152 CAMELOT AND THE CULTURAL REVOLUTION

of his motives in assassinating President Kennedy. If he had in fact cooperated with Soviet intelligence and if indeed the information he provided had played some part in the downing of the U-2, his role in the assassination would have to be viewed in an even more sinister light. Oswald, of course, denied any such cooperation, notwithstanding the written statement he presented to U.S. officials in Moscow. After the assassination, Soviet officials reported to the U.S. government that there had never been any contact between Oswald and Soviet intelligence agencies, and that no one associated with the Soviet government had ever debriefed Oswald when he defected. The Warren Report concluded that "No evidence has been found that [Soviet authorities] used him for any particular propaganda or other political or informational purposes." This was technically true: no such evidence had been found. It was also a conclusion that the FBI, for reasons mentioned above, wished to establish. On the other hand, Oswald's declared intention to reveal secrets should have aroused suspicions about what he did when he disappeared into the Soviet Union in late 1959.[23]

Officials within our own CIA, however, found such denials difficult to believe, since it had been standard practice in both the countries to interview defectors to find out if they might supply useful information (not necessarily of a secret or classified kind). Defectors with military backgrounds were interviewed with particular interest. Oswald, in addition, was perfectly capable of volunteering his services in the most insistent ways in the event that Soviet officials should initially dismiss him as an unstable or unreliable person. In any case, intelligence officials suspected there was more to Oswald's background in the Soviet Union than Soviet authorities were letting on. It was possible, too, they speculated, that Oswald had been sent back to the United States under deep cover as a sleeper agent to be deployed in action at some point in the future, without ever considering that he might take it upon himself to assassinate an American president. Thus the Soviets may have been responsible for using Oswald as an agent but not for this purpose.

Two months after Kennedy's assassination, in January 1964, a Soviet intelligence official, Yuri Nosenko, defected to the United

States, telling CIA agents that he had seen Oswald's file in the course of his duties in Moscow and that it had been clear that Oswald never had any contact with Soviet intelligence. Officials in the counterintelligence division of the CIA did not believe him, thinking instead that he was a double agent sent by the Soviets to circulate disinformation about Oswald that would exonerate the Soviet Union in the Kennedy assassination and thereby mislead the Warren Commission. Hoover and the FBI, however, believed Nosenko and so communicated this conclusion to the Warren Commission. Since the FBI had jurisdiction over the assassination inquiry (because the assassination was a domestic crime), the commission accepted the FBI's conclusion. The CIA, however, kept Nosenko under house arrest for three years, all the while trying to break his story about Oswald and the real purposes behind his own defection. It was also possible that the KGB had prepared a doctored file on Oswald for Nosenko to review, in which case he would pass along disinformation to American intelligence but would not know that it was disinformation—thus making it impossible to "break" his story during interrogation. The counterintelligence division of the CIA was divided internally for years over the question of whether Nosenko was a legitimate defector or a Soviet double agent.[24]

Oswald's wife, Marina, reported that while Oswald may have appeared calm and collected to the FBI agents who interviewed him, he was greatly unnerved by their questions. This was a consistent reaction from Oswald whenever he was approached by one of the FBI agents in the Dallas bureau. Oswald had a bad case of paranoia when it came to the FBI. One associate said he had "an allergy to the FBI." Oswald referred to the agency as "the notorious FBI." He used aliases to evade FBI supervision. He liked to send the FBI on false trails by contacting radical organizations with misleading information about his plans in the knowledge that his letters would be intercepted by the bureau.[25] At the time of the assassination, he was living by himself in a rooming house under a fictitious name. He used postal boxes to receive mail so that the FBI agents could not track his address through his mail. In the summer of 1963, he embarked on his pro-Castro activities in New Orleans so that his name would not be immediately recognized by the local FBI. By the time the Dallas FBI had transferred his file to New Orleans, Oswald had moved back to Dallas again.[26] Just a few weeks before the assassination, he left a threatening note at the FBI headquarters in Dallas warning an agent to stay away from his wife. Later, while in police custody after the assassination, he erupted in anger when that agent appeared in the room where he was being interrogated.

Oswald may have feared the FBI because, in his mind, it fulfilled the same internal security function in the United States as did the KGB in the Soviet Union. He may have been apprehensive that his Russian wife might innocently convey information to FBI agents that would compromise his freedom of action. He may have feared that the FBI might learn something about his wife's background that would raise doubts about her continued residence in the United States. He may have known that if he were placed on an FBI watch list he would have difficulty obtaining a passport. He may have feared arrest. He certainly wished to keep his political activities from coming to the attention of FBI agents. Oswald was playing a cat-and-mouse game with the Dallas FBI and, given the nature of his activities, he had good reason to be wary of their inquiries. After the assassination, Hoover recognized that, to the bureau's everlasting shame, Oswald had succeeded in confusing and evading his agents long enough to pull off the kind of spectacular stunt that he must have been contemplating since he converted to communism as a teenager.

Once Oswald was resettled with his family in Dallas, he wasted little time before plunging into communist-related political activities, as if he had returned to the United States to accomplish some political purpose—not unlike Raymond Shaw, the fictitious character in *The Manchurian Candidate* (a popular film in late 1962), who returned to the United States after being held as a prisoner of war in North Korea with an assignment to assassinate a presidential candidate. In August of 1962, even as the FBI was watching him, he renewed his subscription to *The Worker*, the publication of the U.S. Communist Party, and requested literature from the New York City offices of the Fair Play for Cuba Committee.[27]

In October of 1962, two historic events dominated the national news. Early in the month, violent demonstrations broke out at the University of Mississippi in protest against a federal court order requiring the admission of James Meredith, the first Negro student to seek enrollment at the segregated institution. During the riots on campus, at least three men were killed, fifty were treated for serious injuries at the university infirmary, and six United States marshals were shot, one of them critically wounded. Edwin A. Walker, a retired Army general and leader of the John Birch Society in Dallas, led the protest against the desegregation order and was accused of inciting the violent riots that followed. Five years earlier, General Walker had been the military officer in charge when federal troops were sent to Little Rock, Arkansas, to enforce a similar desegregation order for that city's public schools. Walker, now saying that he was on the wrong side of that contest, urged the governor of Mississippi to defy the newest desegregation order from the federal courts. After calm was restored, and after Meredith was finally enrolled, Walker was arrested for his role in inciting the violence and was later indicted by a U.S. grand jury for interfering with U.S. marshals in the performance of their duties. The charges were dropped in mid-January 1963.[28]

A few weeks after the Mississippi riots, President Kennedy appeared on national television to announce that the Soviet Union had placed offensive nuclear weapons in Cuba and that the United States would impose a naval blockade against the island until they were removed. In the wake of the Bay of Pigs invasion, Castro was able to persuade Soviet leaders to install nuclear weapons in Cuba in order to deter any future invasion from the United States. He was fully aware that the Kennedy administration continued to train and arm Cuban exiles in preparation for some future action against his government. Indeed, exiles had continued to stage hit-and-run sabotage operations against Cuban targets after the Bay of

Pigs fiasco. Following Kennedy's television appearance and the imposition of the naval blockade, Khrushchev was soon persuaded by colleagues within the Soviet government to withdraw the nuclear weapons, since (fortunately) it did not make sense from the Soviet point of view to risk a nuclear war over Cuba. Kennedy, in return, promised to end plans to invade Cuba. Castro, however, was incensed by Khrushchev's move since it implied that Cuba was merely a pawn in a greater match played between the two super-powers. Even in the midst of the crisis, Castro urged the use of nuclear weapons if Kennedy made a move against his island to remove them. Indeed, Khrushchev heard Castro to say that the naval blockade itself was justification for a preemptive attack. The deployment of the weapons in the first place was a sign of the degree to which Castro distrusted and detested Kennedy. Castro was prepared to go to any lengths to defend his revolution—including even nuclear war and, perhaps, assassination of American leaders.[29]

A short time after the crisis ended, Oswald opened a subscription to *The Militant*, a magazine published by the Socialist Workers Party. The SWP was a Trotskyite organization that viewed third-world revolutions like Castro's as the wave of the future and was critical of the Soviet Union as a bureaucratic state with an interest in maintaining the status quo, an ideological position which corresponded with Oswald's outlook. A few months after opening his subscription, Oswald mentioned to an associate that he gathered instructions for approved revolutionary activities by "reading between the lines of the *Militant*." The magazine was also sharply critical of the Kennedy administration's policies in Cuba, calling them criminal and murderous and describing Kennedy as a "pirate." Around this time, Oswald commented to an acquaintance at a social gathering that Kennedy's polices might lead to a nuclear holocaust. He also observed that even though Soviet missiles had been removed from Cuba, the Kennedy administration was still sponsoring acts of sabotage against the Castro government.[30]

At some point in January or February of 1963, perhaps when he read that the charges against General Walker in connection with the Mississippi riots had been dropped, Oswald conceived the idea of assassinating him. The general was a prominent figure in both the local and the national news, not simply for his opposition to court-ordered desegregation plans, but also for his calls for a U.S.-led invasion of Cuba to topple Castro's regime. Oswald's wife, in testimony before the Warren Commission, said that her husband had decided that Walker was a fascist who deserved to be killed, much as Hitler should have been assassinated before he plunged the world into war. It was most certainly Walker's reputation as an anticommunist and as a foe of Castro that provoked Oswald's ire. He carefully scouted the area around Walker's home, took photographs of the area to assist in his preparations and also to offer proof when it might be needed to document his revolutionary bona fides, and memorized the bus routes to and from the scene. On March 12, 1963, with his plan to shoot Walker in mind, Oswald ordered a rifle with a telescopic sight from a sporting goods company in Chicago, using the alias Alek James Hidell on forged identification cards that he may have produced at a photographic firm where he worked at the time. The weapon was soon shipped and was in Oswald's hands by March 25. On March 31, Marina took a photograph of Oswald in the back yard of their home holding up the rifle along with copies of *The Militant* and *The Worker*. She wrote in Russian on the photograph, "hunter of fascists, ha, ha, ha."[31] She seemed to believe that her husband's political activities were faintly ridiculous in view of his status in America as a "nobody." In view of what happened later, however, it is plain that Oswald ordered the rifle for one overriding purpose: to carry out political assassinations.

On the evening of April 10, 1963, Oswald took a position in an alley behind Walker's home and fired a single shot with his new rifle at the general as he sat inside near a window while working on his income tax return. The shot missed after it was deflected by the wooden window frame, sailing over Walker's head before it lodged in a wall of the room where he was sitting. Oswald fled on foot without waiting to see if he had hit his mark, hiding the rifle alongside nearby railroad tracks with the plan of returning a few days later to retrieve it. A police detective investigating the case told reporters that "Whoever shot at the General was playing for keeps. The sniper wasn't trying to scare him, he was shooting to kill."

When Oswald arrived home after the attack, his wife was white with fear, having found a note from him containing instructions about what she should do in case he was arrested. He described to her his attempt on Walker's life, which only magnified her sense of alarm. Oswald was prepared to be captured or even to be killed at the scene or in an attempt to escape, which (if it had happened) would have brought his career as an assassin to an early conclusion. At this time, therefore, he could not have been contemplating further revolutionary deeds beyond the assassination of Walker, a fact which works against the suspicion that he was sent back to the United States as a Soviet agent, since the intelligence services of the Soviet Union were unlikely to send an agent on a mission to kill a relative small-fry like Walker. Oswald's attack on General Walker turned out to be a tryout of sorts, an experiment through which he demonstrated to himself how far he might go in pursuit of his revolutionary objectives. His appetite for violence whetted, Oswald was now on the lookout for other political missions that he might carry out. Dallas police never connected Oswald to the Walker shooting until the note to his wife was discovered among his possessions after the Kennedy assassination.[32]

Oswald's attack on Walker was thus known immediately to his wife. It was also known to, or strongly suspected by, an older couple who had taken an interest in the Oswalds after coming to know them through the Russian community in Dallas. George de Mohrenschildt, with his wife Jeane, met Lee and Marina Oswald through mutual acquaintances the previous year. Because of his Russian background, de Mohrenschildt volunteered to read Oswald's unpublished manuscript on his experience as a worker in Minsk. He knew that Oswald owned a rifle because his wife had seen it in a closet during a previous visit to his apartment. In addition, Oswald had given him a copy of the photo in which he was shown in his yard holding the weapon. Indeed, after de Mohrenschildt had loaned Marina twenty-five dollars some weeks earlier, she told him that her "fool husband" had used it to purchase the rifle. When the couple visited the Oswalds two days after the Walker shooting, and after they read about it in the newspapers, de Mohrenschildt made a wisecrack about it, asking Oswald how he could have missed his target. Surprised and caught off-guard by the remark, Oswald did not respond, thinking perhaps that Marina had told him about the attack. The subject was dropped without further comment.

George and Jeane de Mohrenschildt now strongly suspected that Oswald had fired the shot at Walker. At this point, perhaps now seeing his potential for violence, they broke off contact with Oswald, leaving a few days later on a trip to New York City. When they returned to Dallas, Oswald had moved to New Orleans. In June, the de Mohrenschildts moved to Haiti, where George worked under a contract with the federal government and where they lived when Kennedy was assassinated. They did not report Oswald to the police after the Walker shooting, perhaps because they feared implicating themselves in his crime. De Mohrenschildt, after all, had supplied the funds that Oswald used to purchase the rifle. Though entirely innocent, they may have feared embarrassment by having their name mentioned in the press in connection with Oswald's. They may have feared that such an association would compromise de Mohrenschildt's ability to win the government contracts that were the source of their livelihood. Nevertheless, if they or Marina Oswald had at this time reported Oswald to the police, as they most certainly should have done, he would not have been free seven months later to assassinate President Kennedy.[33]

In the meantime, the war of words between Kennedy and Castro continued to escalate even after the nuclear showdown the previous October. On April 20, Castro delivered a speech in Havana asserting that the United States had given up plans to invade Cuba following the missile crisis but had replaced that tactic with a plot to assassinate Cuban leaders. Taking satisfaction from the fact that his government had so far held off attacks from the United States, Castro still warned, "We cannot rest on our laurels, because the enemy will resort to new measures and new tactics and new plans.

They are now making plans to assassinate the leaders of the revolution." Castro had good reason to understand these moves, since before taking power he had organized Cuban exiles in Mexico City to carry out assassination plots against his predecessor, Fulgencio Batista. His remarks came in response to Kennedy's observation (made the previous day) that Castro would no longer be in power in five years, though Kennedy seemed to be calling more for an internal revolution in Cuba than for an assassination of Castro. Nevertheless, a month earlier the *Wall Street Journal* ran an article under its "Washington Wire" with the title "Castro's Assassination Becomes the Major U.S. Hope for De-communizing Cuba." Citing unnamed administration officials, the article suggested that such assassination attempts would be made by Cubans unhappy with Castro's government rather than through an American-sponsored plot. Kennedy, in addition, ruled out any immediate plans for an invasion or a blockade of Cuba, which placed him at cross-purposes with anti-Castro exile groups in the United States who criticized him for backing out of previous pledges to support a second invasion. Chastened by the catastrophic implications of the missile crisis and trying to make good on his promise not to invade Cuba, Kennedy had in fact moved to phase down support for the Cuban exiles, thus discouraging their hopes that a second U.S.-sponsored invasion might bring down Castro. The assassination plots continued, as did more coordinated plans for an invasion of Cuba under direct U.S. supervision. Castro's statement was thus not all that far off the mark.[34]

Oswald may have followed this international war of words between Castro and President Kennedy, perhaps taking special note of Castro's accusation that Kennedy was organizing plots to assassinate Cuban leaders. Such an accusation might have struck a chord with Oswald, since only days earlier he had tried to assassinate General Walker himself. Now he was thinking of assassination as a tactic in which he had a special interest or capability. After reading in the newspaper some harsh comments that Richard Nixon had made about Cuba, Oswald told his wife that he would like to shoot the former vice president. He was bluffing, as she soon saw, since Nixon was nowhere near Dallas at that time. Still, it was a sign that his line of thinking had changed following the attack on General Walker. If there was a moment when the idea of assassinating President Kennedy entered Oswald's mind as a realistic prospect, this may have been it.[35]

Two weeks after the Walker shooting and only days after Castro's speech, Oswald departed Dallas for New Orleans, leaving his wife and small child behind to stay with an older couple whom they had befriended a few months before. They would rejoin him later in New Orleans once Oswald found employment and rented an apartment. Marina Oswald encouraged her husband to leave Dallas out of fear that the police might connect him with the Walker incident. Oswald himself may have been willing to leave because he saw that he might be at risk for capture if he pursued his above-ground political activities in Dallas. There was another reason as well. Oswald had decided that the time had come for him to enlist as an active soldier in Castro's revolution. He had long sympathized with that revolution. Now he wished to travel there, perhaps to become an advisor to Castro or to join his army to fight the exiles who wanted to overthrow his government, or perhaps even with plans to return to the United States afterwards with instructions from Castro as to how he might advance the revolution. He said to his wife that he could win an appointment in Castro's government. In order to get to Cuba, however, he needed to establish a public record of support for the Cuban revolution. That could not be done in Dallas, where he lived and (sometimes) worked, and where many people, including the local FBI, knew about his defection to the Soviet Union. New Orleans, moreover, was then a hotbed of anti-Castro activity, a locale where anti-Castro exiles plotted hit-and-run raids against Cuba and possibly even another invasion of the island. It was feasible for someone of Oswald's skill operating in New Orleans to gather valuable intelligence about such plans that might later be passed on to Castro's government.[36]

Oswald's first move was to seek permission from the national office of the Fair Play for Cuba Committee to establish a local chapter in New Orleans. Fair Play for Cuba was an organization that promoted diplomatic recognition of the Castro government and peaceful relations between the United States and Cuba. Oswald proposed to rent a small office in the city for use as headquarters of his new chapter. He requested a charter from the national office along with some advice as to how he should proceed with his work on behalf of Castro. The national director of the organization, Vincent T. Lee, responded by sending Oswald a membership card, a copy of the bylaws of the organization, and a word of caution about the resistance he was likely to encounter in the New Orleans area when he advanced Castro's cause. He advised Oswald against opening an office that was accessible to the public, recommending instead that he rent a post office box and work out of a private home. If Oswald could recruit a sufficient number of members and appoint officers for the organization, he suggested, the national office could approve a charter for Oswald's local chapter.[37]

Oswald, however, had no intention of following any such advice, since, as Edward Epstein writes, "his purpose was not to recruit members and build a functioning Fair Play chapter in New Orleans, but to create a dossier of letters, documents and news clippings which would get him to Cuba."[38] Marina Oswald told the Warren Commission, "I only know that his basic desire was to get to Cuba by any means and all the rest of it was window dressing for that purpose."[39] Thus, ignoring instructions from the national director of Fair Play, Oswald rented office space for his fledgling organization, though his landlord soon kicked him out when he discovered the office was being used for a pro-Castro organization. Without waiting for a charter from the national organization, Oswald forged membership cards to which his wife affixed the signature of A. J. Hidell, ostensibly the chapter's president. He sent honorary memberships to two nationally prominent communist figures. Soon, using the name Lee Osborne, he printed up one thousand copies of a leaflet announcing the creation of the "New Orleans Charter Member Branch" of the Fair Play for Cuba Committee. These he planned to distribute on the streets of New Orleans in hopes of creating a public controversy that would come to the attention of the local press. For all appearances, therefore, the New Orleans chapter of Fair Play had three officers—Hidell, Osborne, and Oswald (all obviously the same person), plus two additional members in the persons of the prominent communists to whom he had sent honorary memberships. When Oswald informed him of these activities, the national director of Fair Play concluded that he was an unreliable person and terminated his correspondence with him. Oswald never received his charter, though this was not something that mattered much to him anyway.[40]

The Warren Commission Report called the operation "fictitious," as well as "a very shrewd political operation in which one man single handedly created publicity for his cause or for himself." The report also suggested that these efforts revealed Oswald's propensity to lie and to exaggerate his own importance.[41] In these activities, however, Oswald was not "lying" in the accepted sense of that term, but rather, as Edward Epstein writes, establishing a "legend" or a political identity that might enable him to travel to Cuba. In June of 1963, Oswald applied for a passport for international travel, listing his occupation as "photographer" and giving as reasons for the application his plans to travel to various countries in Europe, including Russia. Since he was not on the FBI's watch list, as J. Edgar Hoover felt he should have been, there was nothing to flag the application in Oswald's State Department file. The application was thus routinely approved. In July, the couple applied to the Soviet embassy in Washington for travel visas to permit their entry into the Soviet Union. Oswald, however, given his hopes to go to Cuba, planned to send his wife back to the Soviet Union without him.[42]

During the summer of 1963, from June to late August, Oswald worked off and on to win attention for himself as a prominent and influential backer of the Castro government. In June, he distributed his leaflets on the wharf in New Orleans near the USS *Wasp*, an Essex-class aircraft carrier that was temporarily docked there after cruising off the coast of Cuba. He was sent away by a policeman after an officer complained. Some weeks later, in August, he appeared on a downtown street to distribute his flyers again, but was arrested after he had an altercation with a group of anti-Castro Cubans. A few days earlier, Oswald had tried to infiltrate the anti-Castro exile community in New Orleans by visiting a place of business known to be operated by one of its members, Carlos Bringuier. Oswald be-friended him, pretended to be a foe of Castro, engaged him in con-versation, and suggested that with his background he could help train exiles in techniques of sabotage. When a few days later Brin-guier and his associates saw Oswald distributing pro-Castro leaflets, they loudly confronted him, drawing the attention of the police.

There is little doubt that Oswald wanted to be arrested and, indeed, that he pretended to befriend the anti-Castro Cubans in order to provoke them into a public altercation. When he was ques-tioned by the local police about his organization, Oswald told one lie after another, telling investigators that his operation had thirty-five members, that it convened monthly meetings, that the president of the local chapter–"Hidell"–asked him to circulate the leaflets, and that he had been born in Cuba. Oswald did not mention his stay in the Soviet Union, though the police learned about this before he was released. While being questioned by the New Orleans police, he requested another interview by the FBI, perhaps to call atten-tion to his residence in New Orleans so that when he moved again, the FBI would be slow to pick up his trail. When Oswald paid his small fine in court a few days later, he was filmed and photographed by the local press corps as he departed.

As a consequence of press reports about his arrest, Oswald was invited to appear on a local radio program that focused on contro-versial political issues. William Stuckey, the director of the program, visited Oswald at his residence after reading the press reports of his arrest and of his pro-Castro activities. It was arranged for Oswald to appear on the program in a debate featuring Mr. Bringuier, the anti-Castro Cuban with whom he had the earlier altercation, and Edward Butler, the director of a conservative organization in New Orleans. Stuckey and Butler, having learned independently of Oswald's previous defection to the Soviet Union and three-year residence there, resolved together to confront him with this infor-mation in the debate. This they did much to Oswald's discomfort, because the information tended to support accusations that Fair Play for Cuba was a communist front and that Castro's regime was a puppet government of the Soviet Union. Stuckey reported afterwards that the confrontation destroyed Oswald's ability to operate as a friend of Castro in the New Orleans area, but he praised Oswald as a "nice, bright boy" who "handled himself very well." Oswald was, he said, "a very logical, intelligent fellow." A short time later, Oswald wrote to an official of the U.S. Communist Party to ask if, in view of his residence in the Soviet Union, it would be advisable for him to compete with "anti-progressive forces" above ground or whether he should remain underground. The reply suggested that it was advisable for a person with Oswald's personal history to remain in the background.[43]

In the meantime, the FBI was trying to track Oswald as he moved from place to place in Dallas, then to New Orleans, then back to the Dallas area once more. In March of 1963, FBI agents in Dallas reopened their file on Oswald when they learned from a former landlady that he was drinking heavily and beating his wife. A check of Oswald's file showed that he had become a subscriber to *The Worker*, the Communist Party publication. In April, the FBI field office in New York City learned that Oswald had been in touch with the Fair Play for Cuba Committee, though this information did not reach the Dallas office for another two months. In May, the agent in charge in Dallas, James Hosty, learned that Oswald had moved again; in June he was located in New Orleans as a result of his contact with Fair Play. The FBI tracked him down in New Orleans in August, just before he was arrested following his altercation with the anti-Castro exiles. An informant with ties to the Communist Party in the New Orleans area told the FBI that Oswald was unknown in these circles, which meant that Oswald, though certainly a suspicious character, was not a threat to the internal security of the country. In September, Oswald's file was transferred from the Dallas to the New Orleans office of the FBI. But the Oswalds, following the embarrassing radio interview, moved again. Lee Harvey Oswald always seemed able to stay one step ahead of the FBI.[44]

On September 7, 1963, Fidel Castro attended a reception at the Brazilian embassy in Havana and submitted to an impromptu interview by an Associated Press reporter. In the course of that interview, Castro made some startling remarks. Referring to hit-and-run raids by exile forces against Cuban territory, he announced, "We are prepared to fight them and answer in kind. United States leaders should be mindful that if they are aiding terrorist plans to eliminate Cuban leaders, they themselves will not be safe." The article describing the interview was carried over the Associated Press wire, appearing in numerous daily papers around the country, including the local paper in New Orleans, where Oswald was then living.[45] Oswald probably saw the article, along with Castro's threatening statement, since he searched out news about Cuba and Castro. A surprising number of people on the East Coast, however, were unaware of Castro's threat against U.S. leaders because this particular quotation was not contained in the articles on the interview that appeared in the *New York Times* and the *Washington Post*.

This was the second statement made by Castro in a period of less than five months in which he accused American officials of planning to assassinate Cuban leaders, though this time, unlike before, he appeared to threaten retaliation against the United States for any such attempt. The same day that Castro made his statement, CIA case officers in Brazil interviewed Rolando Cubella, a potential defector from the Cuban government who had previously offered intelligence about the Castro government. In this meeting, however, Cubella (code named "Amlash" within the CIA) outlined a plan to overthrow Castro's government, beginning with the assassination of Castro himself. He offered to proceed with the operation if it received the blessing of high officials in the U.S. government and if he got the equipment needed to carry out the job. Intelligence officials noted the coincidence of Castro's threatening remarks following so closely on the heels of the meeting with Cubella and they quickly convened a meeting to discuss what Castro might have had in mind. They decided that among various things Castro might do, he was unlikely to direct an assassination attempt at any U.S. leader. Some officials, however, were convinced that Cubella was a double agent working for the Cuban government, which would explain how Castro was able to react so quickly to the meeting in Brazil. Throughout the autumn of 1963, CIA officers continued to meet with "Amlash" to discuss the plan, notwithstanding fears among some agents that the contact was insecure. At one of those meetings, "Amlash" requested rifles, telescopic sights, and explosives to support the operation, and assurance that the Kennedy administration backed the plan.[46]

It can never be known if Oswald heard Castro's threatening statement and then "read between the lines" to draw the conclusion that Castro was calling for the assassination of American leaders, including perhaps President Kennedy himself. This line of reasoning was strongly suggested by Jean Davison and Edward Jay Epstein in their biographical studies of Oswald, by Gus Russo in his 1998 study of the assassination, and by the report on the Kennedy assassination approved by a Senate Select Committee in 1976. This hypothesis is entirely plausible and is perhaps the explanation for Oswald's motives that is most consistent with the facts as we know them. That is to say, it is consistent with Oswald's strong political views regarding Cuba; consistent with his earlier attack on General Walker, which was presumably made because of Walker's anti-Castro views; and consistent with all of Oswald's work in New Orleans during the summer of 1963 on behalf of Castro's government. If Oswald heard Castro's remarks, he would not have been required to think for very long before concluding what steps he was being asked to take. As a member of the Senate Select Committee later said, Castro's statement might have been heard by Oswald much as the words of King Henry II were heard by his deputies when he said of Thomas Becket, "Who will rid me of this meddlesome priest?" The Warren Commission, however, did not reference Castro's speech in its final report, and thus did not connect it to Kennedy's assassination.

Oswald, his work completed in New Orleans, prepared to move again. Now he was desperate to travel to Cuba, even going so far as to plan an airline hijacking before finding out that other Americans had traveled to Cuba through Mexico City. In late September,

Marina headed back to the Dallas area with their daughter, planning to live for the time being with Ruth Paine, an acquaintance who was sympathetic to her plight as a Russian woman in a strange land. Oswald meanwhile had prepared a detailed dossier on all of his recent political activities in support of the Castro government, which he hoped would persuade Cuban authorities to allow him to travel to their country. Among other activities, Oswald wrote, "I infiltrated the Cuban Student Directorate [an anti-Castro group] and then harassed them with information I gained, including having the New Orleans City Attorney call them in and put a restraining order pending a hearing on some so-called bond for invasion they were selling in the New Orleans area." Oswald was well aware of the anti-Castro activities being planned in New Orleans with (as he thought) the support of the Kennedy administration.

He had also obtained a travel visa under one of his aliases, good for a fifteen-day stay in Mexico. On September 25, he got on a bus in New Orleans bound for Mexico City by way of Houston. Arriving there after a two-day trip, he visited the Cuban embassy seeking permission to travel to Cuba on his way to the Soviet Union. Expecting a warm welcome because of his political background as documented by his dossier, Oswald was disappointed to learn that he would first have to obtain a visa for travel to the Soviet Union before an "in-transit" visa to Cuba could be approved. He tried his old tactics of persuasion on the Cuban officials, offering to work on behalf of Castro to fight American imperialism. These appeals were unavailing, perhaps because they were too nonspecific. Oswald then went to the Soviet embassy, where he was told that he would have to wait for a period of three or four months while his application was being processed.

At the Soviet embassy, Oswald met and discussed his situation with Valeriy Kostikov, a Soviet official who was known to be a KGB agent with a network of intelligence sources in the region. The CIA picked up word of this meeting through telephone taps it had placed on the phone lines between the Cuban and Soviet embassies. When Oswald called the Soviet embassy from the Cuban embassy, he mentioned his wish to meet with Kostikov, which set U.S. intelligence officials to work trying to figure out who Oswald was. After being rebuffed by the Soviet officials, Oswald returned to the Cuban embassy, where he argued with the official in charge about his refusal to approve the in-transit visa to Cuba. Oswald was no doubt frustrated by these refusals, given all the hard work he had invested in preparation for the meetings. Castro would later say that during these exchanges Oswald made a threat against President Kennedy, thinking perhaps that such a threat would change the thinking of the Cubans, particularly in view of Castro's recent speech. Oswald's remarks, however, as nearly as can be inferred, further alarmed the officials at the Cuban embassy, reinforcing their determination to turn him away.[47]

U.S. intelligence officials would later express suspicions about what Oswald was really doing in his shuttling back and forth between the Cuban and Soviet embassies in Mexico City. Was he in fact trying to find a way to Cuba, as his wife stated and as his record of activities in New Orleans would suggest? Was he attempting to "come in from the cold"–that is, to abandon his underground activities in the United States in favor of a regular life in a communist country? Was he seeking guidance for future moves from his Soviet "handlers"? Was he seeking approval for future assassination attempts?

After remaining in Mexico City for two weeks and making little progress on his objective of traveling to Cuba, and seeing also that his visa would shortly expire, Oswald headed back to Dallas by bus, arriving there on October 3, no doubt greatly disappointed that his hopes had been frustrated once more by bureaucratic red tape. Somewhat at loose ends after his trip, he rented a small apartment in a rooming house, using the alias O. H. Lee, and resolved to look for a job. The fact that he planned to live apart from his wife and used an alias meant that Oswald still wished to evade the FBI and that he intended to continue with his underground political activities. Within a few weeks, he would receive word in Dallas that his travel visa to Cuba had been approved by Cuban officials, provided that he received his visa to travel to the Soviet Union. The approval of his visa thus suggests that despite the provocative remarks he had made, Oswald would still be welcome in Cuba.

On October 4, the White House announced a series of forthcoming presidential trips, including one to the Dallas-Fort Worth area on November 21-22. News of the scheduled visits appeared in the national press on October 5, receiving major coverage in the Dallas media that same day. With his plans to travel to Cuba now on hold, Oswald may have seen a new opportunity appear magically on the horizon. It may have seemed to Oswald that fate had dealt him a rare opening. A week later, with the help of Ruth Paine, he interviewed for and was offered a position at the Texas School Book Depository on Elm Street in Dallas. He began work on October 16. Oswald's new job, however, seemed not to interfere much with his political activities. Later in the month he wrote again to an official of the Communist Party in New York to say that he had monitored an "ultra-right" rally in Dallas at which General Walker spoke out against the United Nations. This was the speech Walker delivered the day before Adlai Stevenson was heckled in Dallas.[48]

The FBI in Washington was soon informed by the CIA about Oswald's visit to the Soviet and Cuban embassies in Mexico City, along with reports that he had contacted a Soviet intelligence officer. Oswald was already a subject of concern to the bureau because of his contacts with the Fair Play for Cuba Committee and the U.S. Communist Party. Yet the FBI did not know where he was. Agents in New Orleans soon discovered that he had moved from his address in that city. His wife was traced to the Paine residence in Dallas in late October. James Hosty, the FBI agent who was tracking Oswald in Dallas, visited the Paine home on November 1 but did not find Oswald or his wife there. Questioning Ruth Paine, he discovered that Oswald had found a job at the School Book Depository in Dallas. She did not, however, have a place of residence for Oswald. The FBI, as a matter of policy, did not interview persons of interest at their places of employment. Hosty returned four days later and then had an opportunity to speak with Marina. She volunteered no information about Oswald or where he was living. When Oswald learned about Hosty's visit, he was greatly alarmed that the FBI was on his trail once more. A short time later, he barged into the bureau office in Dallas to confront Hosty about the questions posed to his wife. Not finding Hosty in the office, Oswald left a threatening note (which Hosty destroyed after Oswald was killed). This was the last exchange between Oswald and the FBI before November 22.[49]

On November 18, President Kennedy addressed various issues concerning Latin America at a dinner in Miami hosted by the Inter-American Press Association. In the course of these remarks, he pointedly addressed the situation in Cuba. "It is a fact," he said, "that a small band of conspirators has stripped the Cuban people of their freedom and handed over the independence and sovereignty of their Cuban nation to forces beyond the hemisphere." He said that "the conspirators" have made Cuba an instrument of a foreign power that wishes to use it as a weapon "to subvert the other American republics." As if in answer to Castro's speech in September, he went on to say that "Once Cuban sovereignty has been restored, we will extend the hand of friendship and assistance to a Cuba whose political and economic institutions have been shaped by the will of the Cuban people."[50]

These remarks were inserted into the president's speech as a signal to "Amlash," the Cuban agent working with the CIA whose real name was Cubella, that the U.S. government at the highest level approved the planned coup against Castro. The CIA case officer working with "Amlash" arranged a meeting with him in Paris on November 22, at which time he delivered to him a poison pen for use in an assassination attempt. A few hours later President Kennedy was assassinated. CIA officials then ran a check on Kostikov, the KGB agent with whom Oswald met in Mexico City, and were surprised to see the name "Cubella" on the list of contacts that the investigation turned up.[51] It appeared that the CIA had been working with a double agent in its schemes to eliminate Castro.

From 1961 to late 1963, there were two pressing political issues that absorbed the attention of the Kennedy administration and the nation as a whole. The first was the civil rights movement, the historic effort to win equal rights for the American Negro, expressed through such events as the sit-in demonstrations in the South, the desegregation battles at the state universities in Alabama and Mississippi, the March on Washington in 1963, Martin Luther King's "I Have a Dream" speech, the assassination of Medgar Evers in Mississippi, the Birmingham church bombing, and numerous acts of violence against civil rights workers. The second issue was the Cold War, with Cuba as its flashpoint, expressed by the failed Bay of Pigs invasion, the Cuban missile crisis in 1962, the ongoing war of words between Kennedy and Castro, and covert efforts to overthrow Castro's government by invasion, sabotage, or assassination. At this time, other "hot spots" around the world—Vietnam, Laos, and the Congo—were very much on the back burner compared with Cuba. The efforts on behalf of civil rights took place in public and were highly visible to the American people; the Cold War efforts, to a significant degree, were carried out in a clandestine manner, in secret and out of sight of the public.

Jacqueline Kennedy, along with most liberals, was immersed in the first, Lee Harvey Oswald in the second. Liberals were preoccupied with civil rights, Oswald with defending Castro against plots to eliminate him. Oswald assassinated President Kennedy in order to interrupt his administration's efforts to assassinate Castro and overthrow his communist government in Cuba. Oswald was perfectly willing to be captured or killed in this enterprise, just as he was seven months earlier when he made an attempt on General Walker's life. The evidence suggests (but does not prove) that he carried out the act on his own without assistance or guidance from agents of the Cuban or the Soviet government. Nevertheless, Oswald's activities in New Orleans during the summer of 1963 and his visits to the two embassies in Mexico City two months before the assassination remain more than a little suspicious. If there was in fact a conspiracy in the assassination of President

Kennedy, it more than likely involved agents of the Cuban government or pro-Castro activists operating in the United States.

No one with any national influence wished to state this truth at the time, including Mrs. Kennedy, President Johnson, leaders of the U.S. Senate and House, the national press, or the federal government's chief investigative agencies, the FBI and the CIA. Some of the key information needed to document this interpretation was not known to the public at the time, though many national leaders were aware of it. The fact was clear to everyone, however, that Oswald was a communist with sympathies for Castro and the communist government in Cuba. Jack Ruby's unfortunate intervention into the case removed Oswald permanently from the scene, thereby allowing Oswald's political motives to be pushed into the background in a way that would have been impossible if he had survived to face a public trial. As a consequence, those whose political preoccupations centered about civil rights were able to interpret President Kennedy's life and death within that framework and to make that interpretation stick in the public's mind.

Oswald, however, achieved far more by his violent act than he might ever have hoped or expected. Lyndon Johnson, once in power, soon phased out assassination plots against Castro and began to withdraw U.S. support from the Cuban exiles determined to dislodge him from power. Johnson was convinced, according to some, that Kennedy's death was related to the assassination plots against Castro. Plans for another invasion of Cuba were permanently shelved.[52] Johnson soon reoriented Cold War policy away from its focus on Cuba and toward the challenge of communist revolution in Southeast Asia. In fairness, there were some signs that Kennedy had begun to move in this direction in the months before he was assassinated. In any case, Kennedy's assassination led to a "hands off" policy toward Cuba, which provided Castro's government the latitude it needed to survive over these many decades. In that sense, Oswald accomplished what he set out to do.

The civil rights interpretation of the assassination, moreover, provided momentum for the reform agenda that had been held back or bottled up in Congress during the Eisenhower and Kennedy years. A major civil rights bill was soon passed as a memorial or testimonial to President Kennedy. The assassination and its aftermath created a favorable environment for liberal reform, at least in the short run. It lasted long enough to carry President Johnson to a landslide re-election in 1964, which strengthened his support in the Congress sufficiently to allow passage of further liberal legislation under the rubric of the Great Society. The last major era of liberal reform in the United States occurred in the eighteen months following Kennedy's assassination. Before long, however, the deeper implications of Kennedy's death set in, with lasting consequences for the liberal movement.

Yet this interpretation—that Kennedy was a martyr to civil rights or a victim of the nation's culture—also produced some unwanted and unforeseen repercussions. Norman Mailer touched on this point when he wrote that Oswald's deed contributed immensely to "the sludge and smog of the world's spirit" in the following years. This occurred in part because Kennedy's reputation as a liberal was magnified but Oswald's motives as a communist diminished in the aftermath of the assassination—an interpretive coupling that produced disorienting consequences. The first heightened the sense of loss felt on Kennedy's death; the second rendered that loss somewhat meaningless and difficult to understand. The widespread feeling that the nation itself contributed to Kennedy's death encouraged an attitude of anti-Americanism that became a pronounced aspect of the radical and countercultural movements of the 1960s. This was an outlook that, over the years, never entirely disappeared from the worldview of the American left. Among liberals, it left a residue of ambivalence about the use of American power abroad and the worth of traditional institutions that had long received the unquestioned support of the American people.

Oswald thus brought about some surprising consequences by his intrusion into history. From the perspective of more than forty years, it appears that the assassination saved Castro from Kennedy's concentrated efforts to overthrow or assassinate him, led to a change in focus in American foreign policy, and created an environment favorable to liberal reform. At the same time, it also led to confusion and disorientation among the American people, and it played an important part in turning many Americans against their country in the latter half of the 1960s when blame for the assassination was deflected from Oswald to the country more broadly. The effects of the Kennedy assassination, combined with the domestic backlash against the war in Vietnam, were so profound for the United States that for a period of years in the 1960s and 1970s they shifted the ideological momentum of the Cold War in the direction of the Soviet Union. If an assassin is judged by the far-reaching consequences of his act, Lee Harvey Oswald, in contrast to John Wilkes Booth, might rank as one of the more consequential assassins in history.

There was, however, no good reason for Americans to feel guilt or remorse for some imagined role they might have played in President Kennedy's death. The statements made at the time to the effect that "We are all guilty" were entirely wrong-headed. Equally false were the analyses that found bigotry or intolerance or some flaw in the national soul to have been responsible for Kennedy's death. Americans may have felt themselves so powerful that when an enemy committed a crime against them, they imagined that they must have authored the act themselves. Oswald assassinated President Kennedy for political reasons connected to Cuba that were completely unrelated to these other social factors. As with most other assassinations, the "root cause" of the Kennedy assassination was the political controversy that gave rise to it—in this case, the Cold War conflict between Castroism and U.S. policy toward Cuba.

Oswald, moreover, was not representative of any major group or cultural tendency in the United States. He was a communist who hated the United States. He adopted Marxism as his guiding philosophy to express that hatred. When he defected to the Soviet Union, he tried to renounce his American citizenship but was talked out of it by officials at the U.S. embassy in Moscow. He defected in order to do harm to the United States, and he returned for the same purpose. Oswald found the United States to be much inferior to the Soviet Union. His radicalism was entirely un-American and anti-American. Even among communists or radicals he was *sui generis*. Oswald played no significant role in any extremist movement —certainly not in any extremist movement of the right. He recognized no conventional morality by which he might have been bound. He was most certainly not a "nut" or a "crackpot" in the sense that he was insane or mentally unstable. His views were well worked out. He knew exactly what he was doing when he embraced Marxism, defected to the Soviet Union, worked on behalf of Castro, and shot President Kennedy. As an assassin, he worked on his own and may in fact have been incapable of working for any length of time in cooperation with others. Oswald deliberately—not accidentally—worked against the grain of American society.

When Senator Robert Kennedy ran for the presidency in 1968, many liberals (at least those not committed to Senator Eugene McCarthy) looked to his candidacy as an opportunity to redeem liberalism from "the sludge and smog of the spirit" that had descended on it following John F. Kennedy's death. Robert Kennedy seemed able to speak at once to intellectuals, college students, minorities in the urban areas, and traditional working-class voters —the last group, representing the core of the crumbling New Deal coalition, now showing signs of defecting to the Republicans over the emerging issues of crime, lawlessness, and cultural values. If we are to believe the reports of friends and associates, Kennedy acquired a sense of pathos and tragedy as a consequence of his brother's assassination, perhaps because of the role he might have played in causing it or because it demonstrated how fragile our plans and expectations really are. His image as the hatchet-man for his brother was replaced by one that made him appear wounded by life, and thus sensitive to the sufferings of the less fortunate. Kennedy, it was thought, might begin to restore the sense of hope and optimism that was compromised (at least among liberals) by the assassination of President Kennedy and the unanswered questions surrounding his death. Whatever residue of guilt was still felt because of the assassination of President Kennedy might be expiated by the election of his brother to the presidency. At the same time, Senator Kennedy had good reason to know why Oswald killed his brother and he knew it had nothing to do with any "spirit of lawlessness" or "climate of hate" in the nation. Yet he was willing to accept the belief that this was so as an ingredient in his popularity. His candidacy was thus strongly associated with the disorienting emotions that still lingered from his brother's assassination. Some thought—or hoped—that Kennedy's election to the presidency might place the liberal movement back on the hopeful path it had charted from the early victories of the New Deal until the day President Kennedy was killed.

Robert Kennedy's assassination seemed to end such hopes once and for all. It called out emotional reactions that were eerily similar to those expressed in the wake of his brother's assassination. Expressions of national guilt and self-doubt were prominent themes in the national conversation following Senator Kennedy's death; indeed, these expressions were so strongly and insistently pronounced that one senses they might have arisen from deeper cultural sources than the assassinations alone. It must be remembered that Senator Kennedy was assassinated at an especially tumultuous time, just two months after Martin Luther King had been assassinated in Memphis. Pundits and politicians spoke about a climate of violence that had overtaken the country and led to Senator Kennedy's assassination. James Reston wrote in response to Senator Kennedy's assassination much as he did in response to President Kennedy's—that is, he pointed to a spirit of lawlessness in the nation (and in the world) that had claimed still another victim. The playwright Arthur Miller condemned the United States for a climate of violence but also said that acts of violence were deserved because the nation had tolerated injustice and poverty. Jack Newfield, in his biography of Robert Kennedy, lamented the fact that "No one seemed to think that Vietnam, or poverty, or lynchings, or our genocide against the Indians had anything to do with" the assassination. Citizens in the Soviet Union said that Americans were "barbarians" and that they lived in a "frightening country." Europeans feared that Senator Kennedy's assassination meant that

Americans were about to embark on an "orgy of hate."[53] President Johnson immediately appointed a blue-ribbon commission to study the challenge of violence in the United States. Scholars such as Richard Hofstadter began to study violence as a central theme in American history.[54] Jacqueline Kennedy said to relatives, "I despise America and I don't want my children to live here any more. If they are killing Kennedys, my kids are the number one targets."[55] Mrs. Kennedy certainly deserved sympathy both for the loss of her brother-in-law (on top of the loss of her husband) and for her fears for her children. Yet to blame America for Senator Kennedy's assassination was neither a fair nor a rational response. Neither was the claim that Senator Kennedy was a victim of a "climate of violence."

Senator Kennedy was shot during his campaign for the presidency in Los Angeles on the evening of the 1968 California presidential primary. The assassin was Sirhan Sirhan, a Jordanian-born Palestinian who had immigrated to the United States with his family some years earlier. Sirhan was apparently obsessed with the thought of killing Kennedy. The words "Kennedy must die" were scrawled in personal notebooks found in his home. A Palestinian nationalist, he felt anger and betrayal over Kennedy's support for Israel in its wars with Arab states, apparently believing that it was contradictory to his opposition to the war in Vietnam. He had an urge to shoot Kennedy before the one-year anniversary of the Six Day War (which fell on June 5, the day Kennedy was shot), in which Israel waged a short and successful war against Egypt, Syria, and Jordan. The Los Angeles police chief said his department had a long subversive file on Sirhan, which grew out of Arab nationalist activities. Sirhan's notebooks, according to the mayor of Los Angeles (quoted in the *New York Times*), were filled with "pro-communist, anti-capitalist, and anti–United States" statements. One of the prominent slogans found in these notebooks was "Long live Nasser" —a reference to the Egyptian president known for his support for Arab nationalism and opposition to colonialism. Nasser was viewed by some as the "Castro of the Middle East." The leader of a radical group that offered assistance to Sirhan said that Senator Kennedy was "the advocate of sending American jet bombers to Israel so Jews may kill more Arabs." Sirhan operated on the basis of a political template that was unfamiliar to most Americans at the time.[56]

In that sense, Sirhan was even more unrepresentative of the United States and of the nation's culture than was Oswald, who at least was born and raised in the United States and was an American citizen. Sirhan's national loyalties were directed to the Arab world rather than to the United States. Like Oswald, he despised the United States because he objected to American policies abroad. Liberals understood the Kennedys in terms of their domestic liberalism, but Oswald and Sirhan judged them in relation to their foreign policies. Sirhan's act was unrelated to any "climate of violence" or "spirit of lawlessness" in the United States but was a byproduct of national rivalries in another part of the world. There was indeed a climate of lawlessness in the United States in the late 1960s, as reflected in crime rates, disorder on college campuses, and riots in urban centers, but Sirhan's act was quite unrelated to it. Assassins do not always strike according to the logic of popular opinion or the political narratives of pundits and scholars. It might be more justly said that Sirhan was the first of a wave of terrorists from the Middle East to strike out against the United States in retaliation for the nation's policies in that region.

SEVEN · CAMELOT

THE MOST POTENT ELEMENT of the Kennedy legacy is its association with the legend of King Arthur and Camelot. Though it has been dismissed as a sentimental fairy tale, the link between the Arthurian legend and the Kennedy administration has proved to be one of the more enduring symbols of the Kennedy era, one that gained strength through the years following the assassination. If "grief nourishes myth," as has been said, then it is also true that death nourishes grief and is the source of myth and legend. It is through the attempt to give meaning to death, and to maintain a sense of continuity with the dead, that the living create myths and pass them along through the generations. Our most powerful myths are associated with death, particularly the death of heroes.[1]

Modern liberalism bears an uneasy and even antagonistic relationship to myth and legend, as it does to religion. As a doctrine of rational rules, committed to science and rational inquiry, liberalism has sought to banish myth and legend to the netherworld of the supernatural, much as it has tried to contain religion within the area of private conscience. A politics that takes its bearings from myths and legends is, from the standpoint of liberalism, one that is likely to be irrational, detached from reality, perhaps even predisposed to violence. Liberalism, as a theory of history, also tends to debunk the role of heroes in shaping large events, preferring to believe that such events arise from broader and more democratic historical processes. Lionel Trilling, as we have noted earlier, criticized liberalism for this one-dimensional doctrine, suggesting that there is much to be learned about the complexity and tragedy of human life from myth and legend. Yet it is also true that myth and legend may be misused when they are conflated too closely with contemporary persons and events, since their status as idealized images or symbols may be compromised thereby. The tension between liberalism and myth was never revealed so clearly as in the reaction to the Kennedy assassination.

William Manchester, in the conclusion to his authoritative account of the assassination, writes that legends of various kinds began to grow up around President Kennedy within days of his death. The Kennedy legend, however, was different from the legend that grew up around Lincoln, who was understood more as a hero of the common man, Whitman's rough-hewn leader off the frontier, melancholic and deep, paternal savior of the nation in a time of ultimate peril, "Father Abraham" to his loyal troops and, after his death, to his people in general. In a new nation, without a long history of heroes and legends, Lincoln was an original, the nation's first martyred hero. As Whitman wrote, Lincoln by his death filled a void in the folklore of the nation. He provided a flesh-and-blood symbol for Union and liberty, thus proving that even democracies committed to reason and progress have need of heroes, martyrs, and legends. Kennedy, the second of our martyred leaders, was something different—youthful, vigorous, sophisticated, glamorous, modern, idealistic, more princely than paternal. Lincoln's was the death of a father, Kennedy's of a brother. "The Kennedy legend grows and deepens," James Reston later wrote. "It is clear now that he captured the imagination of a whole generation of young people in many parts of the world, particularly in the university communities. Even those who vilified him now canonize him." Both deaths—Lincoln's and Kennedy's—elicited profound national grief, though (as has been said) the one death helped to unify a nation, the second to divide it against itself.[2]

The sudden death of a popular leader (Manchester writes), particularly one so young and vigorous as Kennedy, has provoked strong and emotionally laden reactions in cultures throughout history. In *The Golden Bough*, Sir James Frazier described the practice followed in some cultures of sacrificing the king, the "man-god," as a palliative offering to the gods or in a preemptive measure to ensure that he died before his physical powers were allowed to decay. "By putting him to death before his natural force was abated," Frazier wrote, the people "would secure that the world should not fall into decay with the decay of the man-god."[3] The sacrifice of the man-god led to the martyr, or the great man who would give his life for the safety of his people. Martyrdom in turn generated myth in the form of epic tales about the departed king or man-god. When the king was killed, as Manchester notes, it was often late in the autumn, corresponding to the time of harvest and the onset of winter, when his subjects convinced themselves that an offering to the gods was required to assure the return of a green and abundant spring. Manchester remarks that one of Kennedy's favorite books (perhaps because of the erotic scenes therein) was Mary Renault's *The King Must Die*, which tells the ancient tale of Theseus, who through his struggles challenged the traditional religious practice in his culture of sacrificing the king as a fertility offering to the gods.[4] Manchester's mythic references point to a conclusion that many Americans intuitively felt at the time of President Kennedy's assassination: that he was cut down in some way by his own people.

The legend of King Arthur and his knights is one of the most popular and powerful of these epic tales. According to the legend, which has some basis in historical fact, Arthur was a Celtic warrior-king who lived late in the fifth or early in the sixth century, when the Romans began to withdraw from Britain as their empire collapsed and when Saxons from Scandinavia and the continent began their invasions to fill the vacuum left behind. Arthur, so it is said, defeated the invaders in numerous confrontations and united his kingdom against the Saxons in parts of what are now known as western England and Scotland, converting his people in the process to the new religion of Christianity. Over the generations, the legend grew of Arthur as a "Christ-like" king, one who was at once strong, courageous, and just, and who in the end sacrificed his life for his people. As one historian has said, "King Arthur seems to demonstrate the heroic theory of history, which holds that an individual can permanently alter the course of events."[5] In time the legend of King Arthur would become one of the unifying symbols of the British people, demonstrating both their high ideals and their resolution in defense of their island homeland.

Because the legend was handed down through the ages in impressive works of poetry and prose, we are today familiar with its main features: the magical kingdom of Camelot, Arthur's sword, Excalibur, Queen Guinevere and knight Lancelot, the Knights of the Round Table, the quest for the Holy Grail. Contemporary readers look to Thomas Malory's fifteenth-century epic, *Le Morte d'Arthur*, as an early source of legendary knowledge surrounding the rise and fall of Arthur's kingdom. Tennyson's *Idylls of the King*, dedicated to Prince Albert, the late consort to Queen Victoria for whom Britain mourned as deeply as Americans mourned for Lincoln, altered the legend somewhat by giving it a tragic or elegiac turn. More recently, T. H. White in *The Once and Future King* has rewritten the legend in tune with a contemporary style and sensibility. Tennyson's poem, however, best captures the sense that the hero has died both on behalf of and at the hands of his own people. Near the end of the poem, as Arthur is dying, he reflects on his life and death and speaks to his knight Sir Bedivere:

> The sequel of today unsoldiers all
> The goodliest fellowship of famous knights
> Whereof this world holds record. Such a sleep
> They sleep—the men I loved. I think that we
> Shall never more, at any future time,
> Delight our souls with talk of knightly deeds,

> Walking about the gardens and the halls
> Of Camelot, as in days that were.
> I perish by this people that I made.[6]

Of the many themes contained in the Arthurian legend, this one seemed to stick most powerfully—and perhaps most unreasonably —to the assassination of John F. Kennedy.

As with so many of the myths and legends surrounding President Kennedy and his assassination, the introduction of the Camelot image into the subject was the creative contribution of Jacqueline Kennedy. Within a week of her husband's death, Mrs. Kennedy invited the journalist Theodore H. White to the Kennedy compound in Hyannis for an exclusive interview that would serve as the basis for an essay in a forthcoming issue of *Life* magazine dedicated to President Kennedy. In the course of that interview, she pressed upon White the Camelot image that would prove to be so influential in shaping the public memory of President Kennedy and his administration. Mrs. Kennedy, in her sentimental idealism and fascination with legends and fairy tales, sought to attach a morally uplifting message to one of the uglier events in American history. Her interpretation of the event made no room for a character as unappealing and distasteful as Lee Harvey Oswald.

In deploying this legend as the framework for the understanding of her husband's administration, Mrs. Kennedy was attempting to do something quite different with myth and legend than what was urged by Lionel Trilling when he cited with approval Coleridge's mythic introduction to *The Rime of the Ancient Mariner*. Coleridge, as Trilling said, was trying to remind his readers what a strange and fearful place the world can be, notwithstanding the illusions of order and rationality created by modern polities. Trilling encouraged the reading of myth and legend, along with the novel, as an imaginative exercise that might bring wider perspective to political liberalism. Mrs. Kennedy's deployment of the Arthurian legend served an imaginative purpose to be sure, but one that tended to idealize political life by showing how, under the stewardship of a wise leader, it can be rendered free of strife and conflict. The Arthurian legend so used suggested that ordinary politics might be constructively judged from the standpoint of Camelot. Far from pointing to the complexity and variability of life and thus to the limits of politics, Mrs. Kennedy's use of legend suggested how simple and commonsensical the answers are if only a wise leader can be brought to the helm.

Mrs. Kennedy's use of legend also looked to a different effect than Lincoln sought to achieve when he reinterpreted the history of the nation as a retelling of the ancient biblical epic. Lincoln did so in order to inspire reverence for the country's institutions of self-government so they might be perpetuated into the future. Mrs. Kennedy seemed to be invoking legend to augment reverence for her late husband and his family—perhaps even at the expense of that reverential perspective that Lincoln sacrificed his life to nourish.

White was selected for this assignment, almost certainly on the recommendation of Robert Kennedy, because he had long been an associate of the Kennedy family and was known to be a reliable journalist. A Boston native, White attended Harvard, graduating in 1938 as a classmate of Joseph P. Kennedy Jr., though (on White's telling) the two had little direct contact during their college years. Later, in the 1950s, he came to know John F. Kennedy while he (Kennedy) was the junior senator from Massachusetts and White a political reporter for *Collier's* magazine. During this period, between the mid-1950s and the beginning of Kennedy's campaign for the presidency in 1960, the two met often in Washington, with White gleaning from Kennedy much inside information about the leading personalities in Washington. From these conversations White conceived the idea of writing a book on a presidential election campaign from beginning to end, with an emphasis on the various personalities contesting for the White House.[7]

The challenge for the journalist in executing such a project was to portray the candidates in such a way that the most attractive personality came out on top—though, of course, the writer would have no control over the eventual outcome. As White later acknowledged in his memoirs, he decided to structure the book almost like a novel with its own hero and villain. Given White's friendship with Kennedy, along with his dislike for Richard Nixon, he would (if events worked out the right way) cast the election as a morality play with Kennedy representing the forces of light and Nixon the forces of darkness. When White began the project, his wife wisely noted that "It's probably a good book if Kennedy wins; but if Nixon wins, it's a dog."[8]

True to form, White's best-selling chronicle of the campaign, *The Making of the President, 1960*, which appeared in 1961, portrayed Jack Kennedy as a gallant and visionary leader and Nixon as a cynical and opportunistic figure who sought to play on the fears and prejudices of the voters.[9] Kennedy's victory, narrow though it was, paid off White's gamble as it provided the fitting conclusion to the political thrust of his narrative. Kennedy's victory, moreover, pointed history in a progressive and hopeful direction, for the new president, according to White, would attack the problems of race, economic growth, and Cold War tensions that the previous administration had allowed to fester—an assessment that happened also to fit the broad message of Kennedy's campaign. The book helped cement Kennedy's growing reputation as both a hardnosed politician and a liberal statesman who had taken on the Protestant establishment and had come out on top. Careful to avoid any offense to the Kennedy family, White allowed Robert Kennedy to review the manuscript prior to publication. Given White's general point of view and his friendship with the candidate, the Kennedys had little cause for concern over anything he was likely to write.

The runaway success of this volume encouraged White to sign contracts with his publisher to produce similar chronicles of future presidential campaigns. It is telling that these volumes on the elections of 1964, 1968, and 1972 never approached the popularity and influence of his chronicle of the Kennedy campaign. Skillful writer though he was, White could not assign to Lyndon Johnson or to Richard Nixon the flair and sophistication with which he had portrayed Kennedy. It must have been painful indeed for White to be forced to chronicle Nixon's victories in 1968 and 1972 after having dispatched him as a deserving loser in his book on the 1960 campaign. White, in short, was unable to replicate in these later volumes the moral and political contrasts that were so instrumental to the success of the initial installment of the series (though it can be said that his portrayal of Robert Kennedy's tragically abbreviated campaign in 1968 represented political journalism of a high order). With John F. Kennedy out of the picture, however, White's journalism lost something of its force and optimism.

It was against this background that White was selected as the "friendly journalist" to transmit Mrs. Kennedy's nostalgic image of her husband to the broader public. Notwithstanding his association with the Kennedys, or perhaps because of it, White was then a highly respected and widely read journalist, owing in great part to the success of his campaign chronicle. *Life*, the magazine for which he now wrote following the dissolution of *Collier's*, had a weekly circulation of more than seven million subscribers and a total readership of perhaps thirty million. The commemorative issue dedicated to the late president would reach several million more, as it was intended also to serve as a collector's item.

White later wrote that he regretted the role he had played in transmitting the Camelot image to the public. "Quite inadvertently," he wrote in his memoir, *In Search of History* (1978), "I was her instrument in labeling the myth."[10] Nonetheless, he was a more than willing participant in Mrs. Kennedy's plan to shape the public's memory of her husband. When Mrs. Kennedy reached him by phone in New York on the Friday after Thanksgiving (a full week after the assassination), White dropped everything to make plans to travel to Cape Cod, even though the weather was too miserable to fly and his own mother had suffered a mild heart attack that very day. He arrived via automobile at the Kennedy compound on Saturday evening, where Mrs. Kennedy spoke to him at length about the events in Dallas, reciting along the way painful details about the assassination and its immediate aftermath. Here, during this interview, she inserted her recollections about the late president's fondness for *Camelot*.[11]

Following the extended conversation, White retreated to a guest room to review his notes and compose a draft of his essay. His editors were at this time (late on Saturday evening) holding the presses open at great expense while waiting to receive his copy. When White phoned his editors to dictate his text (with Mrs. Kennedy standing nearby), he must have been surprised by their reaction, for they initially rejected the inclusion of the Camelot reference as excessively maudlin and sentimental. Mrs. Kennedy, interpreting the gist of the conversation between the author and his editors, signaled to White that Camelot must be kept in the text. White's editors quickly relented.[12]

Thus the references to Camelot were included in White's essay in the special issue of *Life* that hit the newsstands on December 3, 1963. The extensive distribution of this issue in the United States and abroad guaranteed that these images would receive the widest possible circulation. Though the Arthurian motif has been ridiculed and derided over the years as a sentimental distortion of the actual record, it has nevertheless served to etch the Kennedy years in the public memory as a magical era that will never be duplicated.

White's short essay, which appeared in *Life* under the title "For President Kennedy: An Epilogue," contained various of Mrs. Kennedy's wistful remembrances of her husband, including his fondness for the title tune from the Lerner and Loewe Broadway hit, *Camelot*.[13] In the evening, she said, the couple often enjoyed listening to a recording of the song before going to bed. His favorite lines, she told White, were these: *Don't let it be forgot, that once there was a spot, for one brief shining moment that was Camelot.* "There will be great presidents again," she continued, "but there will never be another Camelot again." Her husband, she said, was an idealist (which White knew was untrue) who saw history as something made by heroes like Marlborough or King Arthur. "Jack had this hero idea of history," she told White, "the idealistic view." Thus, she wished to have his memory preserved in the form of heroic symbols rather than in the dry and dusty books written by historians, whom she regarded as "bitter old men" who delight in revealing the vices and weaknesses of heroes. Camelot was one of these symbols; the eternal flame that she had placed on her husband's grave was another.

Mrs. Kennedy's effort to frame her husband's legacy in this way was widely regarded as a distorted caricature of the real Kennedy and something he would have laughed at. The heroic conception of history probably reflected more the ideals of Mrs. Kennedy than those of her husband, who would hardly have been surprised to learn that various heroes in history had foibles, vices, and feet of clay. Indeed, it was said that one of Kennedy's favorite books was David Cecil's biography of Lord Melbourne, published in 1939 when he was studying in England, which recounted the infidelities and affairs of Melbourne and his circle.[14] Young John F. Kennedy, moreover, had written in *Why England Slept* that one can expect to find few heroes in democratic systems, where leaders must follow rather than guide popular opinion. Kennedy's aides and associates reported that they had never heard him speak either about *Camelot* the play or about its theme song. Some of Mrs. Kennedy's friends said they had never even heard *her* speak about King Arthur or the play prior to the assassination. There is a sense that this was something she made up after her husband was killed.[15] If so, one has to give her credit for quick and imaginative thinking in the midst of the most profound tragedy and grief; and also for her keen understanding that symbols and images often trump substance in shaping public memory.

There are, however, some reasons to believe that the Arthurian saga meant much more to Mrs. Kennedy than such a verdict would suggest. The great care she took in summoning White to Hyannis a week after the assassination is itself suggestive of the deep meaning she attached to these Arthurian images. The whole point of this interview was, after all, to use the journalist to transmit to the wider public the mythic association between Camelot and the New Frontier. This was not something that was done casually or on the spur of the moment.

Camelot made its debut on Broadway in December 1960 with a star-studded cast featuring Julie Andrews as Guinevere, Richard Burton as Arthur, Robert Goulet as Lancelot, and Roddy McDowall as Mordred. The musical also featured several memorable tunes (in addition to the title song) written and arranged by Alan Jay Lerner and Frederick Loewe, which were shortly collected by Columbia Records into an album for public sale. The play, which received mixed reviews from critics but was a considerable financial success, was based on T. H. White's (no relation to the journalist) now classic Arthurian fantasy, *The Once and Future King*, published in 1958 but made up of four parts that the author wrote separately beginning in 1938.[16]

The Once and Future King, one of the most popular and widely read books of our time, has been termed "a literary miracle" and a "masterpiece," albeit a "queer kind of masterpiece." Reviewing the saga in the *New York Times*, Orville Prescott called it "a glorious dream of the Middle Ages as they never were but as they ought to have been, an inspired and exhilarating mixture of farce, fantasy, psychological insight, medieval lore and satire all involved in a marvelously peculiar retelling of the Arthurian legend."[17] White's imaginative version of the Arthurian legend was not only a bestseller but also an important cultural statement in its own right.

The Once and Future King is a twentieth-century retelling of Sir Thomas Malory's fifteenth-century classic, *Le Morte d'Arthur*. Malory's story also inspired Tennyson's Victorian version of the Arthurian legend, *Idylls of the King*, and countless other variations through the centuries. Unlike its predecessors, which celebrated knighthood and chivalry and portrayed Arthur as a brave warrior, White's modern version pokes fun at the pretensions of knighthood and pointedly criticizes war, militarism, and nationalism. Lancelot, for example, portrayed as a brave and handsome knight in the traditional tales, is here seen as an ugly and ungainly figure. In a similar vein, White presents Arthur less as a brave warrior than as an idealistic peacemaker who sought to tame the war-making passions of mankind. White's telling of the saga is also more didactic in purpose and mirthful in tone than the heroic versions of Arthur produced by

Malory and Tennyson (and countless other storytellers). This, however, is his point: the traditional ideal of heroism celebrated war and violence. A new understanding was needed to bring about lasting peace and justice, one that rejected boundaries, frontiers, and nationalities. The moral outlook implicit in White's saga was presumably one of its aspects that most appealed to Mrs. Kennedy.

White succeeded brilliantly in reinterpreting the traditional Arthurian romance as a modern allegory demonstrating the futility of war and the pointlessness of nationalism and national rivalries. He came of age in the years after World War I in a culture that, as a consequence of the wholesale slaughter on the killing fields of France and Belgium, now repudiated war as a futile exercise that should be banned for all time. Much as C. S. Lewis (his contemporary) deployed fantasy to represent Christian teachings and to encourage an appreciation of the supernatural, White used the Arthurian fantasy to teach the progressive ideals of peace and justice as advanced through the leadership of wise statesmen. The moral message of White's saga is, however, somewhat ambiguous. On the one hand, it teaches that innocence and good intentions are not sufficient to establish peace and harmony unless they are instructed by wisdom. At the same time, since Arthur is a wise king but fails nonetheless to head off discord and war, the story suggests that wisdom joined to power may not suffice either. It is not clear if White was recasting the legend to teach us the possibilities or the limits of politics.

As a fantasy or a romance, *The Once and Future King* is necessarily difficult to translate into the real world of political conflict where the statesman does his work. Arthur is an example of a medieval archetype: the Christ-like king. Jesus Christ did not seek kingship over the secular world. His kingdom was not of this world. Yet the romantic king who tries to govern in his image must deal with the unwieldy and often amoral or immoral forces of this world. The wise leader, progressive and farsighted as he might be, cannot wave away personal ambitions, national interests, or artificial boundaries as irrational or destructive forces, but must accept them as elements of reality that limit his choices and range of action. Such realities define the limits of good intentions; wisdom consists in recognizing such realities, ameliorating them as far as possible, but recognizing also the limits of statecraft as a means of getting rid of them altogether. For those who are charmed by the idyllic world of Camelot, or whose views of the political world are shaped by it, there is bound to be a tendency to judge the real world of politics from the standpoint of the fantasy or to flee the real world entirely in favor of an ideal world where enduring problems seem easier to solve. White's fantasy sets up an ideal polity that stands in judgment of the real world of conflict and war. This is hardly the point of view that White sought to establish in his stories, but it is a sensibility that some readers have taken away from *The Once and Future King*.

The Sword in the Stone, the initial installment of the tetralogy, traces the upbringing of the young Arthur (called "Wart") and his education under the guidance of the wizard Merlyn, who in White's telling lives his life backwards through time, which enables him to foretell the future and to drop observations throughout the story about events in modern times. Here White introduces into the Arthurian legend the idea of education as crucial to the formation of the wise leader. Merlyn teaches young Wart about power, statecraft, and the absurdity of war by exposing him to the ways of birds and animals, for whom national boundaries are entirely artificial. Wart learns from Merlyn that the principle of "might makes right" is responsible for the ills of the world, and that the duty of a wise king is to introduce the noble ideal that "right makes might." Following this education, Wart becomes King Arthur when he alone is able to pull the magic sword from the stone in which it is embedded.

White's King Arthur seeks to implement his ideal through various measures, for example, by inventing chivalry and the Round Table, by seeking the Holy Grail, and, finally, by creating the rule of law. The saga has a tragic ending when Arthur's kingdom is finally torn apart by civil war, due in large part to conflicts originating in his own household. He is betrayed by Queen Guinevere and favored knight Lancelot, who carry on a poorly concealed love affair. He is seduced by his half-sister, who produces a son, Mordred, who as a grown man turns on Arthur when he takes no action in response to the betrayal by Lancelot and the queen. Sensing weakness and irresolution, Mordred challenges Arthur's kingship.

The closing chapter, titled *The Candle in the Wind*, ends on the eve of the final battle as Arthur broods about his legacy and wonders why things have gone so far wrong. Ruminating on his education under Merlyn, he concludes that mankind's infatuation with war arises from the existence of artificial boundaries that divide men and women into factions and nations. "The imaginary lines on the earth's surface need only to be unimagined," he concludes.

Deep in thought, Arthur looks up to see a young boy, no more than thirteen, prepared with his bow for the battle to come the next day. The boy, modeled by White on Thomas Malory himself, is eager to enter the fray, to kill and perhaps be killed in service to his sovereign king.

Arthur, now searching for another way to perpetuate Merlyn's teaching, talks the boy out of going into battle and urges him instead to go forward in life and spread the noble ideals that Arthur and his knights have stood for. The boy, Arthur says, is "a kind of a vessel" to carry forth the ideal of peace through law and the rightful use of power.

"Thomas," Arthur says, "my idea of those knights was a sort of candle, like these ones here. I have carried it for many years with a hand to shield it from the wind. It has flickered often. I am giving you the candle now—you won't let it out?"

"It will burn," the boy answers and pledges to go out as an ambassador to promote Arthur's ideals of peace and justice. Arthur prepares for battle, now hopeful that a day might come when the world will again see "a new Round Table which had no corners, just as the world had none—a table without boundaries between the nations who would sit to feast there."[18] The volume ends on this note. Arthur —the once and future king—will die, but he (or one like him) will return at an unknown time to carry forward once again the flame of idealism.

The broad message of White's modern saga, and of the Broadway play and the Hollywood film it inspired, must have resonated deeply with Jacqueline Kennedy, and perhaps with President

Kennedy as well. There were, of course, biting ironies in Mrs. Kennedy's attachment to a legend that unravels the consequences of seduction, betrayal, and infidelity. There were further ironies in the association of the central myth of English nationality with the nation's first Irish president. Still, the larger message was one that she sought to associate with her husband's political legacy. He was not, in this telling, the King Arthur of medieval legend, but the modern knight who sought peace by subordinating force to right.

In these ways, the Camelot image that Mrs. Kennedy employed seems to have been more carefully constructed than some have suggested. It is entirely believable that President Kennedy and Mrs. Kennedy listened to and enjoyed the musical track of *Camelot*. Mr. Kennedy had known Alan Jay Lerner (who wrote the lyrics) since they attended Choate and Harvard together as young men, and Lerner had maintained a relationship with him. In May of 1963, shortly after *Camelot* ended its successful run on Broadway, Lerner produced a lighthearted musical review for a birthday party in New York honoring President Kennedy. Various celebrity performers—such as Carol Channing, Ann-Margaret, Louis Armstrong, Henry Fonda, and Tony Randall—participated in the proceedings.[19] Mrs. Kennedy very likely read *The Once and Future King* and perhaps saw or showed to her children the cartoon version of *The Sword and the Stone* that was produced by Walt Disney in 1963. President Kennedy himself was not above using themes possibly drawn from *The Once and Future King*.

During a press conference in March of 1962, President Kennedy was asked about complaints that had been heard from Army reservists who had been called back to duty because of the crises in Berlin and Vietnam. His response has been widely quoted: "There is always inequity in life," he said. "Some men are killed in war and some men are wounded and some men never leave the country, and some men are stationed in the Antarctic and some are stationed in San Francisco. It is very hard in military or in personal life to assure complete equality. Life is unfair." This philosophical comment was the subject of much commentary at the time, but it may well have been informed by a lengthy exchange in *The Sword and the Stone* in which Merlyn teaches exactly this lesson to young Arthur. Life often seems unfair, he says, because what is good for one person may be bad for another.[20]

Then there is the matter of the eternal flame. According to William Manchester in *The Death of a President*, the symbol occurred to Mrs. Kennedy two days after the assassination as her husband's body was being taken to lie in state at the Capitol. "It just came into my head," she said.[21] Mrs. Kennedy said at the time that her idea was inspired by the flame burning over the memorial to the Unknown Soldier in Paris, which she had seen in 1961 when she and President Kennedy made a state visit to the French capital. Advisors and counselors to the family were at first concerned that such a symbol might appear undignified or that the rules of Arlington National Cemetery might forbid it. Mrs. Kennedy, however, every bit as insistent here as she was later with Theodore White and his editors, declared that, regardless of any obstacles, the eternal flame must be made part of the gravesite as a perpetual reminder of the ideals for which President Kennedy lived and died.

The concept of the eternal flame, then, held some deep meaning for Mrs. Kennedy. There is little doubt that it was her own invention, much like the Camelot image she imparted to Theodore White. The flame burning in Arlington National Cemetery certainly bears a strong resemblance to that burning over the memorial in Paris, though the flame in Paris is ceremonially rekindled on a daily basis. In ancient times, an eternal flame burned at the Temple of Apollo at Delphi, and another burned later at the Temple of Vesta on the Roman Forum. But up to the time of President Kennedy's death, an eternal flame had never before been dedicated to an individual.

Yet there was also a suggestive association between the eternal flame and the Camelot legend, which must have occurred to Mrs. Kennedy as she thought of the most appropriate ways to honor her late husband. When judged in the context of that emotional time, and in view of the line of thinking she was following, the eternal flame at the Kennedy gravesite is more evocative of the Camelot legend than of the memorial to the Unknown Soldier in Paris. This association was one that Mrs. Kennedy was understandably reluctant to declare, for it would have been difficult to state openly that a symbol from a legend or from a Broadway play was affixed to the grave of the fallen president. Still, given her attachment to the Camelot legend, and the link she drew in the interview with Theodore White between the Arthurian legend and the eternal flame, one is justified in concluding that the flame burning over President Kennedy's grave is in fact King Arthur's candle in the wind.

One has to admire Mrs. Kennedy for the skill and imagination with which she deployed these images in the immediate aftermath of the assassination, and also her brave and clearheaded conduct in the difficult days following the assassination, a vivid contrast to the hopelessly distraught emotional state into which Mrs. Lincoln fell after her husband's assassination. Here Mrs. Kennedy acted for her husband in the role of Lincoln's Stanton, organizing his mourning and funeral rites for subtle (and not so subtle) political purposes. Because of these acts of imagination, our retrospective view of President Kennedy was filtered through the symbols and images she put forward during that politically influential time. Kennedy, the hardnosed cold warrior who would "bear any burden and pay any price to insure the survival and success of liberty," was viewed after his death as a dedicated peacemaker in the image of T. H. White's King Arthur. The president who hesitated on civil rights for fear of antagonizing his supporters in the South was turned into a martyr for equal rights. The hardheaded liberal devoted to incremental progress was suddenly viewed after his death as the consummate liberal idealist.

Much of this was a consequence of Mrs. Kennedy's deliberate and carefully calculated image-making. Hard as it may be to accept, the posthumous image of John F. Kennedy reflected more the sentimental beliefs of Jacqueline Kennedy than the practical political liberalism of the man himself. To the extent that after 1963 the liberal movement reshaped itself in terms of this image, it absorbed in great degree the sentimental liberalism of Jacqueline Kennedy. By this route the excessively idealistic version of liberalism that earned the rebuke of all the leading postwar liberals in the 1950s, including Kennedy himself on many occasions and Arthur Schlesinger Jr. in *The Vital Center*, moved into the mainstream of liberal thought in the 1960s and thereafter.

But by turning John F. Kennedy into a liberal idealist, Mrs. Kennedy inadvertently contributed to the unwinding of the tradition of American liberalism that her husband represented in life. The symbols and images she advanced were intended to have, and indeed did have, a double effect: first, to establish Kennedy as a transcendent figure beyond judgment in terms of conventional categories and far superior to any contemporary political figure in skill, understanding, and idealism; second, in so doing, to highlight what the nation had lost when he was killed. The two elements were mirror images of one another. The Camelot myth was contrived to magnify the sense of loss felt as a consequence of Kennedy's death and the dashing of liberal hopes and possibilities. If one accepted the image (and many did), then the best times were now in the past and would not soon be recovered. Life would go on, but the future could not match the magical chapter that had been brought to a premature end. As Mrs. Kennedy said, "there will never be another Camelot again."

Such a view challenged the liberal ideal of history as a progressive enterprise, always moving forward, despite setbacks here and there, toward the goal of improving and perfecting the American experiment in democracy and self-government. The Camelot image fostered nostalgia for the past with the thought that the Kennedy administration represented a peak of achievement that would not soon be replicated. The nation, after all, had lost its best opportunity to meet its as yet unrealized potential. The Camelot image, moreover, by implying that great periods of achievement occur episodically in history, further contradicted the liberal assumption of steady historical progress. Some confusion and disorientation are bound to result from the attempt to apply myth and legend to real historical circumstances instead of understanding them as idealized representations that are meant to inspire people to higher standards of conduct and aspiration. This is perhaps a fine line to maintain, especially for those whose views of politics are informed by myths and legends and for whom there must be a strong urge to see those myths and legends brought into actual existence.

The legend of the Kennedy years as unique or magical was, in addition, divorced from real accomplishments as measured by important programs passed or difficult problems solved. The magical aspect of the New Frontier was located, by contrast, in its style and sophistication rather than in its concrete achievements. Postwar liberalism, known for its emphasis on rationality, practical accomplishment, and optimism about the future, was turned on its head by the retrospective image of the Kennedy years that developed after the assassination. If, as many believed, the nation itself was in some way responsible for Kennedy's death, it followed that a mood of punishment and chastisement was more appropriate than one of self-confidence and optimism. Mrs. Kennedy, without ever intending to do so and without fully understanding the consequences of her image-making, thus put forth an interpretation of her husband's life and death that posed still further challenges to mid-century liberalism.

EIGHT · THE OLD LIBERALISM AND THE NEW

KENNEDY'S ASSASSINATION opened up a break with the American past and a rupture in the evolving world of liberal ideas and idealism. Unlike Lincoln's assassination, which united the nation around the symbols for which the Civil War was fought, the Kennedy assassination broke up the postwar consensus and opened new divisions in American life over the health of the nation's culture and the worth of its key institutions.

In the years and decades after the assassination, nearly all the elements of the far right that had so unnerved the liberals of the 1950s moved across the political spectrum to the far left, including a fascination with conspiracies, the use of overheated and abusive rhetoric to characterize foes, and expressions of hatred for the United States. By the late 1960s, Americans had gotten used to seeing left-wing college students heckling speakers, denouncing them as Nazis and fascists, and attacking the police as "pigs" in such a way as to make the right-wing demonstration against Adlai Stevenson in Dallas look like a tame and mannerly affair. In one of those odd turnabouts that seemed to characterize the period, Grayson Kirk, the president of Columbia University who in 1963 called for a crackdown on the far right as a consequence of the Kennedy assassination, watched helplessly in 1968 as radical students took over his campus and occupied his own office, joyfully rifling through his private files and scrawling obscenities on the walls. The uprising at Columbia turned out to be a model for what would transpire on dozens of other campuses in the months and years to follow.

The anti-Americanism that marked the new radicalism of the 1960s was one of the distinguishing features that most clearly marked its break with the liberal reformism of the preceding era. The United States—"Amerika" in the lexicon of the New Left—was now an out-of-control colossus, a world superpower that suppressed the aspirations of third-world peoples abroad and minorities at home. The attributes that most Americans (and also the postwar liberals) thought were most valuable about their nation—its prosperity, its free economy, its representative political institutions, its tradition of liberty, its conquest of the American continent—the radicals denounced as wicked, gross, or disreputable. Prosperity (they said) was based on greed, the so-called free economy on capitalist exploitation, democracy on the suppression of minorities, freedom on materialism and false choices, and the conquest of the continent on the genocide of indigenous peoples. The friction between the new radicalism and the older liberalism led to a new synthesis on the political left that carried forward these essential features of the radical mood under the umbrella of a "new" liberalism, which is still with us today.

Meanwhile, the activities of the radical right, which were prominent in the headlines in the years leading up to the assassination, were soon pushed into the background by the antics of the radical left. By the late 1960s, the far right's fascination with plots concerning fluoridated water, federal aid to education, or even communism seemed quaint in comparison with the fevered doctrines put forward by the denizens of the New Left. As with the far right in the 1950s and early 1960s, the heated rhetoric of the far left in the later 1960s led inevitably to acts of political violence. The riots in urban centers and on college campuses flowed from the violent language adopted by the far left in the wake of Kennedy's assassination and during the years of the Vietnam War. From the end of World War II up to the time Kennedy was killed, political violence in the United States generally emanated from the far right; after that event, for the next generation, it came largely from the left. This sudden and generally unanticipated reversal caught the postwar liberals badly off-guard.

At the same time, the Kennedy assassination and its aftermath discredited the central ideas and assumptions of the postwar liberal movement. The claim that the far right represented the main threat to progress and democratic order was no longer credible after a Marxist had assassinated an American president. According to liberal writers like Richard Hofstadter, Daniel Bell, and others, the far right was disconnected from reality, its followers semi-delusional in their belief that communism represented a domestic threat to the United States. After Oswald assassinated Kennedy, the leaders of the far right did not appear quite so deranged after all—or at least it was now far more difficult for intellectuals to make that case. The various interpretive metaphors that the liberal theorists had developed to account for the rise of the far right appeared increasingly ineffectual as the radical right receded in importance in the 1960s and as the New Left arose to take its place as the focus of public attention. The concepts of status anxiety, class resentment, the paranoid style, and the war against modernity—which had been applied with so much success to the radical right—were rarely deployed to account for the new radicalism of the 1960s. The sudden eruption of radical politics and cultural criticism also discredited the "end of ideology" thesis, which held that ideological conflicts would wane in advanced societies as a consequence of affluence. The events of the 1960s suggested that the reverse might be the case: affluence begets a new kind of radical politics that revolves around questions of culture. To be fair, Daniel Bell had suggested as much in his influential "End of Ideology" essay, though his caveat about the thesis was rarely noted. In any case, the shattering of the theoretical framework that had been carefully constructed by liberal thinkers in the postwar era posed a genuine intellectual crisis for the liberal movement. The Kennedy assassination and its aftermath seemed to call for some kind of intellectual reconstruction.

The legacy of the liberal movement of the 1950s, however, was picked up somewhat later by that loose collection of intellectuals called neoconservatives. The neoconservatives—"liberals who had been mugged by reality," as Irving Kristol described them—carried forward the central idea of postwar liberalism: the deployment of conservative principles in defense of liberal institutions. The neo-conservatives sought (much as did their predecessors in the 1950s) to represent the enduring ideals of both liberalism and conservatism in the intellectual arena.

What especially distinguished the neoconservatives, however, was precisely their willingness to attack the New Left of the post-Kennedy era with the same sophistication and principled argument as they and their predecessors deployed against the radical right of the 1950s. The neoconservatives were unsparing in their criticisms of the New Left in part because of the way its leaders mocked and sabotaged democratic procedures, but also because of the anti-Americanism that was a striking feature of their rhetoric. In a remarkable article that appeared in the November 1970 issue of *Commentary* magazine, Dennis Wrong pointed out that by the late 1960s many prominent intellectuals had begun to adopt in their writings "a tone of extravagant, querulous, self-righteous anti-Americanism." Wrong was writing about the views that were being expressed in the *New York Review of Books*, though his conclusions were applicable to the world of liberal and left-wing thought in general. Most of this, as he wrote, was focused on the war in Vietnam, but the new anti-Americanism received a somewhat earlier expression in the form of several articles that appeared in the mid-1960s claiming that President Kennedy had been assassinated through an elaborate right-wing conspiracy.[1]

There were, in addition, some clear links between the liberals of the 1950s and the neoconservatives of the 1970s and the decades thereafter. For one thing, the liberals of that earlier period were occasionally described as "neoconservatives" themselves because of their concern for defending liberal institutions against attacks from the radical right–just as their successors were so described because of their defense of the same institutions against attacks from the radical left.[2] As a consequence of this linkage, some of those earlier liberals eventually found themselves in the neoconservative camp in the 1960s and 1970s. Daniel Bell, for example, was an early neoconservative, a founder (along with Irving Kristol and Nathan Glazer) of *The Public Interest* in 1965. Seymour Martin Lipset was another of those earlier liberals who later made common cause with the neoconservatives. Richard Hofstadter, who described the 1960s as the "age of rubbish," might eventually have found his way into the neoconservative camp had he not died prematurely in 1970 at age fifty-four.

It is not impossible to imagine how the prominent neoconservatives of the 1970s might have become leaders of a reinvigorated liberal movement in reaction to the disorder and confusion that marked the 1960s. After all, many neoconservatives were Democrats and remained so, at least until the 1980s, when it was clear that their cause was hopeless in a party that had moved permanently to the left on the major issues of the day. Some of the younger neoconservatives were nurtured in their careers by influential Democrats like Senator Henry Jackson and Senator Daniel Patrick Moynihan. Their views on communism, civil rights, and the welfare state were not all that distant from John F. Kennedy's. Yet even though Democrats looked to Kennedy as a hero, they regarded neoconservatives as pariahs and their ideas generally beyond the pale for self-respecting liberals. In terms of the liberal movement, therefore, the neoconservatives eventually found themselves to be in a distinct minority, which is a measure of the degree to which liberal ideas were reformulated and reconstructed in response to the upheavals and disorienting events of the 1960s.

The reason to connect the Kennedy assassination with the rise of the new radicalism–and the eclipse of the older liberalism–is that some of the most striking features of this new political mood were present in the reaction to Kennedy's death. These we have already had occasion to mention: the assignment of guilt for Kennedy's death to the nation at large, the sense that there must be something deeply wrong with the country in order for such an event to have occurred, the search for conspiracies emanating from the far right to account for the tragedy, the denial that communism could have played any role in the death of the president, the emphasis on civil rights (rather than the Cold War) as the context within which Kennedy's death should be understood. The Camelot idea, more-over, introduced a sense of pointlessness to political activity since—according to the logic of the Arthurian metaphor—the best of times were irretrievably lost in the past. The manner by which the assassination was investigated and explained contributed further to this sense of confusion and disorientation. The fact that the official investigations could not assign a motive to Oswald led to a suspicion that some important facts were being held back by the national authorities (which was true), leading in turn to feelings of distrust for the federal government. This potent package of misunderstandings and exaggerations was nourished by a profound sense of grief felt by the public on the loss of such an attractive leader, but also by outright deceptions promoted by national leaders, including the Kennedy family, President Johnson, and the chief investigative bodies of the national government. All these factors combined to reinforce the radical mood that, for additional reasons, was gathering force in the nation in the years after Kennedy's death.

Thus it was that President Kennedy was shot by a communist, but out of the confusion and disorientation surrounding his death, radical doctrines gained new adherents and greater influence in American life than ever before. Even as Kennedy was lionized after his death, the ideas for which he stood were soon eclipsed by the changed mood that was overtaking the nation, or at least significant parts of it.

Kennedy's anticommunism, for example, was turned on its head by the radicals of the 1960s and by the liberals who eventually took command of the reform movement. They argued that the Cold

War was a diversion from urgent domestic issues and represented a false conflict spurred on by military and industrial interests in the United States. In 1972, the national Democratic Party, led by its presidential candidate, George McGovern, essentially withdrew from the Cold War, leaving that battle to be fought in the years afterwards by a coalition of Republicans and conservative Democrats. In 1977, a Democratic president, no doubt thinking of Kennedy's efforts to oust Castro, apologized for national policies that had been crafted out of an "inordinate fear of communism." Such claims had been part of the worldview of the far left going back to the 1940s, but until Kennedy's death they had not played any prominent role in liberal politics. Kennedy's assassination, traumatic as it was for Americans in general and for liberals in particular, provided an occasion for these ideas to enter the mainstream of the liberal movement. The denial that a communist could have killed the president was an extension of earlier left-wing claims that, for example, the United States started the Cold War, Alger Hiss could not have been a Soviet spy, Whittaker Chambers lied in saying so, the Rosenbergs were innocent, and Castro was an idealistic reformer.

The distrust and suspicion of the national government that developed in the years after Kennedy's death represented an especially important adjustment in approach by the reform movement. From Roosevelt to Lyndon Johnson, including most especially John F. Kennedy, liberals expressed great faith in the capacity of the national government to carry out programs to improve the lives of a majority of Americans. The countless programs they promoted are ample testimony to that faith. Yet such a faith could not help but be undermined by accusations that elements of the national government might have engineered the assassination of a president and then conspired with prominent leaders to cover it up. It was perhaps not well understood that such accusations, when not backed up by hard facts and evidence, struck at the heart of the welfare state that liberals over the preceding generation had worked so hard and intelligently to construct. After all, one can hardly argue before a perceptive audience that the national government is so corrupt as to engineer the assassination of a president but at the same time sufficiently competent and trustworthy to administer the pensions and health care of the American people. This ambivalence about national power—that is, the idea that the government is at once deeply corrupt and potentially beneficent—entered into the mainstream of liberal thinking in the aftermath of the Kennedy assassination. Such ambivalence compromised the case for the welfare state; indeed, it may have opened the way somewhat later for potent attacks on it from a conservative direction.

But the most far-reaching, though subtle, adjustment in the liberal worldview in the wake of the assassination concerned its assumptions about history, progress, and the uses of reform and the connection of these to the liberal sense of American nationality. From the Progressive era through the New Deal and down to the Kennedy-Johnson years, reform was understood as an instrument of progress, a means by which the American experiment in democracy was progressively improved and perfected. The past, from the standpoint of twentieth-century liberalism, was a record of continuous struggle and improvement for the vast majority of Americans, with farsighted reformers like Jefferson, Jackson, Lincoln, and FDR leading the way. The liberal agenda, like the American experiment itself, was ever unfinished. Liberals might therefore look to the future with a sense of optimism that their ideas for reform would in time be enacted into law. The conservatives, on the other hand, were stuck in the past, always trying to preserve worn-out ways but with no vision for an American future. Kennedy himself frequently mocked Republicans for what he felt was their head-in-the-sand attitude.

This, then, was the liberal "narrative" (to borrow a term favored by academics), an interpretation of the nation's history that allowed liberals to project the achievements of the past into the future. There is a marked tendency for political movements to establish compelling narratives that place the present into the perspective of the past and the future. Lincoln, as we have seen, advanced a view of history that incorporated a strong biblical element. Americans, he said, were "the almost chosen people," living in a promised land but corrupted by the taint of slavery. Martin Luther King framed the Negro struggle for freedom in America in Old Testament terms. Jacqueline Kennedy had her own imaginative interpretation of her husband's place in history. The liberal view was different from all of these in that it was entirely secular in terms of the rhetoric it deployed, the reforms it contemplated, and the future it envisioned.

In the years after Kennedy's death, liberals recast their understanding of reform from an instrument of progress to an instrument for punishment. They did not reject reform but did change their understanding of its purpose. The concept of national guilt that developed so powerfully in the immediate aftermath of Kennedy's assassination turned out to be a much more durable emotion than it was conceived to be at that painful time. If the nation deserved to bear some guilt for Kennedy's death, as many said at the time, and if Kennedy's death was a stand-in for the suffering of countless innocents, then perhaps the nation was in need of reforms that went well beyond legislative proposals like the Civil Rights Act or the Medicare program. The idea developed that the nation deserved punishment and chastisement for its manifold failures to live up to its stated ideals. From this point of view, reform was called for as an instrument for correction. Such an assumption resurrected for a secular purpose the traditional Protestant idea of reform as the means by which a community is purged of its sins.

Between the time of Kennedy's assassination in 1963 and Jimmy Carter's election in 1976, the liberal movement was gradually taken over by a new doctrine that might be called (for want of a better term) Punitive Liberalism, an influential point of view that emerged directly from the cultural upheavals of the 1960s. This doctrine took as its point of departure the assumption (described above) that the United States was responsible for numerous crimes and misdeeds through its history that called for some kind of official recognition and punishment. White Americans had enslaved blacks and committed genocide against Native Americans. They had oppressed women and ill-treated minority groups, like the Japanese who had been unjustly interned as a security measure during World War II. Americans had been harsh and unfeeling toward the poor. By its greed, the nation had despoiled the environment and consumed a disproportionate share of the world's resources. Americans had coddled dictators abroad and violated human rights out of an irrational fear of communism. Jack Newfield instinctively expressed such a view when he attributed Robert Kennedy's assassination to "poverty, lynchings, or our genocide against the Indians."

This was a version of history, too, a "narrative," albeit of a negative kind. For the Punitive Liberals, American history was a story of sin and corruption going all the way back to the initial European visitations to North American shores. This view was impossible to reconcile with the progressive narrative of the liberal movement as it developed through the course of American history, and especially through the twentieth century. In its distrust of America—that is, in its anti-Americanism—it incorporated a set of assumptions that was earlier associated with left-wing critiques of American capitalism. It could not have been predicted that this radical cultural critique, once incorporated into the mainstream of the liberal movement, would yield a new political outlook that represented a significant break with the liberal tradition in America.

This new version of the American past was quite the opposite of the old Whig interpretation of history that found its way into the writings of some of the leading American historians of the postwar period. The Whig interpretation held that history is a benign process marked by successive improvements over time in the direction of liberty, equality, and representative government. The Punitive Liberals, as we have called them, saw American history as a malignant process by which capitalist institutions and white males gained the upper hand over workers, women, and minority groups. Their indictment implicitly applied to the writing of the Constitution itself, which they said (here echoing Charles Beard but differing with Abraham Lincoln) was still another act by which entrenched economic interests perpetuated their power. The purpose of reform was to begin to even the historical score against those who had previously tilted the game unfairly in their own favor.

With such a bill of indictment, the new liberals now held that Americans had no good reason to feel pride in their country's past or optimism about its future. They began to argue that the purpose of national policy was more to punish the nation for its sins than to build a brighter and more secure future for all. The focus of reform was to find ways of compensating those groups that had suffered as a consequence of the cruel policies and customs of the past. In terms of policy, such a vision pointed in the direction of employment and educational preferences for women and designated minority groups, and toward programs that would promote the expression of their distinctive interests and points of view in government, journalism, textbooks, and educational institutions. This latter emphasis, in turn, pointed toward cultural criticism as a key aspect of reform in view of its possibilities for laying bare the discriminatory assumptions of traditional cultural practices. Thus the concept of "cultural politics" was a centerpiece of the new liberalism.

Given their punitive assumptions, the proponents of this view tended to be somewhat dour and pessimistic. Reform, after all, was now a grim business of parceling out punishments and redressing grievances inherited from the past. This was not, however, a platform that could be sold effectively to a majority of voters, since presumably it was precisely such a majority that was in need of reformation and punishment. Thus the punitive liberals chose to advance their causes more in the courts and the regulatory bodies—these being more appropriate venues for leveling blame and exacting punishment. Instead of looking to the possibilities of the future, punitive liberals were preoccupied with the crimes and misdemeanors of the past.

This point of view, however, despite its influence in some precincts of American life, carried with it some significant liabilities when it was translated into the political arena. Because the movement sought to cultivate guilt as a means of leveraging policy and influence, it proved incapable or uninterested in promoting practical measures to strengthen the economy or to advance American power in the world. Such goals in any case would have been contradictory to deeper cultural longings, which were to dispel American pride and to shrink national ambitions at home and abroad. The Cold War, as has been noted, seemed like an especially pointless struggle between two deeply flawed empires. The advances made by third-world revolutionaries like Castro appeared as appropriate rebukes to the arrogant misuse of American power. A strong and growing national economy, meanwhile, was definitely a mixed blessing from this point of view, since the wealth so created would disproportionately reward the rich and self-centered middle classes —the very groups that deserved chastisement in the eyes of the new liberals and radicals.

Thus the punitive outlook of a Jimmy Carter could not have been more at odds with the forward-looking optimism of a John F. Kennedy, the liberal cold-warrior and advocate for the idea that "a rising tide lifts all boats." For example, Kennedy would never have taken on the role of reprimanding the voters for their "malaise," as Carter did, but instead would have exercised leadership to lift the public's spirits, just as Roosevelt had done in the midst of the Great Depression. The new liberalism that was crafted in response to Kennedy's assassination and the disorder of the 1960s did not bring with it the old optimism and self-confidence that were required to lead the nation, these traits having been lost somewhere along the way.

In the most surprising turnabout of all, it was finally the Republicans led by the conservative Ronald Reagan who moved in to fill the void left behind by the retreat of the liberals. The conservatives had never before been known for their optimism about the future or their devotion to progress. Leaders of the conservative intellectual movement that took shape in the 1950s were reasonably clear and consistent on this point: there was no good reason to expect the future to be better than the past. Whittaker Chambers, certainly a good representative of this outlook, said when he abandoned communism that he was leaving the winning side to join the losers. William F. Buckley Jr., the founder and publisher of *National Review*, wrote when he started the magazine in 1955 that its purpose was "to stand athwart history yelling stop!" Conservatives attacked the "myth" of progress so dear to liberals. When Lyndon Johnson defeated Barry Goldwater in the 1964 landslide election, most observers concluded that conservatism in America had been discredited once and for all.

Yet by 1980 the conservatives, led by Ronald Reagan, were able to seize the mantle of optimism and progress that had been abandoned by the liberals. Reagan, in great part because of these advantages, had little difficulty in dispatching the Democrats who challenged him. In the span of years between Kennedy's assassination and Reagan's election in 1980, the liberal consensus that Kennedy represented was shattered beyond recognition and was gradually replaced by a set of ideas that bore but a tangential relationship to the tradition of liberal reform that had evolved over the first two-thirds of the twentieth century.

In his memoir of the Kennedy administration, Arthur Schlesinger Jr. wrote that among the important features of Kennedy's legacy was his willingness "to fight for reason against extremism and mythology."[3] This was accurate as it was applied to Kennedy himself but it was most untrue of his legacy as it was shaped from his assassination and its disorienting aftermath. Kennedy's legacy, as things turned out, could not be separated from the manner of his death, the myths and legends that came to surround it, and the extremism that it provoked. In trying to turn Kennedy into a legendary figure and by interpreting his assassination as an indictment of the nation, his admirers and supporters inadvertently turned him into something else: the last articulate spokesman for the now lost world of post-war American liberalism.

ACKNOWLEDGMENTS

The author is grateful to Roger Kimball, editor and publisher of Encounter Books, for his encouragement in undertaking the project and for his patience while awaiting its completion. The book could not have been written without his wise editorial counsel. Carol Staswick of Encounter Books edited the manuscript with admirable professional care and attention. The late Michael Joyce, a close friend of many years, initially suggested that my thoughts about the Kennedy assassination should be shaped into a book. Neal Kozodoy, editor of *Commentary* magazine, provided invaluable editorial guidance for an earlier essay on this subject, which appeared in the May 2006 issue of *Commentary* under the title "Lee Harvey Oswald and the Liberal Crack-Up." Gabriel Schoenfeld, senior editor of *Commentary*, also provided helpful suggestions for expanding the scope of that essay.

Sheila Mulcahy, Jennifer Wotochek, Alice Newton, and Sara Fay offered encouragement and assistance at critical times as the manuscript was nearing completion. Larry Mone, president of the Manhattan Institute, contributed helpful suggestions in connection with the history of American liberalism. The author is especially grateful to his wife, Patricia, his son, Will, and to an anonymous friend for their patience in listening to my theories and for other indulgences too numerous and varied to catalog.

Any merits or demerits that may be attached to the book, however, should be assigned to the author alone.

NOTES

INTRODUCTION

1 Robert Dallek, *An Unfinished Life: John F. Kennedy, 1917-1963* (New York: Little, Brown & Co., 2003). See also Barbara Leaming, Jack *Kennedy: The Education of a Statesman* (New York: W. W. Norton & Co., 2006); Michael O'Brien, *John F. Kennedy: A Biography* (New York: Thomas Dunne Books, 2005); Seymour M. Hersh, *The Dark Side of Camelot* (New York: Little, Brown & Co., 1997); Geoffrey Perret, *Jack: A Life Like No Other* (New York: Random House, 2001); Thomas C. Reeves, *A Question of Character: A Life of John F. Kennedy* (New York: Macmillan, 1991); and John Hellmann, *The Kennedy Obsession: The American Myth of JFK* (New York: Columbia University Press, 1997).

2 On Jacqueline Kennedy Onassis, see, for example, Sarah Bradford, *America's Queen: The Life of Jacqueline Kennedy Onassis* (New York: Penguin Books, 2000); C. David Heymann, *A Woman Named Jackie* (New York: Birch Lane Press, 1995); Christopher Andersen, *Jackie after Jack: Portrait of the Lady* (New York: William Morrow, 1998); Edward Klein, *Just Jackie: Her Private Years* (New York: Ballantine Books, 1998); John H. Davis, *Jacqueline Bouvier: An Intimate Memoir* (New York: John Wiley & Sons, 1996).

3 An ABC News poll in 2003 found that 22 percent of respondents believed that Oswald acted alone, while 70 percent said that a wider conspiracy was responsible. A Gallup Poll taken the same year placed the proportion believing in a conspiracy at 76 percent.

4 On Oswald's anti-American outlook, see Norman Mailer, *Oswald's Tale* (New York: Random House, 1997); and Jean Davison, *Oswald's Game* (New York: W. W. Norton & Co., 1983), pp. 29-40, esp. pp. 38-39.

5 Arthur Schlesinger Jr., *A Thousand Days* (Boston: Houghton Mifflin, 1965); and Theodore C. Sorensen, *Kennedy* (New York: Bantam Books, 1966). Other works of this genre include Paul B. Fay, *The Pleasure of His Company* (New York: Harper & Row, 1966); and Pierre Salinger, *With Kennedy* (New York: Doubleday, 1966).

6 Schlesinger, *A Thousand Days*, p. 1031.

7 Merrill D. Peterson, *Lincoln in American Memory* (New York: Oxford University Press, 1994), p. 35.

One: Liberalism

1 Richard Hofstadter, *The Age of Reform* (New York: Vintage Books, 1955), p. 14.

2 Summaries of the Progressive point of view (especially the twin emphases on democracy and expertise) may be gleaned from several works of the period, especially: Walter Weyl, *The New Democracy* (New York; Macmillan, 1912).; Herbert Croly, *The Promise of American Life* (1909; New York: Capricorn Books, 1964); Walter Lippmann, *Drift and Mastery* (1913; Madison: University of Wisconsin Press, 1986).

3 Hofstadter, *The Age of Reform*, p. 18.

4 On the differences between Progressive and New Deal reform, see Hofstadter, *The Age of Reform*, ch. 7; and Arthur Schlesinger Jr., *The Vital Center* (Boston: Houghton Mifflin, 1948), ch. 8.

5 For an insightful critique of postwar liberalism, see Christopher Lasch, *The New Radicalism in America, 1889-1963* (New York: W. W. Norton & Co., 1965), ch. 9.

6 Schlesinger, *The Vital Center*, p. 182.

7 Ibid., ch. 6.

8 Sen. Joseph McCarthy, "Enemies from Within," speech at Wheeling, West Virginia, February 9, 1950; reproduced at http://historymatters.gmu.edu/d/6456/.

9 Quotation from Daniel Bell, "Interpretations of American Politics, 1955," in *The Radical Right*, ed. Bell (New York: Doubleday & Co., 1963), p. 58.

10 Quoted in Clinton Rossiter, *Conservatism in America: The Thankless Persuasion* (New York: Vintage Books, 1962), p. 93.

11 Louis Hartz, *The Liberal Tradition in America* (New York: Harcourt, Brace & World, 1955).

12 On these points, see ibid., ch. 11.

13 Daniel Bell, ed., *The Radical Right* (New York: Doubleday & Co., 1963). This volume was an expanded and updated version of *The New American Right* (Criterion Books, 1955).

14 Richard Hofstadter, "The Pseudo-Conservative Revolt," 1955, in *The Radical Right*, ed. Bell, p. 76. Hofstadter's harsh treatment of American conservatism suggests why Clinton Rossiter subtitled his book on this subject (cited above), "The Thankless Persuasion."

15 Hofstadter, "The Pseudo-Conservative Revolt," p. 85.

16 Ibid., p. 83.

17 Daniel Bell, "The Dispossessed," in *The Radical Right*, ed. Bell, pp. 3-8.

18 On the subject of status and its link to radicalism, see Bell, "The Dispossessed"; and Hofstadter, "The Pseudo-Conservative Revolt."

19 Bell, "The Dispossessed," p. 10.

20 Richard Hofstadter, "The Paranoid Style in American Politics," in *The Paranoid Style in American Politics and Other Essays* (Cambridge, Mass.: Harvard University Press, 1965). The article originally appeared in *Harper's*, October 1964, based on a lecture delivered at Oxford University in November 1963. For a more general discussion of Hofstadter's thought, see David S. Brown, *Richard Hofstadter: An Intellectual Biography* (Chicago: University of Chicago Press, 2006).

21 See Hofstadter, *The Paranoid Style in American* Politics, p. 37.

22 On Goldwater and the Republicans, see Hofstadter, "The Paranoid Style in American Politics," p. 3.

23 Richard Hofstadter, *Anti-Intellectualism in American Life* (New York: Random House, 1964).

24 Daniel Bell, *The End of Ideology: On the Exhaustion of Political Ideas in the 1950s* (New York: The Free Press, 1962), pp. 402-3. Bell's argument drew heavily from an earlier suggestive essay by Edward Shils, "The End of Ideology," *Encounter*, November 1955, pp. 52-58. The theme is also taken up in Seymour Martin Lipset, *Political Man* (Garden City, N.Y.: Anchor Books, 1963), ch. 13, "The End of Ideology?"

25 Herbert Butterfield, *The Whig Interpretation of History* (London, 1931; New York: W. W. Norton & Co., 1965). See also George Orwell, "Looking Back on the Spanish War," in *The Collected Essays, Journalism, and Letters of George Orwell*, Vol. 2, *My Country Right or Left, 1940-43*, ed. Sonia Orwell and Ian Angus (Boston: David R. Godine, 2004), p. 259.

26 Richard Hofstadter, *The Progressive Historians: Turner, Beard, Parrington* (1968; New York: Vintage Books, 1970), pp. 42-43.

27 Arthur Schlesinger Jr., *The Age of Jackson* (Boston: Little Brown, 1945). For a critique of Schlesinger's interpretation of Jackson, see Lee Benson, *The Concept of Jacksonian Democracy* (Princeton, N.J.: Princeton University Press, 1961).

28 Hofstadter, *The Progressive Historians* (first published by Random House, 1968).

29 See Peter Viereck, "The Revolt against the Elite," in *The Radical Right*, ed. Bell, p. 169.

30 See Lasch, *The New Radicalism in America*.

31 Ibid., p. 90.

32 Lionel Trilling, *The Liberal Imagination* (New York: Anchor Books, 1950).
Quotations cited are from the Preface, pp. xi-xii. On Trilling see also
Gertrude Himmelfarb, *The Moral Imagination: From Edmund Burke to Lionel
Trilling* (Chicago: Ivan R. Dee, 2006), pp. 219-29.

33 Trilling, *The Liberal Imagination*, p. xii.

Two: Kennedy

1 Kennedy's approval rating was at 58 percent according to a Gallup Poll
taken November 8-10, 1963.

2 Victor Lasky, *J.F.K.: The Man and the Myth* (New York: Macmillan, 1963).
Lasky's was the first comprehensive and critical study of Kennedy's
career. His book laid the foundation for subsequent Kennedy biographies.
Kennedy was killed before he and his aides could mount a counter-
campaign against the book. After the assassination, Lasky's publisher
withdrew the book from circulation. However, subsequent biographies
by members of Kennedy's inner circle, particularly Schlesinger's *A Thousand Days*, can be read as official answers to the main points made in
Lasky's book.

3 The *Atlantic Monthly* recently commissioned a group of historians to rank
the one hundred most influential Americans since the time of the Revolution. The list was led by Lincoln, Washington, Jefferson, and Franklin
Roosevelt. Among contemporaries of John F. Kennedy, Presidents Truman, Eisenhower, Johnson, Nixon, and Reagan made the list. Kennedy
did not. See *Atlantic Monthly*, December 2006. This is, however, a highly
disputable assessment. Mark Gillespie, "JFK Ranked as Greatest U.S.
President," Gallup News Service, February 21, 2000.

4 Quoted in Arthur Schlesinger Jr., *A Thousand Days: John F. Kennedy in the
White House* (1965; Boston: Houghton Mifflin, 2002), p. xi.

5 See Theodore C. Sorensen, *Kennedy* (New York: Bantam Books, 1966),
pp. 751, 758; and Schlesinger, *A Thousand Days*, p. 1031.

6 See also Paul Healy, "The Senate's Gay Young Bachelor," *Saturday Evening
Post*, June 13, 1953, p. 127.

7 Many sources document Kennedy's efforts to position himself as a
moderate during his congressional career. See Thomas C. Reeves,
A Question of Character: A Life of John F. Kennedy (New York: Macmillan,
1991), chs. 8 and 9. Also, Schlesinger, *A Thousand Days*, pp. 9-14; John P.
Avlon, *Independent Nation: How Centrists Can Change American Politics* (New
York: Three Rivers Press, 2004), pp. 137-61; and Robert Dallek, *An
Unfinished Life: John F. Kennedy, 1917-1963* (New York: Little, Brown & Co.,

2003), ch. 6. References to *Time* and *Newsweek* articles in Reeves, *A Question of Character*, pp. 141, 151.

8 On Kennedy's record in the Senate, see (for example) Dallek, who concludes that "his Senate career had produced no major legislation that contributed substantially to the national well being." *An Unfinished Life*, ch. 6, quotation on p. 226.

9 Lasky, *J.F.K.: The Man and the Myth*, pp. 212-13.

10 On the Kennedy family's association with McCarthy, see Michael O'Brien, *John F. Kennedy: A Biography* (New York: Thomas Dunne Books, 2005), pp. 252-53; Lasky, *J.F.K.: The Man and the Myth*, pp. 141-43; Reeves, *A Question of Character*, pp. 87-88; Dallek, *An Unfinished Life*, pp. 162-63, 191; Joan Blair and Clay Blair Jr., *The Search for JFK* (New York: G. P. Putnam's Sons, 1976), pp. 522, 526.

11 Quotation cited in Lasky, *J.F.K.: The Man and the Myth*, p. 238.

12 Ibid., p. 27.

13 The elder Kennedy's business activities (especially his interests in liquor and film companies) are described in Richard J. Whalen, *The Founding Father: The Story of Joseph P. Kennedy* (New York: New American Library, 1964), chs. 4-7. See also Seymour M. Hersh, *The Dark Side of Camelot* (New York: Little, Brown & Co., 1997), chs. 4, 5 and 6.

14 Joseph Kennedy's diplomatic and political career is discussed in several places, including Barbara Leaming, *Jack Kennedy: The Education of a Statesman* (New York: W. W. Norton & Co., 2006), chs. 3 and 4. See also Dallek, *An Unfinished Life*, ch. 2; and Hersh, *The Dark Side of Camelot*, ch. 3.

15 On insinuations of anti-Semitism, see Dallek, *An Unfinished Life*, p. 175; and Hersh, *The Dark Side of Camelot*, pp. 63-64.

16 On Kennedy's master's thesis, see Leaming, *Jack Kennedy: The Education of a Statesman*, ch. 4.

17 Dallek, *An Unfinished Life*, p. 63.

18 On the revisions to Kennedy's thesis, see Leaming, *Jack Kennedy: The Education of a Statesman*, pp. 104-8; and Dallek, *An Unfinished Life*, p. 65. See also Arthur Schlesinger's discussion in *A Thousand Days*, pp. 84-85.

19 Kennedy's treatment of Chamberlain was questionable because Chamberlain went to Munich to secure "peace in our time," not to buy time to prepare for an unavoidable war. Churchill, however, did acknowledge later that Britain was not ready to confront Hitler in 1938 owing to earlier failures to prepare. See Winston Churchill, *The Gathering Storm* (New York: Houghton Mifflin, 1948), ch. 18, "Munich Winter," pp. 326-27.

20 On the publication and reviews of Kennedy's book, see once again Leam-
    ing, *Jack Kennedy: The Education of a Statesman*, p. 109; Dallek, *An Unfin-
    ished Life*, pp. 65-66; Whalen, *The Founding Father*, pp. 294-95; and
    Thomas C. Reeves, *A Question of Character: A Life of John F. Kennedy* (New
    York: The Free Press, 1991), pp. 49-51.

21 On Churchill and Kennedy, see Schlesinger, *A Thousand Days*, pp. 83-84.
    Also Leaming, *Jack Kennedy: The Education of a Statesman*, esp. ch. 11.
    Kennedy's father, however, did not give up his resentment of Churchill.
    When Churchill published *The Gathering Storm* (1948), the first volume
    of his war memoirs, Kennedy wrote a long letter to the *New York Times*
    claiming that his treatment of the Prague and Munich crises was filled
    with errors. See David Reynolds, *In Command of History: Churchill Fighting
    and Writing the Second World War* (New York: Random House, 2005),
    pp. 136-37.

22 The book diverged substantially in style from Kennedy's master's thesis.
    Arthur Krock contributed his editorial skills to the project. As the pub-
    lisher's deadline closed in, the senior Kennedy assigned to the project his
    personal speechwriter, who spent two weeks turning the manuscript into
    publishable form. Up to that point, the manuscript was (in the speech-
    writer's description) a "mishmash" of ungrammatical sentences and news
    clippings. See Reeves, *A Question of Character*, p. 49; also, Herbert Parmet,
    Jack: The Struggles of John F. Kennedy (New York: Doubleday Books, 1983),
    pp. 77-78.

23 John F. Kennedy, *Profiles in Courage* (1956; New York: HarperCollins,
    2003). Biographers who have examined Kennedy's notes for *Profiles in
    Courage* suggest that Theodore Sorensen actually wrote the bulk of the
    manuscript based on Kennedy's oral comments and rough notes, supple-
    mented by Sorensen's own research. This judgment is based on the lack
    of correspondence between Kennedy's handwritten notes and the con-
    tents of the book itself. Sorensen drew on the assistance of several others,
    including historians Allan Nevins, Arthur Schlesinger Jr., and Jules Davids.
    See especially Herbert Parmet, *Jack: The Struggles of John F. Kennedy*,
    pp. 320-33; and Reeves, *A Question of Character*, pp. 126-28. Sorensen,
    however, has consistently maintained that, though he assisted in the
    drafting of the book, Kennedy is its true author. See Sorensen, *Kennedy*,
    pp. 68-70.

24 Kennedy, *Profiles in Courage*, p. 5.

25 Quoted in Lasky, *J.F.K.: The Man and the Myth*, p. 144.

26 Parmet, *Jack: The Struggles of John F. Kennedy*, pp. 240-41; Lasky, *J.F.K.: The
    Man and the Myth*, pp. 144-45.

27 Dallek, *An Unfinished Life*, pp. 288-89; Leaming, *Jack Kennedy: The Education of a Statesman*, ch. 11.

28 Leaming, *Jack Kennedy: The Education of a Statesman*, ch. 11, quotation on p. 244.

29 Lasky, *J.F.K.: The Man and the Myth*, pp. 510-13; Reeves, *A Question of Character*, pp. 249, 365; Dallek, *An Unfinished Life*, p. 289.

30 Richard Rovere, "Letter from Washington," *New Yorker*, November 30, 1963.

31 On plans to assassinate Castro, see Hersh, *The Dark Side of Camelot*, chs. 13 and 14; Reeves, *A Question of Character*, ch. 12; and Dallek, *An Unfinished Life*, pp. 439-40.

32 On Kennedy's rhetorical debt to Churchill, see Leaming, *Jack Kennedy: The Education of a Statesman*, chs. 11 and 12. With respect to his Inaugural Address, see esp. pp. 258-60.

33 Quoted in Dallek, *An Unfinished Life*, p. 583.

34 Schlesinger, *A Thousand Days* (2002), pp. 725-29; Robert Frost, "For John F. Kennedy, His Inauguration," in *The Poetry of Robert Frost*, ed. Edward Connery Lathem (New York: Holt, Rinehart & Winston, 1969), pp. 422-25.

35 Daniel J. Boorstin, *The Image: A Guide to Pseudo-Events in America* (New York: Atheneum, 1978), p. 61.

36 Norman Mailer, "Superman Comes to the Supermarket," *Esquire*, November 1960, reprinted in *Smiling Through the Apocalypse: Esquire's History of the Sixties*, ed. Harold Hayes (New York: McCall Publishing Co., 1970), pp. 3-30.

37 Sorensen, *Kennedy*, pp. 244-45.

38 Schlesinger, *A Thousand Days* (2002), pp. 115-16.

39 Mailer, "Superman Comes to the Supermarket," p. 17.

40 Garry Wills, *The Kennedy Imprisonment* (New York: Houghton Mifflin, 1981).

Three: Martyr: Lincoln

1 Arnold Epstein and Benjamin R. Forester, *Danger on the Right* (New York: Random House, 1964).

2 President Kennedy's speech may be found on the Internet site of the John F. Kennedy Library, www.jfklibrary.org, under "Remarks Prepared for Delivery at the Trade Mart in Dallas, November 22, 1963." His frequent speeches against the radical right are summarized in Arthur M.

Schlesinger Jr., *A Thousand Days: John F. Kennedy in the White House* (1965; Boston: Houghton Mifflin, 2002), pp. 749-58.

3 Tom Wicker, "Kennedy Decries Racial Bombings; Impugns Wallace," *New York Times*, September 17, 1963, p. 1; James Reston, "The Crisis of Lawlessness in Alabama," *New York Times*, September 18, 1963, p. 38.

4 "Dallas Leaders Apologize to Stevenson for 'Outrage,'" *New York Times*, October 26, 1963, p. 1; Schlesinger, *A Thousand Days*, pp. 1020-21; *Life*, John F. Kennedy Memorial Edition, December 3, 1963, p. 59.

5 Schlesinger, *A Thousand Days*, pp. 1021-22; Jim Bishop, *The Day the President Was Shot* (New York: Bantam Books, 1968), p. 128.

6 William Manchester, *The Death of a President* (New York: Harper & Row, 1967), p. 265.

7 Ibid., pp. 354, 259.

8 James Hosty, an FBI agent in Dallas who had monitored Oswald's activities, told a Dallas police officer on the afternoon of the assassination that he and other agents knew of Oswald and felt he was "possibly capable" of committing such an act. See Bishop, *The Day the President Was Shot*, pp. 276-77. Hosty later denied making this statement.

9 Manchester, p. 365.

10 Quotation is from Christopher Andersen, *Jackie after Jack* (New York: William Morrow & Co., 1998), p. 23. See also Bishop, *The Day the President Was Shot*, p. 374.

11 Bishop, *The Day the President Was Shot*, p. 339.

12 On Lincoln's funeral, see Lloyd Lewis, *Myths after Lincoln* (New York: Harcourt, Brace & Co., 1929).

13 See Perry Miller, *The Life of the Mind in America* (New York: Harcourt, Brace & World, 1965), p. 6.

14 See Russell B. Nye, *Society and Culture in America: 1830-1860* (New York: Harper & Row, 1974), p. 287; Miller, *The Life of the Mind in America*, p. 11. See ch. 8 in Nye's volume for an insightful discussion of the character and influence of the Protestant revival.

15 Quoted in Miller, *The Life of the Mind in America*, pp. 68-69.

16 See Edmund Wilson, *Patriotic Gore* (New York: Oxford University Press, 1962), pp. 107-8. Also, Abraham Lincoln, "Address Before the Young Men's Lyceum of Springfield, Illinois, January 27, 1838," in *The Collected Works of Abraham Lincoln*, ed. Roy P. Basler, vol. 1 (New Brunswick, N.J.: Rutgers University Press, 1953).

17 Wilson, *Patriotic Gore*, pp. 129-30.

18 For the best commentary on Lincoln's Lyceum speech, see Harry V. Jaffa, *The Crisis of the House Divided: An Interpretation of the Issues in the Lincoln-Douglas Debates* (Chicago: University of Chicago Press, 1972), ch. 9.

19 See Richard J. Carwardine, *Evangelicals and Politics in Antebellum America* (New Haven: Yale University Press, 1993). Also, James Moorhead, *American Apocalypse: Yankee Protestants and the Civil War* (New Haven: Yale University Press, 1978).

20 Allen C. Guelzo, *Abraham Lincoln: Redeemer President* (Grand Rapids, Mich.: Eerdmans, 2003), p. 246.

21 On the Gettysburg Address and its themes, see Harry V. Jaffa, *A New Birth of Freedom: Abraham Lincoln and the Coming of the Civil War* (Oxford, U.K.: Rowman & Littlefield, 2000), ch. 2. See also Garry Wills, *Lincoln at Gettysburg: The Words That Remade America* (New York: Simon & Schuster, 1992), chs. 2 and 3.

22 Lincoln to Mrs. Lydia Bixby, November 21, 1864, in *The Collected Works of Abraham Lincoln*, ed. Basler, vol. 8, pp. 116-17.

23 See Jaffa, *The Crisis of the House Divided*, p. 316.

24 Lewis, *Myths after Lincoln*, p. 87; Richard Carwardine, *Lincoln: A Life of Purpose and Power* (New York: Vintage Books, 2006), p. 132. On Lincoln's religious thought, see Guelzo, *Abraham Lincoln: Redeemer President*, ch. 8.

25 Michael W. Kaufmann, *American Brutus: John Wilkes Booth and the Lincoln Conspiracies* (New York: Random House, 2004). Quotation from Booth's diary on p. 400.

26 Quotation is from the *New York Times*, April 26, 1865, p. 2. On the reaction to Lincoln's assassination, see Guelzo, *Abraham Lincoln: Redeemer President*, pp. 339-41; Lewis, *Myths after Lincoln*, chs. 9 and 10. See also Thomas Goodrich, *The Darkest Dawn: Lincoln, Booth, and the Great American Tragedy* (Bloomington: Indiana University Press, 2005), chs. 16-18; Harry S. Stout, *Upon the Altar of the Nation: A Moral History of the Civil War* (New York: Viking Press, 2006), ch. 45; and Barry Schwartz, *Abraham Lincoln and the Forge of National Memory* (Chicago: University of Chicago Press, 2000), pp. 34-39.

27 Quoted in Lewis, *Myths after Lincoln*, p. 94.

28 *New York Times*, April 23, 1865, p. 2.

29 See Lewis, *Myths after Lincoln*, pp. 97-98. A few ministers, dissenting somewhat from this consensus, wondered why Lincoln should have sought entertainment in a public theater on the evening of Good Friday. See Guelzo, *Abraham Lincoln: Redeemer President*, pp. 246 ff.

30 *New York Times*, April 23, 1865, p. 2; *New York Times*, April 21, 1865, p. 2; Lewis, *Myths after Lincoln*, p. 69.

31 Edward Steers Jr., *Blood on the Moon: The Assassination of Abraham Lincoln* (Lexington: University of Kentucky Press, 2001), pp. 268-69. "Immediately after the President's death, a cabinet meeting was called by Secretary Stanton and held in the room where the corpse lay." *New York Times*, April 16, 1865, p. 1. The report went on to say that it was not known what was discussed at that meeting. It has been inferred that Stanton discussed funeral arrangements with his associates in the cabinet.

32 Lewis, *Myths after Lincoln*, p. 106.

33 The information on Lincoln's funeral in the paragraphs to follow is gleaned from the following sources: *New York Times*, April 17-30, 1865; Lewis, *Myths after Lincoln*, chs. 11 and 12; Carl Sandburg, *Abraham Lincoln: The War Years* (New York: Harcourt Brace Jovanovich, 1926), ch. 53; Merrill Peterson, *Lincoln in American Memory* (New York: Oxford University Press, 1994), pp. 14-23; Goodrich, *The Darkest Dawn*, chs. 24, 26, and 29; and Guelzo, *Abraham Lincoln: Redeemer President*, pp. 450-63.

34 Lewis, *Myths after Lincoln*, p. 124.

35 Walt Whitman, "When Lilacs Last in the Door-yard Bloom'd," Verse 6, from *Leaves of Grass* (Philadelphia: David McKay Publishers, 1900). Also, Whitman, "Death of Abraham Lincoln," Lecture delivered in New York City, April 14, 1879 (same collection).

36 Charles Beard, *An Economic Interpretation of the Constitution of the United States* (New York: Macmillan, 1913). On Progressives and the Constitution, see Richard Hofstadter, *The Progressive Historians* (New York: Anchor Books, 1970), pp. 268-69.

37 Carl Becker, *The Declaration of Independence: A Study on the History of Political Ideas* (New York: Harcourt, Brace & Co., 1922).

38 Ibid., pp. 278-79. Becker here is directly at odds with Lincoln, who wrote in a letter in 1859: "All honor to Jefferson—to the man who, in the concrete pressure of a struggle for national independence by a single people, had the coolness, forecast, and capacity to introduce into a merely revolutionary document an abstract truth, applicable to all men and all times, and so to embalm it there, that today, and in all coming days, it shall be a rebuke and a stumbling block to the very harbingers of re-appearing tyranny and oppression." Lincoln to Henry Pierce, April 11, 1859, in *The Collected Works of Abraham Lincoln*, ed. Basler, vol. 3, pp. 374-76.

39 Well stated expressions of this approach can be found in James Mac-Gregor Burns, *The Deadlock of Democracy* (New York: Prentice-Hall, 1963); and E. E. Schattschneider, *Party Government* (Holt, Rinehart & Co., 1959).

Four: Martyr: Kennedy

1 See Jim Bishop, *The Day the President Was Shot* (New York: Bantam Books, 1968), pp. 306-7; and William Manchester, *The Death of a President* (New York: Harper & Row, 1967), pp. 316, 348. Mrs. Kennedy sought to stop publication of the Bishop and Manchester books, at least until they were revised according to her wishes. She was sensitive to reports contained in these books about her conduct in the hours immediately following the assassination. She may have felt that such conduct (brushing off President Johnson, displaying the bloody dress) was not in keeping with the poise, dignity, and bravery with which she conducted herself once she regained her composure.

2 James Reston, "Why America Weeps," *New York Times*, November 23, 1963, p. 1.

3 James Reston, "A Portion of Guilt for All," *New York Times*, November 25, 1963, p. 5.

4 Editorial, *New York Times*, November 24, 1963, p. 18.

5 Jim Newton, *Justice for All: Earl Warren and the Nation He Made* (New York: Riverhead Books, 2006), p. 410; *New York Times*, November 25, 1963, p. 4.

6 *New York Times*, November 25, p. 4. For a summary of Oswald's views on race and integration, see Jean Davison, *Oswald's Game* (New York: W. W. Norton & Co., 1983), p. 112. See also Oswald's statements on race and segregation in Norman Mailer, *Oswald's Tale* (New York: Random House, 1995), pp. 506-7. Oswald wrote that "racial segregation or discrimination should be abolished."

7 *New York Times*, November 29, 1963, pp. 1, 20.

8 Drew Pearson, "Kennedy a Victim of Hate Drive," *Washington Post*, November 29, 1963, p. C3; *New York Times*, November 25, 1963, p. 8; November 26, 1963, p. 9.

9 "Tass Accuses Racists," *New York Times*, November 24, 1963, p. 4; Henry Tanner, "Mikoyan Flies to Washington as Russians Praise Kennedy," *New York Times*, November 25, 1963; "Rightists, Not Reds, to Blame, Moscow Says," *Chicago Tribune*, November 24, 1963, p. 14. Castro's comments on the assassination are quoted in Davison, *Oswald's Game*, p. 256. See also Jules Dubois, "U.S. Reactionaries Plotted Killing: Fidel," *Chicago Tribune*, November 24, 1963, p. 9. Later, during the 1970s, Soviet intelligence would fabricate documents to suggest a link between Oswald and E. Howard Hunt, who in 1963 was an officer in the CIA but later was implicated in a bungled attempt to break into the headquarters of the

Democratic National Committee. The purpose of the forgery was to suggest a link between the CIA and the Kennedy assassination and to throw a cloud of confusion over Oswald's communist background. See Christopher Andrew and Vasili Mitrokhin, *The Sword and the Shield: The Mitrokhin Archive and the Secret History of the KGB* (New York: Basic Books, 1999), pp. 228-29.

10 James Reston, "A Time to Heal," *New York Times*, November 26, 1963, p. 7.

11 *New York Times*, November 26, 1963, p. 36.

12 Anthony Lewis, "Congressional GOP Deplores Linking Assassination to 'Hate,'" *New York Times*, December 7, 1963, p. 12.

13 Arthur M. Schlesinger Jr., *A Thousand Days* (Boston: Houghton Mifflin, 1965), pp. 1020-25; quotations on pp. 1026 and 1027.

14 Russell Baker, "Silence Is Everywhere as Thronged Capital Bids Farewell to President Kennedy," *New York Times*, November 26, 1963, p. 4. Baker also noted in this article that, in the midst of national mourning, "the cranks and haters continued to operate in the night." A police official in Washington, D.C., reported that many phone calls had been received threatening just about every dignitary who planned to appear at the funeral, with Chief Justice Earl Warren a prominent target of such threats.

15 Theodore H. White, *The Making of the President, 1964* (New York: Atheneum, 1964), p. 13.

16 C. David Heymann, *A Woman Named Jackie* (New York: Birch Lane Press, 1994), p. 417.

17 Taylor Branch, *Parting the Waters: America in the King Years, 1955-1963* (New York: Simon & Schuster, 1988), p. 917.

18 Ibid., p. 918.

19 Ibid., p. 920.

20 Leon Festinger, *A Theory of Cognitive Dissonance* (Stanford, Calif.: Stanford University Press, 1957), pp. 246-59. On millenarian movements of the type discussed by Festinger, see Norman Cohn, *The Pursuit of the Millennium* (New York: Oxford University Press, 1970). Hofstadter cited Cohn's book on millenarian movements in the Middle Ages as evidence for the persistence of the paranoid style.

21 Reston, "A Time to Heal."

CHAPTER 5: CONSPIRACY

1 See Edward Steers Jr., *Blood on the Moon: The Assassination of Abraham Lincoln* (Lexington: University of Kentucky Press, 2001); William A. Tidwell,

James O. Hall and David W. Gaddy, *Come Retribution: The Confederate Secret Service and the Assassination of Abraham Lincoln* (Jackson: University of Mississippi Press, 1989).

2 Steers, *Blood on the Moon*, ch. 6.

3 See William Hanchett, *The Lincoln Murder Conspiracies* (Chicago: University of Illinois Press, 1983).

4 Daniel Pipes, *Conspiracy: How the Paranoid Style Flourishes and Where It Comes From* (New York: The Free Press, 1997), pp. 22-23.

5 See ibid., chs. 4 and 5; and Richard Hofstadter, *The Paranoid Style in American Politics and Other Essays* (Cambridge, Mass.: Harvard University Press, 1965), pp. 10-18.

6 Quoted in Hofstadter, *The Paranoid Style in American Politics*, p. 12.

7 J. M. Roberts, *The Mythology of Secret Societies* (London: Secker & Warburg, 1972), pp. 119-21.

8 Ibid., p. 7.

9 Pipes, *Conspiracy: How the Paranoid Style Flourishes*, p. 82.

10 Ibid., p. 80.

11 Edward Jay Epstein, *The Assassination Chronicles: Inquest, Counterplot, and Legend* (New York: Carroll & Graf, 1992), pp. 523-24.

12 *New York Times*, November 24, 1963, p. 1; "Oswald Evidence Was Piling Up," *Washington Post*, November 25, 1963, p. A13.

13 *New York Times*, November 24, 1963, p. 2.

14 On Warren's reluctance to lead the commission and on Johnson's fears of an international crisis in the wake of the assassination, see William Manchester, *The Death of a President* (New York: Harper & Row, 1967), p. 630. On the FBI's preliminary report, see *New York Times*, December 3, 1963, p. 1.

15 *The Warren Commission Report* (U.S. Government Printing Office, 1964; New York: Barnes & Noble Books, 2003). See also coverage of the report in *New York Times*, September 28, 1964.

16 See *The Warren Commission* Report, pp. 105-9; U.S. House of Representatives, *Report of the Select Committee on Assassinations* (New York: Bantam Books, 1979), p. 45. Investigators never found any bullet fragments from any other weapon besides the one owned by Oswald. If a second gunman had fired on the presidential limousine, then presumably bullet fragments from another weapon would have been found somewhere in the car or in the bodies of the two men who were hit. In its investigation carried out in the late 1970s, the House Committee on Assassinations commissioned

a precise chemical analysis (called a neutron activation analysis) on the various bullet fragments found in the presidential limousine, in Governor Connally's thigh, and on his stretcher at Parkland Memorial Hospital. This analysis strongly suggested that these fragments came from just two bullets, one which hit President Kennedy in the head and a second which went through his upper back and then into Connally, and that both came from Oswald's weapon. This analysis provided additional confirmation for the so-called single-bullet theory.

17 Ibid., pp. 421-24.

18 James Reston, "A New Chapter Unfolds in the Kennedy Legend," *New York Times*, September 28, 1964, p. 1; Tom Wicker, "American Tragedy: The Terrible Toll of Violence," *New York Times*, June 9, 1968, p. E1.

19 C. L. Sulzberger, "A Time for Hot Lines, Not Assassins," *New York Times*, September, 28, 1964, p. 28.

20 "Soviet Papers Call Warren Data False," *New York Times*, September 30, 1964, p. 31.

21 Thomas Buchanan, *Who Killed Kennedy?* (New York: G. P. Putnam, 1964); Joachim Joesten, *Oswald: Assassin or Fall Guy?* (New York: Marzani & Munsell, 1964). See also Christopher Andrew and Vasili Mitrokhin, *The Sword and the Shield: The Mitrokhin Archive and the Secret History of the KGB* (New York: Basic Books, 1999), pp. 226-27. The authors, citing evidence from Soviet files, report that Joesten's publisher, Marzani & Munsell, received subsidies from the Soviet Union from 1960 onward.

22 *New York Times*, September 29, 1964, p. 29.

23 Mark Lane, *Rush to Judgment: A Critique of the Warren Commission Inquiry* (New York: Holt, Rinehart & Winston, 1966); Sylvia Meagher, *Accessories after the Fact: The Warren Commission, the Authorities, and the Report* (New York: Bobbs-Merrill, 1967); Josiah Thompson, *Six Seconds in Dallas: A Microstudy of the Kennedy Assassination* (New York: Geis Publishers, 1967); Richard H. Popkin, *The Second Oswald* (New York: Avon Books, 1967).

24 Quoted by Edward Jay Epstein, "Counterplot," in *The Assassination Chronicles*, p. 264.

25 Edward Jay Epstein, "Who's Afraid of the Warren Report?" *Esquire*, December 1966.

26 Todd Gitlin, *The Sixties: Years of Hope, Days of Rage* (New York: Bantam Books, 1993), p. 313.

27 See G. Robert Blakey and Richard Billings, *The Plot to Kill the President* (New York: Times Books, 1981).

28 A Gallup Poll taken in 2003 suggested that 76 percent of Americans

believed in a conspiracy theory in the assassination of President
Kennedy, with the CIA and the Mafia being favored sources of the plot.

29 CBS News Special Report, "The Warren Report," June 1967; U.S. House
of Representatives, *Report of the Select Committee on Assassinations* (New
York: Bantam Books, 1979), pp. 1-2. For a summary of the findings of the
autopsy reanalysis, see pp. 41-46. The House report, while concluding
that Oswald fired the lethal shots that killed President Kennedy, concluded also that a fourth shot may have been fired by an unknown gunman from the grassy knoll area, a conclusion that pointed to a conspiracy.
This conclusion was based on an analysis of a recording made by a motor-
cycle policeman in or near Dealey Plaza at the time the shots were fired.
This conclusion was subsequently discredited by further analysis, thus
eliminating any evidence of a second gunman.

30 Gerald Posner, *Case Closed: Lee Harvey Oswald and the Assassination of JFK*
(New York: Random House, 1993), chs. 17-19.

31 Norman Mailer, *Oswald's Tale* (New York: Random House, 1995), p. 778.

32 Ibid., p. 783.

33 On the theory of the altered wounds, see David S. Lifton, *Best Evidence:
Disguise and Deception in the Assassination of John F. Kennedy* (New York:
Macmillan, 1981). See also Jim Marrs, *Crossfire: The Plot That Killed
Kennedy* (New York: Carroll & Graf, 1989). Marrs has also written a book
alleging a government conspiracy in the terrorist attacks of September 11,
2001, and another on the secret links between the Freemasons and the
Trilateral Commission.

34 U.S. Senate, *The Investigation of the Assassination of President John F. Kennedy:
Performance of the Intelligence Agencies*, Book V (Washington: U.S. Government Printing Office, 1976), pp. 2-7, 32-45. Quotation from Hoover on
the FBI's reputation is on p. 55. On Hoover's motivations in promoting the
"lone nut" theory, see Epstein, "Legend," in *The Assassination Chronicles*,
pp. 305-9. See *The Warren Commission Report*, pp. 457-58, for the commission's criticisms of the FBI.

35 See U.S. Senate, *The Investigation of the Assassination of President John F.
Kennedy*, Book V, pp. 5-6, 23-31; Posner, *Case Closed*, pp. 454-55. The
Senate report did conclude that President Eisenhower probably authorized
attempts by the CIA in 1960 to assassinate Premier Patrice Lumumba
of the Belgian Congo. These efforts did not succeed and Lumumba was
shortly killed by rivals for power in the Congo. Associates of Eisenhower
disputed this conclusion, however, claiming that he would never have
authorized assassination as an instrument of foreign policy. See U.S.
Senate, Select Committee to Study Governmental Operations with

Respect to Intelligence Activities, *Alleged Assassination Plots Involving Foreign Leaders* (Washington: U.S. Government Printing Office, 1975), pp. 51-52. For a rebuttal in defense of Eisenhower, see Stephen E. Ambrose, *Ike's Spies: Eisenhower and the Espionage Establishment* (Jackson: University of Mississippi Press, 1981), ch. 21.

36 On Kennedy's knowledge of assassination plots, see Seymour Hersh, *The Dark Side of Camelot* (New York: Little, Brown & Co., 1997), ch. 13; David C. Martin, *Wilderness of Mirrors* (New York: Harper & Row, 1980), pp. 120-47; John Prados, *Safe for Democracy: The Secret Wars of the CIA* (Chicago: Ivan R. Dee, 2006), pp. 298-321; John Ranelagh, *The Agency: The Rise and Decline of the CIA* (New York: Simon & Schuster, 1986), pp. 383-400, esp. p. 385.

37 On the Warren Commission and the intelligence agencies, see U.S. Senate, *The Investigation of the Assassination of President John F. Kennedy*, Book V, pp. 9-21. See also U.S. House of Representatives, *Report of the Select Committee on Assassinations* (1979), pp. 252-56. The House report was highly critical of the CIA's level of cooperation with the Warren Commission.

CHAPTER 6: ASSASSIN

1 On Oswald's politically charged character, see Edward Jay Epstein, "Legend," in *The Assassination Chronicles: Inquest, Counterplot, and Legend* (New York: Carroll & Graf, 1992); and Epstein, "Who Was Lee Harvey Oswald?" *Wall Street Journal*, November 22, 1983. Also, Jean Davison, *Oswald's Game* (New York: W. W. Norton & Co., 1983), esp. chs. 1, 2, and 18. The comment in description of Oswald was made by Aline Mosby, a UPI reporter stationed in Moscow when Oswald defected. See Epstein, "Legend," p. 385; and *The Warren Commission Report* (U.S. Government Printing Office, 1964; New York: Barnes & Noble Books, 2003), p. 414.

2 *The Warren Commission Report*, Appendix VIII.

3 *The Warren Commission Report*, p. 677. See also Gus Russo, *Live by the Sword: The Secret War against Castro and the Death of JFK* (Baltimore: Bancroft Press, 1998), pp. 87-97; Davison, *Oswald's Game*, ch. 2.

4 Davison, *Oswald's Game*, pp. 54-56.

5 Ibid., ch. 3.

6 *The Warren Commission Report*, pp. 678-81.

7 On Oswald's Marine Corps training, see Epstein, "Legend," pp. 351-55; *The Warren Commission Report*, pp. 681-83; Davison, *Oswald's Game*, ch. 4; Russo, *Live by the Sword*, pp. 97-100.

8 See Davison, *Oswald's Game*, pp. 71-72; Epstein, "Legend," pp. 343-46, 388-89.

9 Epstein, "Legend," pp. 620, 387; *The Warren Commission Report*, p. 256.

10 *The Warren Commission Report*, pp. 684-85.

11 Davison, *Oswald's Game*, pp. 81-82; *The Warren Commission Report*, pp. 687-89.

12 *Washington Post*, November 1, 1959, p. A7.

13 "Texan Thru with U.S., Aims to Be Russian," *Chicago Tribune*, November 1, 1959, p. A13; *Washington Post*, June 9, 1962, p. A7.

14 *The Warren Commission Report*, pp. 692-93.

15 Quoted in Epstein, "Legend," p. 383.

16 Ibid., chs. 3 and 4.

17 Francis Gary Powers, *Operation Overflight* (New York: Holt, Rinehart & Winston, 1970), pp. 356-58.

18 Stephen E. Ambrose, *Ike's Spies: Eisenhower and the Espionage Establishment* (Jackson: University of Mississippi Press, 1981), pp. 289-91.

19 On Oswald and the U-2, see also Epstein, "Legend," ch. 5. Epstein writes that it is probable that Oswald supplied the Soviets with information useful to bringing down the U-2, owing to security lapses at Atsugi Air Base that may have given him access to classified information about the U-2 program.

20 *Washington Post*, June 9, 1962, p. A7; *Chicago Daily Tribune*, June 9, 1962, p. C9.

21 Warren Commission Exhibits, vol. 16; *The Warren Commission Report*, p. 399; Norman Mailer, *Oswald's Tale* (New York: Random House, 1995), pp. 299-301. For a summary of some of Oswald's political views, see Mailer's book, pp. 505-9.

22 *The Warren Commission Report*, pp. 434-35, p. 393; Epstein, "Legend," pp. 445-47; U.S. Senate, *Investigation of the Assassination of President John F. Kennedy*, Book V, p. 88.

23 *The Warren Commission Report*, p. 393. On Oswald in the Soviet Union, see Russo, *Live by the Sword*, pp. 102-11; Priscilla Johnson McMillan, *Marina and Lee* (New York: Harper & Row, 1977), pp. 106-81.

24 Epstein, "Legend," pp. 295-339; David C. Martin, *Wilderness of Mirrors* (New York: Harper & Row, 1980), ch. 9; John Ranelagh, *The Agency: The Rise and Decline of the CIA* (New York: Simon & Schuster, 1986), pp. 402-9. See also Edward Jay Epstein, *Deception: The Invisible War*

between the KGB and the CIA (New York: Simon & Schuster, 1989),
pp. 285-89.

25 *The Warren Commission Report*, p. 435; Epstein, "Legend," p. 508.

26 Ibid., p. 490.

27 Ibid., pp. 287-88.

28 *New York Times*, October 1, 1962, p. 1; *New York Times*, January 15, 1963,
p. 1.

29 See, among many sources, Don Munton and David A. Welch, *The Cuban
Missile Crisis: A Concise History* (New York: Oxford University Press, 2007),
esp. pp. 80-83 on Castro and the use of nuclear weapons. See also the
award-winning film *The Fog of War: Eleven Lessons from the Life of Robert S.
McNamara* (2003). In the section on the missile crisis, McNamara
describes Castro's willingness to use nuclear weapons.

30 See Epstein, "Legend," pp. 484, 490, 647n.4; also *The Warren Commission
Report*, pp. 289, 414-15; Davison, *Oswald's Game*, pp. 119-20.

31 *The Warren Commission Report*, pp. 723-24; Davison, *Oswald's Game*, p. 127.
Oswald probably developed these photographs himself (along with his
reconnaissance photographs of the layout around General Walker's home)
while employed at the photographic firm Jaggers-Stiles-Stovall. He held a
position there from October 1962 until April 1963, when he was dismissed for poor performance on the job.

32 "Shot Fired at Walker Was to Kill," *Washington Post*, April 12, 1963, p. A6;
The Warren Commission Report, p. 724, 404-6; Davison, *Oswald's Game*,
pp. 128-29; Epstein, "Legend," pp. 488-93; McMillan, *Marina and Lee*,
ch. 24.

33 See *The Warren Commission Report*, pp. 282-83, 404-5, 723-24; Epstein,
"Legend," pp. 488-93; Mailer, *Oswald's Tale*, pp. 497-525; McMillan,
Marina and Lee, pp. 360-74. Edward Jay Epstein suspects that de Mohrenschildt may have reported Oswald's attempt on Walker's life to contacts
within the CIA, who maintained an interest in Oswald due to his stay in
the Soviet Union. If this in fact was so, the CIA at this time was also
aware of the potential threat posed by Oswald—another reason why the
agency may have preferred a tightly circumscribed investigation of the
Kennedy assassination. See Epstein, pp. 555-69. The Walker shooting
also sheds further light on Oswald's motives in attacking Kennedy.
Walker opposed the civil rights movement but Kennedy supported it.
Both, however, opposed Castro and sought to bring him down.

34 "Castro Says U.S. Plans Slayings," *New York Times*, April 21, 1963, p. 26;

"Exile Leader Accuses President of Breaking Vow to Invade Cuba," *New York Times*, April, 16, 1963, p. 1; Max Frankel, "President Denies That U.S. Pledged 2nd Cuba Invasion," *New York Times*, April 20, 1963, p. 1; *Wall Street Journal*, March 15, 1963, p. 1; John Prados, *Safe for Democracy: The Secret Wars of the CIA* (Chicago: Ivan R. Dee, 2006), pp. 302-12. Gus Russo writes with evidence to back up the claim that Kennedy continued to develop plans for an invasion of Cuba after the missile crisis, but with leadership coming from the CIA rather than from the Cuban exiles. See Russo, *Live by the Sword*, chs. 7 and 8.

35 *The Warren Commission Report*, p. 188.

36 *The Warren Commission Report*, pp. 725-29; Epstein, "Legend," pp. 497-99; Davison, *Oswald's Game*, pp. 132-33; Russo, *Live by the Sword*, ch. 6. The source for Oswald's comment that he could gain an appointment in Castro's government is in Epstein, p. 497.

37 *The Warren Commission Report*, pp. 290-91; Davison, *Oswald's Game*, pp. 139-45; Epstein, "Legend," pp. 497-99.

38 Epstein, "Legend," p. 498.

39 *The Warren Commission Report*, p. 412.

40 *The Warren Commission Report*, pp. 406-12 and pp. 290-93; Epstein, "Legend," pp. 498-99.

41 *The Warren Commission Report*, pp. 291, 407.

42 *The Warren Commission Report*, pp. 436, 727; Epstein, "Legend," p. 500.

43 *The Warren Commission Report*, pp. 406-11, 288; Davison, *Oswald's Game*, ch. 10; Epstein, "Legend," pp. 504-8.

44 *The Warren Commission Report*, pp. 435-38.

45 Daniel Harker, "Castro Warns U.S. Not to Aid His Foes," *Chicago Tribune*, September 9, 1963, p. A10.

46 Ranelagh, *The Agency: The Rise and Decline of the CIA*, pp. 402-3; Epstein, "Legend," pp. 509-12; Davison, *Oswald's Game*, pp. 182-84; U.S. Senate, *Investigation of the Assassination of John F. Kennedy: Final Report*, Book V, pp. 14-21, 36-39.

47 On Oswald's trip to Mexico City and his visits to the Cuban and Soviet embassies, see *The Warren Commission Report*, pp. 299-311, 730-36; U.S. Senate, *The Investigation of the Assassination of President John F. Kennedy: Final Report*, Book V, Section III; Epstein, "Legend," ch. 14; Davison, *Oswald's Game*, ch. 12. Castro's report that Oswald had made a threat against President Kennedy is discussed in Davison, pp. 210-11, and

Epstein, "Legend," pp. 515-16. Further information along these lines is contained in the U.S. Senate report cited above, pp. 77-86. See also Russo, *Live by the Sword*, ch. 10.

48 *The Warren Commission Report*, pp. 735, 738.

49 *The Warren Commission Report*, pp. 437-44, 739; Davison, *Oswald's Game*, ch. 14.

50 *New York Times*, November 19, 1963, p. 1.

51 U.S. Senate, *The Investigation of the Assassination of President John F. Kennedy: Final Report*, pp. 18-20, 25-26; Epstein, "Legend," pp. 517-18.

52 See Prados, *The Secret Wars of the CIA*, pp. 319-23; Russo, *Live by the Sword*, pp. 390-91.

53 James Reston, "World Morality Crisis," *New York Times*, June 6, 1968, p. 20; Arthur Miller, "On the Shooting of Robert Kennedy," *New York Times*, June 8, 1968, p. 30; Jack Newfield, *RFK: A Memoir* (New York: Nation Books, 2003), p. 302; Raymond G. Anderson, "Russians Discern Sign of U.S. Decay," *New York Times*, June 6, 1968, p. 19.

54 David S. Brown, *Richard Hofstadter: An Intellectual Biography* (Chicago: University of Chicago Press, 2006), ch. 10.

55 Christopher Andersen, *Jackie after Jack: Portrait of a Lady* (New York: William Morrow & Co.), 1998, p. 182.

56 Peter Kihss, "Notes on Kennedy in Suspect's Home," *New York Times*, June 6, 1968, p 1.

SEVEN: CAMELOT

1 See Karen Armstrong, *A Short History of Myth* (New York: Canongate Books, 2005), pp. 3-4.

2 William Manchester, *The Death of a President: November 22, 1963* (New York: Harper & Row, 1966), pp. 623-24. Lloyd Lewis makes the point about the young nation in need of heroes in *Myths after Lincoln* (New York: Harcourt, Brace & Co., 1929), "Epilogue," pp. 347-56. Reston quoted in Manchester, p. 625.

3 Sir James Frazier, *The Golden Bough* (1890; New York: Macmillan, 1951), p. 310.

4 Mary Renault, *The King Must Die* (New York: Pantheon Books, 1958).

5 Norma Lorre Goodrich, *King Arthur* (New York: Harper & Row, 1986), p. 11.

6 Alfred Lord Tennyson, *Idylls of the King* (New York: Penguin Books, 1983), p. 293.

7 Theodore H. White, *In Search of History: A Personal Adventure* (New York: Harper & Row, 1978), pp. 471-73.

8 Ibid., p. 471.

9 Theodore H. White, *The Making of the President, 1960* (New York: Atheneum, 1961).

10 White, *In Search of History*, p. 538.

11 Ibid., pp. 538-44.

12 Ibid., p. 545.

13 *Life*, John F. Kennedy Memorial Edition, December 3, 1963.

14 Lord David Cecil, *Melbourne* (New York: Bobbs-Merrill, 1939).

15 Arthur M. Schlesinger Jr., *A Thousand Days: John F. Kennedy in the White House* (1965; Boston: Houghton Mifflin, 2002), p. xi.

16 T. H. White, *The Once and Future King* (1958; New York: G. P. Putnam's Sons, 1987). On the reviews of Camelot, see Sylvia Townsend Warner, *T. H. White: A Biography* (New York: Viking Press, 1967), pp. 300-2. Writing in the *New York Times*, reviewer Howard Taubman said that the play was only "partly enchanted" owing to its conflicting themes of romance and tragedy that are never resolved. See *New York Times*, December 11, 1960, p. X5.

17 See Orville Prescott, "Books of the Times," *New York Times*, June 1, 1959, p. 25; and December 30, 1959, p. 19.

18 T. H. White, *The Once and Future King*, pp. 634-37.

19 Richard P. Hunt, "President Given Birthday Party," *New York Times*, May 24, 1963, p. 14.

20 White, *The Once and Future King*, pp. 88-89.

21 Manchester, *The Death of a President*, p. 550.

EIGHT: THE OLD LIBERALISM AND THE NEW

1 Dennis Wrong, "The Case of The New York Review," *Commentary*, November 1970. See also the numerous letters published in response to his article in the March 1971 issue of the magazine.

2 For the use of the term "neoconservatism" in the 1950s, see David S. Brown, *Richard Hofstadter: An Intellectual Biography* (Chicago: University of Chicago Press, 2006), pp. 87-89.

3 Arthur Schlesinger Jr., *A Thousand Days* (1965; Boston: Houghton Mifflin, 2002), p. 1030.

BIBLIOGRAPHY

Ambrose, Stephen E. *Ike's Spies: Eisenhower and the Espionage Establishment.* Jackson: University of Mississippi Press, 1981.

Andersen, Christopher. *Jackie after Jack: Portrait of the Lady.* New York: William Morrow, 1998.

Andrew, Christopher, and Vasili Mitrokhin. *The Sword and the Shield: The Mitrokhin Archive and the Secret History of the KGB.* New York: Basic Books, 1999.

Armstrong, Karen. *A Short History of Myth.* New York: Canongate Books, 2005.

Avlon, John P. *Independent Nation: How Centrists Can Change American Politics.* New York: Three Rivers Press, 2004.

Beard, Charles. *An Economic Interpretation of the Constitution of the United States.* New York: Macmillan, 1913.

Becker, Carl. *The Declaration of Independence: A Study on the History of Political Ideas.* New York: Harcourt, Brace & Co., 1922.

Bell, Daniel. *The End of Ideology: On the Exhaustion of Political Ideas in the 1950s.* New York: The Free Press, 1962.

Bell, Daniel, ed. *The Radical Right.* New York: Doubleday & Co., 1963.

Benson, Lee. *The Concept of Jacksonian Democracy.* Princeton, New Jersey: Princeton University Press, 1961.

Bishop, Jim. *The Day Kennedy Was Shot.* New York: Bantam Books, 1968.

Blair, Joan, and Clay Blair Jr. *The Search for JFK.* New York: G. P. Putnam's Sons, 1976.

Boorstin, Daniel J. *The Image: A Guide to Pseudo-Events in America.* New York: Atheneum, 1978.

Bradford, Sarah. *America's Queen: The Life of Jacqueline Kennedy Onassis.* New York: Penguin Books, 2000.

Branch, Taylor. *Parting the Waters: America in the King Years, 1955-1963.* New York: Simon & Schuster, 1988.

Brown, David S. *Richard Hofstadter: An Intellectual Biography.* Chicago: University of Chicago Press, 2006.

Buchanan, Thomas. *Who Killed Kennedy?* New York: G. P. Putnam, 1964.

Burns, James MacGregor. *The Deadlock of Democracy.* New York: Prentice-Hall, 1963.

Butterfield, Herbert. *The Whig Interpretation of History*. New York: W. W. Norton & Co., 1965. First published in London, 1931.

Carwardine, Richard J. *Evangelicals and Politics in Antebellum America*. New Haven: Yale University Press, 1993.

Carwardine, Richard. *Lincoln: A Life of Purpose and Power*. New York: Vintage Books, 2006.

Cecil, Lord David. *Melbourne*. New York: Bobbs-Merrill Co., 1939.

Churchill, Winston. *The Gathering Storm*. New York: Houghton Mifflin, 1948.

Cohn, Norman. *The Pursuit of the Millennium*. New York: Oxford University Press, 1970.

Croly, Herbert. *The Promise of American Life*. New York: Capricorn Books, 1964. First published in 1909.

Dallek, Robert. *An Unfinished Life: John F. Kennedy, 1917-1963*. New York: Little, Brown & Co., 2003.

Davis, John H. *Jacqueline Bouvier: An Intimate Memoir*. New York: John Wiley & Sons, 1996.

Davison, Jean. *Oswald's Game*. New York: W. W. Norton & Co., 1983.

Epstein, Arnold, and Benjamin R. Forester. *Danger on the Right*. New York: Random House, 1964.

Epstein, Edward Jay. *The Assassination Chronicles: Inquest, Counterplot, and Legend*. New York: Carroll & Graf Publishers, 1992.

Epstein, Edward Jay. *Deception: The Secret War between the KGB and the CIA*. New York: Simon & Schuster, 1989.

Epstein, Edward Jay. "Who's Afraid of the Warren Report?" *Esquire*, December 1966.

Epstein, Edward Jay. "Who Was Lee Harvey Oswald?" *Wall Street Journal*, November 22, 1983.

Fay, Paul B. *The Pleasure of His Company*. New York: Harper & Row, 1966.

Festinger, Leon. *A Theory of Cognitive Dissonance*. Stanford, California: Stanford University Press, 1957.

Frazier, Sir James. *The Golden Bough*. New York: Macmillan, 1951. First published in 1890.

Frost, Robert. *The Poetry of Robert Frost*. Edited by Edward Connery Lathem. New York: Holt, Rinehart & Winston, 1969.

Gitlin, Todd. *The Sixties: Years of Hope, Days of Rage*. New York: Bantam Books, 1993.

Goodrich, Norma Lorre. *King Arthur*. New York: Harper & Row, 1986.

Goodrich, Thomas. *The Darkest Dawn: Lincoln, Booth, and the Great American Tragedy*. Bloomington: Indiana University Press, 2005.

Guelzo, Allen C. *Abraham Lincoln: Redeemer President*. Grand Rapids, Michigan: Eerdmans, 2003.

Hanchett, William. *The Lincoln Murder Conspiracies*. Chicago: University of Illinois Press, 1983.

Hartz, Louis. *The Liberal Tradition in America*. New York: Harcourt, Brace & World, 1955.

Hayes, Harold, ed. *Smiling Through the Apocalypse: Esquire's History of the Sixties*. New York: McCall Publishing Co., 1970.

Hellmann, John. *The Kennedy Obsession: The American Myth of JFK*. New York: Columbia University Press, 1997.

Hersh, Seymour. *The Dark Side of Camelot*. New York: Little, Brown & Co., 1997.

Heymann, C. David. *A Woman Named Jackie*. New York: Birch Lane Press, 1995.

Himmelfarb, Gertrude. *The Moral Imagination: From Edmund Burke to Lionel Trilling*. Chicago: Ivan R. Dee, 2006.

Hofstadter, Richard. *The Age of Reform*. New York: Vintage Books, 1955.

Hofstadter, Richard. *Anti-Intellectualism in American Life*. New York: Random House, 1964.

Hofstadter, Richard. *The Paranoid Style in American Politics and Other Essays*. Cambridge, Massachusetts: Harvard University Press, 1965.

Hofstadter, Richard. *The Progressive Historians: Turner, Beard, Parrington*. New York: Vintage Books, 1970. First published in 1968.

Jaffa, Harry V. *The Crisis of the House Divided: An Interpretation of the Issues in the Lincoln-Douglas Debates*. Chicago: University of Chicago Press, 1972.

Jaffa, Harry V. *A New Birth of Freedom: Abraham Lincoln and the Coming of the Civil War*. Oxford, U.K.: Rowman & Littlefield, 2000.

Joesten, Joachim. *Oswald: Assassin or Fall Guy?* New York: Marzani & Munsell, 1964.

Kaufmann, Michael W. *American Brutus: John Wilkes Booth and the Lincoln Conspiracies*. New York: Random House, 2004.

Kennedy, John F. *Profiles in Courage*. New York: HarperCollins, 2003. First published in 1956.

Kennedy, John F. *Why England Slept*. Garden City, New York: Doubleday & Co., 1962. First published in 1940.

Klein, Edward. *Just Jackie: Her Private Years*. New York: Ballantine Books, 1998.

Lasch, Christopher. *The New Radicalism in America, 1889-1963*. New York: W. W. Norton & Co., 1965.

Lasky, Victor. *J.F.K.: The Man and the Myth*. New York: Macmillan, 1963.

Leaming, Barbara. *Jack Kennedy: The Education of a Statesman*. New York: W. W. Norton & Co., 2006.

Lewis, Lloyd. *Myths after Lincoln*. New York: Harcourt, Brace & Co., 1929.

Life. John F. Kennedy Memorial Edition. December 3, 1963.

Lifton, David S. *Best Evidence: Disguise and Deception in the Assassination of John F. Kennedy*. New York: Macmillan, 1981.

Lincoln, Abraham. *The Collected Works of Abraham Lincoln*. Edited by Roy P. Basler. 8 vols. New Brunswick, New Jersey: Rutgers University Press, 1953-1955.

Lippmann, Walter. *Drift and Mastery*. Madison: University of Wisconsin Press, 1986. First published in 1913.

Lipset, Seymour Martin. *Political Man*. Garden City, New York: Anchor Books, 1963.

Mailer, Norman. *Oswald's Tale*. New York: Random House, 1997.

Mailer, Norman. *The Presidential Papers*. New York: Bantam Books, 1964.

Manchester, William. *The Death of a President: November 22, 1963*. New York: Harper & Row, 1966.

Marrs, Jim. *Crossfire: The Plot That Killed Kennedy*. New York: Carroll & Graf Publishers, 1989.

Martin, David C. *Wilderness of Mirrors*. New York: Harper & Row, 1980.

McMillan, Priscilla Johnson. *Marina and Lee*. New York: Harper & Row, 1977.

Miller, Perry. *The Life of the Mind in America*. New York: Harcourt, Brace & World, 1965.

Moorhead, James. *American Apocalypse: Yankee Protestants and the Civil War*. New Haven: Yale University Press, 1978.

Munton, Don, and David A. Welch. *The Cuban Missile Crisis: A Concise History*. New York: Oxford University Press, 2007.

Newfield, Jack. *RFK: A Memoir*. New York: Nation Books, 2003.

Newton, Jim. *Justice for All: Earl Warren and the Nation He Made*. New York: Riverhead Books, 2006.

Nye, Russel Blaine. *Society and Culture in America: 1830-1860*. New York: Harper & Row, 1974.

O'Brien, Michael. *John F. Kennedy: A Biography*. New York: Thomas Dunne Books, 2005.

Orwell, Sonia, and Ian Angus, editors. *The Collected Essays, Journalism, and Letters of George Orwell*, Vol. 2, *My Country Right or Left, 1940-43*. Boston: David R. Godine, Publisher, 2004.

Perret, Geoffrey. *Jack: A Life Like No Other*. New York: Random House, 2002.

Peterson, Merrill D. *Lincoln in American Memory*. New York: Oxford University Press, 1994.

Pipes, Daniel. *Conspiracy: How the Paranoid Style Flourishes and Where It Comes From*. New York: The Free Press, 1997.

Popkin, Richard H. *The Second Oswald*. New York: Avon Books, 1966.

Posner, Gerald. *Case Closed: Lee Harvey Oswald and the Assassination of JFK*. New York: Random House, 1993.

Powers, Francis Gary. *Operation Overflight*. New York: Holt, Rinehart & Winston, 1970.

Prados, John. *Safe for Democracy: The Secret Wars of the CIA*. Chicago: Ivan R. Dee, 2006.

Ranelagh, John. *The Agency: The Rise and Decline of the CIA*. New York: Simon & Schuster, 1986.

Reeves, Thomas C. *A Question of Character: A Life of John F. Kennedy*. New York: Macmillan, 1991.

Renault, Mary. *The King Must Die*. New York: Pantheon Books, 1958.

Reynolds, David. *In Command of History: Churchill Fighting and Writing the Second World War*. New York: Random House, 2005.

Rossiter, Clinton. *Conservatism in America: The Thankless Persuasion*. New York: Vintage Books, 1962.

Russo, Gus. *Live by the Sword: The Secret War against Castro and the Death of JFK*. Baltimore: Bancroft Press, 1998.

Salinger, Pierre. *With Kennedy*. New York: Doubleday, 1966.

Schattschneider, E. E. *Party Government*. New York: Holt, Rinehart & Co., 1959.

Schlesinger, Arthur M., Jr. *The Age of Jackson*. Boston: Little, Brown & Co., 1945.

Schlesinger, Arthur M., Jr. *A Thousand Days: John F. Kennedy in the White House*. Boston: Houghton Mifflin, 1965.

Schlesinger, Arthur M., Jr. *A Thousand Days: John F. Kennedy in the White House*. 2nd edition, with a new Foreword. Boston: Houghton Mifflin, 2002.

Schlesinger, Arthur M., Jr. *The Vital Center*. Boston: Houghton Mifflin, 1948.

Schwartz, Barry. *Abraham Lincoln and the Forge of National Memory*. Chicago: University of Chicago Press, 2000.

Sorensen, Theodore C. *Kennedy*. New York: Bantam Books, 1966.

Steers, Edward. *Blood on the Moon: The Assassination of Abraham Lincoln*. Lexington: University of Kentucky Press, 2001.

Stout, Harry S. *Upon the Altar of the Nation: A Moral History of the Civil War*. New York: Viking Press, 2006.

Tennyson, Alfred Lord. *Idylls of the King*. New York: Penguin Books, 1983.

Tidwell, William A., James O. Hall, and David W. Gaddy. *Come Retribution: The Confederate Secret Service and the Assassination of Abraham Lincoln*. Jackson: University of Mississippi Press, 1989.

Trilling, Lionel. *The Liberal Imagination*. New York: Anchor Books, 1950.

U.S. House of Representatives. *Report of the Select Committee on Assassinations*. New York: Bantam Books, 1979.

U.S. Senate, Select Committee to Study Governmental Operations with Respect to Intelligence Activities. *Alleged Assassination Plots Involving Foreign Leaders*. Washington: U.S. Government Printing Office, 1975.

U.S. Senate, Select Committee to Study Governmental Operations with Respect to Intelligence Activities. *The Investigation of the Assassination of President John F. Kennedy: Performance of the Intelligence Agencies*. Book V. Washington: U.S. Government Printing Office, 1976.

Warner, Sylvia Townsend. *T. H. White: A Biography*. New York: Viking Press, 1967.

The Warren Commission Report. New York: Barnes & Noble Books, 2003. First published by the U.S. Government Printing Office, 1964.

Weyl, Walter. *The New Democracy*. New York: Macmillan, 1912.

Whalen, Richard J. *The Founding Father: The Story of Joseph P. Kennedy*. New York: New American Library, 1964.

White, T. H. *The Once and Future King*. New York: G. P. Putnam's Sons, 1987. First published in 1958.

White, Theodore H. *The Making of the President, 1960*. New York: Atheneum, 1961,

White, Theodore H. *The Making of the President, 1964*. New York: Atheneum, 1965.

White, Theodore H. *The Making of the President, 1968*. New York: Atheneum, 1969.

White, Theodore H. *In Search of History: A Personal Adventure*. New York: Harper & Row, 1978.

Whitman, Walt. *Leaves of Grass*. Philadelphia: David McKay Publishers, 1900.

Wills, Garry. *The Kennedy Imprisonment: A Meditation on Power*. New York: Houghton Mifflin, 1981.

Wills, Garry. *Lincoln at Gettysburg: The Words That Remade America*. New York: Simon & Schuster, 1992.

Wilson, Edmund. *Patriotic Gore*. New York: Oxford University Press, 1962.

INDEX

245

DESIGN AND COMPOSITION BY CARL W. SCARBROUGH